The Early Life and Times of a
Glen Tanar Exile

Published by

Librario Publishing Ltd.

ISBN No: 1-904440-42-8

Copies can be ordered from retail
or via the internet at:
www.librario.com

or from:

Brough House
Milton Brodie
Kinloss
Moray
IV36 2UA
Tel / Fax: 01343 850617

Printed in Times (11pt)

Cover design and layout by Steven James
www.chimeracreations.co.uk

Printed and bound by
Antony Rowe Ltd., Eastbourne

The Early Life and Times of a

GLEN TANAR
EXILE

Memoirs of an
Anglo-French Scot

Francois Louis Pierre Fouin

Librario

Dedication

In loving memory of my parents.
Without a tombstone to mark their lives,
this book is their epitaph.

The Author - 1947.
Aberdeen Grammar School.

The Author - 2003.
Happy Retirement.

" View From The Golf Course, Glen Tanar " by Sir W Russell Flint
(commissioned by Lord Thomas Glentanar in the 1930's).

*Taken from a set of prints, given to the author by his godfather, Lord
Glentanar. It is featured in memory of the Laird's many kindnesses to him
throughout those early years.*

Acknowledgements

My grateful thanks to Mrs Jan McLaren for nurturing my early ideas for this memoir. For information relating to Glen Tanar and the Coat's family, thanks are due to the Hon. Mrs Jean Bruce. Jimmy Oswald and Ian Smith, with their intimate knowledge, as head gamekeepers on the estate, also provided many helpful comments. I am also greatly indebted to Mrs Betty Scace, née Robertson, who has come to my rescue by providing names from the past that I could scarcely recall, together with her memories of my mother. Thanks are also due to the librarians in the Aberdeen Central Library who were always pleasant and went out of their way to supply or direct me to necessary background information. My old buddy Alfie Dawson has shared in many of my experiences and has relived with me the saga of the Glen, while renewing and amending many memories, for which I am very grateful. To Charles and Aileen Jason, my admiration as well as thanks for their unstinting determination in keeping my nose to the grindstone. Without Aileen's input and proof reading and Charles' computer skills this book would probably never have been completed.

Dedication

Acknowledgements

Contents

Glen Tanar from the air - 1938

Lake, boathouse and policies in the foreground with mansion house behind. To the left of the "big house" can be seen the flagpole which was less than one hundred yards from our front door. To the right of the circular field lies the golf course with the Chapel of St. Lesmo just visible on the edge of the trees on the far right. The High Road, in the background, sweeps round from the left in a semi-circle to the Belrorie wood on the right. From here the road then leads on over the hill by the Fir Mounth Pass to the Glen Tanar School.

Introduction

We all pass through life only seeing it in its contemporary setting, forgetting that in fifty to a hundred years' time the world will have moved on, and that unless some of us describe our way of life, the knowledge will be totally lost to our great great grandchildren forever. Consequently, this record of a relatively unremarkable early career is the result of a strong desire on my part to set down my experiences in the form of a Memoir.

I wish to leave behind a small cameo of life in my time; the richness and variety of a rural upbringing in an idyllic environment as a boy, enjoying a way of life, which is already history. Additionally, I wish to record a little of the life and times of my parents who made everything possible for me to progress in my career. I regret that I did not start this labour of love while my parents were still alive. Despite having recorded some of the events in their past, it is only now when I get down to the fine details that I find I am short of certain facts. With more detailed information, I could then have done full justice to them. I feel that this is necessary because they have passed on, with no gravestone, plaque, or any sign that they both lived for all of ninety-seven years through momentous times.

Why then do I feel that I have anything special to offer in the way of reminiscences, when generations come and go leaving almost nothing behind to say they have passed this way? I suppose it is something to do with, if not a sense of self-importance, then a sense of my being unusual and set apart due to the fact that I bore this fancy name in a very Scottish parochial setting. Some might say it is because I am an only child, with the implication that I have had a spoilt upbringing with too much attention being focused on me alone. There is an element of truth in this, but I prefer to see it otherwise.

Some readers may wonder why, in a career that has been spent totally in the North-east of Scotland, I have confined these memoirs largely to the period up to my father's retirement from Glen Tanar around 1956. This was not my original intention as I had meant to write purely a family record. However, with both local and widespread interest in our feudal past so obvious, I felt that, as this was where my real passion lay, I should confine myself mainly to this early period. My reader should expect no earth-shattering philosophical analysis or the recording of any great events in these memoirs. However, if read in the context of slightly atypical individuals living through changing times in a Scottish setting, it may add a further flavour to other documented histories of this same era.

The optional title 'Memoirs of an Anglo-French Scot' highlights the fact that these memoirs are written, not as a continuous tale, but as a series of chapters dealing with specific subjects or periods in my life. This method allowed me to give an in-depth view of many areas that would not have been possible, if dealing with them in strict sequence. It also allows the reader to browse through the chapters at random without losing the overall thread of events. This is not a gallant story of working class hardship with barren living and parental sacrifice forming the basis for future success. There are no handed down second-hand clothes, no meatless days, no shivering over a miserable fire. Any hardships that appear in this story have been mainly the result of my own shortcomings.

The early years contained the halcyon days, when the sun always shone, when the snow was whiter than white and the thrill of new experiences took one's breath away. The dawning of a new spring when the birds started their mating songs, when the first shoots appeared on the trees and the daffodils opened their petals to a warming sun, was an entrancing experience. This was a time when the word 'euphoria' summed up all my feelings. On a cloudless summer's day, lying in the warm heather of a hillside overlooking an eagle's eyrie on the Allachy River in Glen Tanar - this whole experience seems now as close to heaven as I shall ever achieve.

The purpose of this book therefore stems from a wish to leave behind a record of some of my experiences for future generations to browse over. It is not intended to be a descriptive work of art but more a practical reliving of events set down in the straightforward way that is both the strength and weakness of our own North-east culture. However, to be really meaningful, it also requires insights and an honesty of recall that may be painful for me while perhaps surprising many of my friends. Also present is a great yearning for the charmed life of my childhood, which neither of my children have ever had the opportunity to savour. Certainly, there was a lot of anxiety and some misery present back in those days which memory has partially blotted out. But our values and appreciation of simple things and events was greater for me, then, than it is for the present generation. Nowadays, affluence, the influence of the media and world travel, have removed much of the mystery experienced in those earlier days.

When dealing with episodes occurring later in my life, I trust that I have been mindful of the feelings of others. If some facts may be incorrect or some of my memories flawed, I hope that those who are affected will accept my sincere apologies. The scene is set; the memories have been brushed down, so prepare to be transported back into that idyllic world of the nineteenth and twentieth centuries.

Maps of Deeside and Brittany in France.

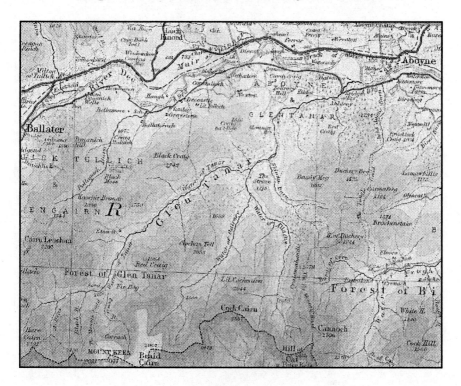

Glen Tanar Estate

Lying between Ballater to the West
and Aboyne to the East.

To the South its main Feature is Mount Keen
which rises to 3077feet.

*(Taken from a John Bartholomew & Son Ltd.,
Edinburgh, Map of Deeside.)*

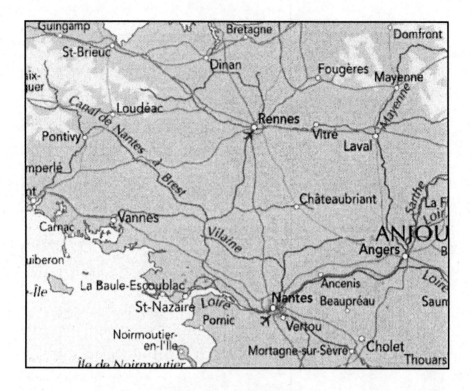

Britanny, France

Father's home farm and village were on the
outskirts of Chateaubriant.

La Baule – scene of our regular holidays, is just north
of St Nazaire, once the location of the huge German
submarine pens.

(Download from multiMap.com)

Chapter 1
Family Background

My father was born Francois Louis Fouin, on 12th May 1881, on the farm of La Plonnais, which is just outside the small Breton village of St Julien de Vouvantes about fifty miles from St Nazaire. The nearest market town is Chateaubriant - not the one famous for the steaks - and the nearest city is Rennes. The farm was probably less than one hundred acres and had been farmed by the Fouins for three generations. From my father's records, it would seem that they would have been tenant farmers. His mother, who was a Tessier, lived on a farm that the family had also occupied for generations. My great grandmother's family were textile manufacturers of a very rough cloth, made up from flax grown locally on the surrounding farms and turned into shirts etc for the workers. Otherwise the family tree, followed back to the 1600's, all seemed to be folk of the soil.

As the eldest son, my father left school at the age of ten, to help his father. But he was never enthralled by the life. He told of the floods, cattle deaths and anthrax among the pig stock, which hardships finally convinced him that a farmer's life was not for him. Luckily there were younger brothers to take his place so that his father agreed to release him. Even as a small boy I was much moved by my father's description of the year the harvest failed and the impact it had on him as an eight-year old which changed forever his attitude to the Roman Catholic Church - but more of this later.

Other tales that come to mind, are the clattering of hooves on the road, as the armed gendarmes went hunting down any suspected Royalists. Despite the French Revolution having been well past, there were still many active Royalists in the country districts and my father used to express the children's terror on their way home from school, when they would dash into the hedgerows on hearing the troopers approach.

Seeing his first car was also something very memorable. What appeared a moving cart without a horse seemed a miracle to the local people, as they gathered round a doctor's car, which had arrived from Nantes, with the doctor's servant visiting her family. My father remembers the doctor using nearly a whole box of matches, before he could get the engine to fire, such was the strength of the breeze.

His first venture away from home at age fourteen, was walking the twenty-five miles to Nantes, to apply, unsuccessfully, for a job in a biscuit factory.

Having eventually turned to domestic service and gathering experience as he went, he soon landed up in Paris working in hotels and then as a butler/valet to the moneyed and titled rich.

Called up for his army service in 1900, Father was found medically unfit for active duty, due to the flattest feet that I have ever seen. However, attached to Les Chasseurs, he was drafted as a batman to a senior officer, who tried hard to keep him in the army after his three years' service. He felt, however, that having cut his ties with the farm, he had to get out and see the world. Becoming employed by an American, he then went back and fore to the USA on a number of occasions. Over the years, further changes of employer followed, always with travel as the main theme. By now he was employed as a valet/courier.

In 1912 an event occurred which almost cost my father his life. By then he was working for a Mr Malloch, a rich New York publisher. Having returned to the states, Mr Malloch told my father to pack everything up and to follow him across a couple of weeks later. As a special treat, he had bought Father a ticket to sail on the *Titanic* on its maiden voyage. Excited at the prospect of this luxury cruise to America, Father boarded the *Titanic* in Southampton. Having seen his baggage stowed in his cabin, he was standing by the rail when a purser came on deck, calling his name and requesting him to come quickly to the telegraph office where an urgent telegram waited him.

1903 - Father aged 22, in the French Cavalry.

Imagine his disappointment when he discovered that his employer had been summoned back to London on business with the result that my father's voyage was cancelled and he was to await Mr Malloch's arrival in this country. Getting all the gear ashore and then standing watching, as the mighty liner slid down Southampton Water, nearly made him weep. He does not record how he felt when the dreadful news of the disaster became known. Sixty years later found me standing reading the headstones of the *Titanic* victims in the graveyard in Halifax, Nova Scotia. This gave me the oddest sensation when I considered how fate controls our lives.

London 1912.

Peasant Boy to "Man about Town"

My father looked back on the years before the First World War with some nostalgia, but also as a time when he had to spend hours, trying to learn English properly. Realising that to make the most of life in the USA, he had to be fluent, he described how night after night he would sit in his little room in London, with a book and a dictionary translating, sometimes until four o'clock in the morning. Strength of will and determination were the admirable qualities which enabled this relatively uneducated man to improve his grasp of English. Nevertheless, even after years in Britain he would still use 'which' instead of 'who' and also 'sheeps' instead of 'sheep', as if determined to keep some of his individuality. At the outbreak of war in 1914, having volunteered for the French army, he was turned down, on account of his defective feet and chronic bronchitis. Told that the British needed interpreters urgently, he went for a further London medical, but was again turned down, even after a senior officer had told him he was accepted.

Unemployed, because having given his notice to his American benefactor, on being told the army service was a certainty, he went to Bellisle House in Ayrshire, for an interview with a Mr George Coats, of the thread empire of J and P Coats. Employed by him as his personal servant/masseur/courier, he was to be with that family for the next forty years.

19

Glen Tanar Exile

My father was a travel addict and he had great tales to tell of life in St Petersburg in 1905, where he saw poverty, starvation and death, such as he had never witnessed anywhere else. Ever after, he maintained that not even Stalin could have treated the Russian people more cruelly than did the Tsar and he had great sympathy for the Revolution. His travels through South America, and over the high Andes in 1926, always gave me a yen to follow in his footsteps, but the chance now seems to have slipped past, without me ever pursuing the opportunity when I was younger. I have always felt a great admiration for my father's drive and initiative, which enabled him to escape from a conventional background. His younger brother Henry joined him in Paris as a footman, under my father. Henry then went on to become a steward on the transatlantic liners, before returning home and joining the French railways, where he ended up as a stationmaster.

As a postscript to this background, I loved my father's tale about Uncle Henry in service. As a footman he was expected to ride up on the box of the carriage when the marchioness went out visiting. Henry was a bundle of roguish energy and was not one to bend the knee to anyone. Seated on high, he liked to draw attention to himself by bowing and smiling to the ladies as the carriage drove along the Bois de Boulogne. This behaviour drove the marchioness frantic, so that by the time they returned, Dad was instructed to discipline Henry or get rid of him. There is no record of the outcome, but getting to know Uncle Henry much later, I surmise that he would only ever have doffed his hat to her ladyship in mock apology.

My mother was Rebecca Watson who was born on 5th January 1892 in Newcastle-on-Tyne. She was the youngest of three daughters whose parents were William Watson and Eliza Hudson. Her father had joined the police, but left soon after her birth to join his brother Robert, running a small land sale colliery on the Longhurst estate, two miles from Morpeth. There appears to be no mining history in the family as, prior to this, all were farmers or estate workers, except for my great grandmother Mary Lambert. She was supposedly the estranged daughter of Squire Lambert of Kirkheaton, who had married William Watson, the head forester on Sir George Swinburne's estate at Capheaton Hall. I have never been able to fully authenticate this piece of family folk lore and feel the actual picture is more complicated than the family's bland version. According to my mother, however, the brains in the family came down this line, as my aunt Isobel was very clever academically and my aunt Molly was an extremely shrewd businesswoman.

When mother was four, the family moved to Morpeth and my grandparents lived out their lives at 5 Bennett's Walk on the banks of the River Wansbeck.

Family Background

My grandfather went on to become a deputy, i.e. a mine's inspector, at Netherton colliery and seems to have retired from there. I inherited various characteristics from my grandfather, one of which was his red-green colour blindness. In addition, he was six feet one inch tall, a half-inch taller than I was. My grandmother was the boss in the family and, according to my mother, was extremely ambitious. She was noted as the person everyone in the district turned to in emergencies. Attending at deliveries, deaths and to anyone in need – according to my quiet grandfather – she was happier to be in anyone else's house than she was in her own.

My mother never really enjoyed school and said the only things she really liked were singing, poetry and sewing, although she had a great love of reading. She was noted as having a fine contralto voice, to develop which she attended lessons for three years as a teenager. She was also encouraged to have piano lessons, so that she could accompany her singing. Her most bitter memory of school was when, aged fourteen, she unexpectedly received four of the best from Mr Bullock the headmaster. During a silent reading class, she was absent-mindedly toying with the window cord, when suddenly Mr Bullock's deep booming voice called her up to the dais in the middle of the room. Then, without a word of explanation, he proceeded to punish her before the whole class. Deeply shamed to be so treated at her age and in front of her peers, she was left with a feeling of legitimate grievance at the injustice of her punishment – a feeling that the headmaster's comforting words later on did little to dispel.

Her account of the death of little Caroline Osborne left a deep and lasting impression on me. I still have a lock of her hair, which I found among my mother's possessions. It is a constant reminder of that sad tale. Caroline, living a few doors from my mother, was probably four years old and a really loveable child. She was greatly attached to Mother, then aged 14, regarding her as her own special friend. Late in the afternoon of 31st of October 1906, Caroline came in to 5, Bennett's Walk to ask Becca to come out and play with her. Mother remembers sitting taking her tea of banana sandwiches and saying, "Not just now Caroline". The little girl was apprehensive in the dark and was known to pull up her pinnie in front of her face in a gesture of self-protection.

In the fading light she ran off home and no one is certain whether it was then, or a little later, that she went missing. With the River Wansbeck in spate and no barrier between path and river, it must be surmised that she ran straight into the turbulent water, as her body was recovered at a weir downstream some days later. My mother asked for and was given a lock of her hair in remembrance of her little friend. But over the years, she never forgave herself for that needless death.

My mother left school at fourteen, going on to serve her apprenticeship as a dressmaker. Her close friend in those days was Hannah Charlton, daughter of the prominent market gardeners in Morpeth. Mother felt that she may have been initially mistaken for one of the Charlton family and that this may have opened the way for her to obtain her first job at Rutherfords. She was paid five shillings (25p) a week after she served her apprenticeship there. Thereafter, Williamsons, the high-class tailors, employed her in Morpeth, where she undertook gentlemen's and ladies' tailoring. In due course her salary was increased to ten shillings (50p) a week and she stayed with the firm for four years.The highlight of her social life at this time was playing Portia in *The Merchant of Venice*; a production put on by the local theatre-company to celebrate a Shakespearean anniversary. She continued to be able to recite her lines to the end of her life. Becoming restless with the monotony of small-town life in Morpeth, Mother took up a post

Morpeth 1908 -
Mother aged 16.
*Early dress-
making days.*

as dressmaker to the Garnet-Williams, a mother and two daughters in Hay-on-Wye. The year was 1913 and she was aged twenty-one. While there, she was to meet my father for the first time as a guest in the house and he left her his forwarding address at the Bachelor's Club in Piccadilly, hoping she would visit him if she were ever in London.

Upon the outbreak of war in 1914 Colonel Garnet-Williams, a reservist, volunteered for active service and Mother, sensing changing circumstances, decided to leave. Returning home, she took courses in hairdressing and as a beautician, feeling these would widen her options for future employment. Restless, she then applied with two friends to go to Roehampton House Orthopaedic Hospital in 1916, to work as gardener's assistants in the large greenhouses. She had harrowing tales to tell of the limbless soldiers whom she met at this time. She herself had experienced the tragedy of war when her own special friend was killed.

Captain Cecil Swinney of the Seventh Northumberland Fusiliers, was the son of the local wealthy owners of the iron foundry in Morpeth and it appears that he was very fond of my mother. After spending his last leave with her, he left, feeling extremely despondent. He told her that he had a premonition that he would never come back.

Officers of that rank were the first to die on the battlefields, often leading their men over-the-top and into battle. Tragically his premonition proved to be well founded and the romance was blown away. The carnage from those battles left scarcely a family untouched in Northumberland. While researching this part of our family history, I came upon a book in my mother's collection entitled *'War History of the Seventh Northumberland Fusiliers'*. There his name is listed in the Roll of Honour as 'Acting Captain Swinney, J.H.C. (M.C.)'. On page fifty-nine the following excerpt describes a German attack just south of Arras in treacherous weather conditions of rain sleet and snow, with no one very clear what was happening. The message reads, '19th April.1917 (Beaurains). In the meantime, we learnt that Captain Swinney was missing. He was last seen standing on the parapet firing at the Bosches with his revolver when they closed round him. We did not find any trace of him afterwards.' Then, falling from between the pages of this book, was a letter addressed to my mother from Swinney Bros.Ltd, Wansbeck Ironworks, Morpeth. From Cecil's father, it reads 'A Minute of my gallant Son. Thanking you for all you did for him – Father.'

The Great War - 1917.
A Father's Heartfelt Appreciation.

In 1918, she returned to service in the employ of Miss Luna Ezzra, at 22 Hill Street, London where she was to meet many of the influential Jewish families of the time, such as the Sassoons and Rothschilds. With my father at 11 Hill Street, it is not surprising that my parents met again there for the first time since 1913 and it would appear that their marriage on 3rd June 1926, was the outcome of this chance meeting. My mother moved on to work for Lady Tweedale at Yesterhouse, Gifford in 1922, on the very day that my Aunt Isobel married Will Halley in Edinburgh. Here, while in this post, she seemed to do most of her travelling, notably to Prague to stay in the American Embassy for almost a year, where her employer's stepfather was chargé-d'affaires.

London 1919.
City Lady - Mother aged 27.

On then to Bohemia for the winter sports, with spells in Dresden and Berlin. Changing jobs in 1923, she then went to Lady Mewkes, wife of Sir Hedworth Mewkes. With houses in Newmarket, London and Cannes, my mother was in her element. As a close friend of the Royal Family, there was always pressure on her mistress to be turned out exquisitely. Paris in March was when Lady Mewkes got fitted out in the latest fashions for the season at Ascot. Attending Ascot, Goodwood and living in Newmarket, bred in my mother a real interest in and love of horse-racing - something that leaves me cold.

On 3rd June 1926, she left the Mewkes' household to be married in Henrietta Street Registry Office, then on for three weeks' honeymoon in the Paris Hotel, Southsea. During this time they visited the Royal Yacht Squadron, where my father was well known through his various connections. It was never explained to me by my parents why a gap of twelve years elapsed before they got around to marriage, although I sensed that it was probably because my mother was having too good a time.

This life in the magnificent mansions of the titled and famous came to a juddering halt at the end of June 1926. When Mother got off the train at

Aberdeen Station she viewed for the first time the grey, cold environment with some dismay. Little did she know that she had committed herself to these hostile surroundings for the rest of her life. When they moved into their little furnished house at the top of the Stable Yard on the Glen Tanar estate, she was just thirty-four years old and my father was forty-five.

She recalls with pleasure the days before the war when Royalty and many well-connected guests were entertained on the estate. Among these were the Prince of Wales and his brother, Albert (George), the future king, who both enjoyed local events such as the annual Ghillies Ball. My father thought a lot of the future Duke of Windsor, who used to seek out my father as soon as he arrived in order to ensure that his extra supply of whisky had been laid aside. Mother recalls often seeing the young princesses passing her gate, when they came to play with the laird's only child Jean or when they went out in the donkey-cart. The future Queen accompanied them at times and Queen Mary also came down from Balmoral. My father seemed unruffled by the importance of the company, as he had been accustomed to it all from his Paris days.

It would appear from my mother's tapes that my father had felt from the outset that he might not live to see his children grow up. Consequently, they both agreed that they would not embark on raising a family. However, after a year my mother felt so very lonely at the Glen, that she asked him to reconsider his opposition to having children. And so it came about that in November 1928 I was born. Otherwise, if estate workers had been allowed to keep dogs, my mother's love for her four-legged friends would probably have meant that I would have been born as a golden Labrador!

Mother paints a picture of the happiness of life at Glen Tanar, but I remember that the situation was rather different for her. This will become more apparent in later chapters. I feel that having a child was the only thing that really kept her there and that my subsequent development did not make her totally regret her decision.

There is a story, occasionally repeated over the years by both parents, about my father's lack of inheritance on the death of the first Lord Glentanar in 1918. George Coats, knighted in 1916, was a severe chronic asthmatic, who latterly required the frequent use of oxygen, which he would allow only my father to administer. Lady Glentanar took the greatest exception to a servant usurping her place and, as her husband's condition became more debilitating my father felt her animosity very strongly. When Lord Glentanar became still weaker, he would scarcely let my father out of his sight either by day or night.

Some months before this, Mr James Cameron, the Head Gamekeeper had been called in to witness the signature of the laird on his latest will. Coming through to my father's room for the usual refreshment, he had told Father that he, my father, was to be left £1,000 in the will. On the laird's death, all that Father received from Lady Glentanar was a framed photograph of the laird, while the Head Gamekeeper did receive £1,000. It would seem rather odd that this should have occurred, as so highly did the laird appear to value my father that it was unlikely that a photograph was to be the only memento. In those far off days of autocratic behaviour however, it is not difficult to imagine the disdainful wave of her Ladyship's hand towards the family lawyer, in dismissing such an unwarranted trivial bequest. On the positive side my father retained his job by simply transferring his duties to the young laird, so nothing in the end was either gained or lost. The Dowager Lady Glentanar eventually died in 1935, but my father, although never liking her and probably in return, never being forgiven, seemed quite resigned to the fact that this was the sort of outcome one might have expected.

George Coats Esq.
1st Baron Glentanar.
That Famous Photograph.

My father, was an utterly honest and straightforward man, so that any thoughts of retribution towards his employer for such an apparently high-handed act would have been dismissed with a Gallic shrug of the shoulders. On the other hand Mother, in a similar situation, might not have been so accommodating and would probably have extracted her pound of flesh over the years. That my father probably made full use of the perks of the job, I do not doubt, but equally I am sure those liberties were never excessive. While my mother obviously scrimped and saved for the day when they would no longer enjoy the benefit of a tied house Father seemed always to maintain a carefree attitude of relaxed affluence.

This record is taken from the tapes I recorded of my father in May 1967 when he was eighty-six and of my mother recorded in February 1985 at the age of ninety-three. Both lived on to their ninety-eighth year, but mother seemed much more mentally alert then, than was my father. Listening to her at the age of ninety-three, reciting Shakespeare and various poems, and singing all the songs from our past, it is difficult to believe she was other than a young woman with an astounding memory.

The interesting postscript to this chapter poses the question of how life might have changed had the phantom legacy materialised. My father always believed that education was the greatest blessing he could hand down to his children. When I was born he speculated as to whether a public school education would give his son a better start in life. On obtaining the application forms for Merchiston Castle School in Edinburgh, it became obvious that this was quite beyond his means. But that £1000 was a fortune in the 1920's and could well have financed such a venture.

I have absolutely no regrets that my life developed in the way it did. Placed in the same situation as my father, but with greater resources, I too opted for the head start that was to take my son to Fettes College in Edinburgh six years behind Tony Blair and into the same school-house, Arniston. Despite all that, it remains a moot point whether this option is warranted with the pros and cons balancing one another out in my opinion. But, like my father, I felt that education is the greatest asset I could provide, in addition, of course, to a loving and caring home.

Finally, I often wondered about my mother's relationship with her own mother, as little warmth seemed to exist between them. Yet among my mother's papers, after she died, were these scribbled lines. Were they perhaps a lament or even more likely a regret?

"To Her"

Who smiles for me though I essay no jest?
Whose eyes are glad at my coming, though I bring her no gift?
Who suffers me readily, though I do her no honour?
My Mother.

Chapter 2
Setting The Scene

I was born on the 20th November 1928 in the tiny cottage hospital at Torphins in Aberdeenshire. In due course I was christened Francois Louis Pierre Fouin on the whim of my mother who liked the names but failed to appreciate the implications of saddling a child with these foreign words in a Scottish setting.

My father was in the employ of the Honourable Lord Glentanar at Glentanar House, four and a half miles from the village of Aboyne in Aberdeenshire. We lived in a pleasant end-terrace house, with a small walled flower garden and lawn, at the top of what was called the Stable Yard. This was only two hundred yards from the mansion house that was always referred to locally as 'the big house'. My father would disappear there before eight in the morning, not to return before ten in the evening. Some afternoons, however, he would pop in for a cup of tea with my mother while the gentry were taking their tea, but would be back within twenty minutes

1929 and all's well
with the world.

to attend at table. In the late twenties and through the thirties, life on these private estates was one of tranquillity. They had a routine unaffected by the momentous times of the Stock Exchange crash. There then followed the depression of the thirties, with millions in Britain existing on the starvation line with no jobs or prospects.

Glen Tanar, compounded of the Gaelic words Glean-tan-ar, signifying the glen of scanty arable land, was for me, always a world in itself. Being an estate, it had its own home farm nearby, so that dairy products were always available, milk being free to employees, as also were kindling, logs and coal. The game larder was fifty yards away and somehow rabbit and, at times, venison appeared on our dinner table. Occasionally grouse was also on the menu and this is still my favourite game bird, closely followed by partridge. The large mansion house gardens backed on to our house and with apple trees growing against our back wall, we regularly plundered the orchard as small boys. Our next door neighbours, the Dawsons, had one of their bedrooms directly over our living-room. They must have been excellent neighbours, as we seemed quite unaware of their close proximity. The father was the estate joiner - a man with marvellous hands, but with a rather gruff manner, while his wife was the garner of all the local gossip. She was a most kindly person and I spent many happy hours in their house over the years. They had two children, Alfie, who was two years younger than I was and Evelyn, who was probably about four years younger. They were pleasant friendly children, while Alfie was my constant buddy in the Glen during all those early years until I left for school in Aberdeen at age fifteen.

Living next to them in the Stable Yard were the Archibalds with their four children, Willie, George, Mabel and James. The father, George, small of stature, was the odd-job-man at the mansion house, capable of turning his hand to innumerable jobs. He was, moreover, a superb fisherman, as I was to learn in later years. Mrs Archibald, cheery, small and rotund, but with a waspish tongue at times, had a peculiar obsession. Her doorstep of slate was washed down daily before having a coat of red brick lovingly applied and God help anyone defacing it! One day, a dusty footprint resulted in a frantic inquisition before she noticed that it was my sandal-print that was the culprit and never again did I enter through her front door. The brass doorknob and fittings were also burnished to perfection, with a pride which seems so at odds with our present-day values. Their eldest son Willie, known as Bill in later life, was probably about a year younger than me and a much more gregarious character than either Alfie or myself. From the early days Willie shared with me a love of fishing. He would be our occasional companion and then would disappear for weeks on end, to join up with other boys on the estate. He was also a master at working his way into favour with people, such as the dairyman or the fishing ghillie and he would get all the benefits of such associations. Occasionally, I was to come across this trait again in my professional life, when I observed certain colleagues currying favour in order to advance their careers. I found this attitude disturbing, although I would not totally shun such opportunities; but I never felt comfortable doing it and my independent streak usually surfaced at the first excuse.

Further down the yard, was a bothy for two single gardeners and next to them a coach-house full of the lovely horse-traps and harnesses, which had sadly become obsolete with the coming of the motor car. Occasionally the laird and his family would have a coach and horses harnessed to go off up the Tanar valley to Eitnach, reliving an era of sedate stately pleasure. Next to the coach-house lived the Silvers. Mr Silver looked after the recreation hall, which was a stylish wooden building, with shingle type wooden roofing and situated on a green area overlooking the Stable Yard. Next to them were further bothies, where the servants or chauffeurs of the laird's house guests could be housed; while next to that, round the bottom of the yard, were all the stables for the riding ponies and a large glass-roofed garage for the Rolls Royces. Garden plots for the employees abutted the recreation hall and were the pride and joy for many, much time and thought going into them to show off their owner's prowess.

| 1932 - | 1933 - | 1934 - |
| Alfie, Self and Willie. | Alfie and Willie. | Willie and Scooter. |

Opposite our house, at the top of the yard, stood the Estate Office and outside on the flat wall stood the red box containing the press-button for the hooter, which dominated the roof of the garage at the other end of the yard. The hooter signalled the end of the week at midday on a Saturday, but its other purpose was to alert the employees to forest fires or other emergencies. Sitting on this wall, Alfie and I, when just at school, would delight in shouting mild or not so mild obscenities down the yard, when the echo would come bouncing back in full volume. After a time, an irate Mrs Dawson put a stop to all that, by brandishing a sweeping brush in our direction and threatening dire consequences if we did not desist.

A further hooter-point was situated at the home farm and on one of our naughty outings, when aged about six, we dared Willie Archibald to try pressing the button. Imagine our anxiety and Willie's panic when the hooter started up with its deafening howling wail, bringing all and sundry running to deal with some catastrophe. Time has blotted out my memory of the consequences, but I bet if we asked Willie after all these years, he would certainly remember the heavy hand of his father on a bare bottom.

This area of the farm has also painful memories for me and I can still see myself kitted out in a lovely light blue coat, wearing my Sunday-best *'Little Dukes'* black shoes, accompanying my mother to collect the milk. While she stopped to speak to the dairyman, I, being only four years old and easily bored, drifted off to the bull house. This was a stylish circular building rising quite shallowly to a central peak and well within my ability to scale in order to sit on the top. Sharply admonished by my mother, I hastily descended, unfortunately scuffing the toes of the expensive *Dukes*. Little was said on the way home, but a sharp smacking resulted, which was a lesson I have obviously remembered to this day. The other estate buildings, such as the larder, the Clerk of Works office, the joiner's shop and the paint shop, were a stone's throw further up the hill from our house and radiated the sense of a small village community.

The Stable Yard - 2003.
The Joiner's Cottage first right.

People often reminisce about their very first memory and I have a sense of sitting up in my high pram; but whether this is true or stimulated by pictures of me at this stage, I am uncertain. Similarly, a very traumatic episode in my life which took place when I was two years old, stirs some vague images. The medical profession at that time and up until the Second World War, had two bees in its bonnet and all and sundry were caught up in this popular fad. Tonsillectomy was advised almost as a routine, whether the child suffered any throat symptoms or not, while circumcision was a must. I had my tonsils and adenoids removed in the old St John's Nursing Home in Aberdeen when I was about six, while circumcision was carried out on me aged two, on the dining table in our living room. Apparently old Dr Brodie Brown, assisted by his son

Dr Willie, carried out the deed, much to my mother's consternation. It is unclear if any local anaesthetic was used, but seemingly I suffered great pain and my mother felt that I failed to thrive for many months after the operation. I have a vague memory of lying on the table in considerable agony, but again whether this is imagined or real is difficult to ascertain, as it was often mentioned in later years as a particularly barbaric act. Probably my bull-house experience is the sharpest early memory, although looking back through old picture albums, I have a sense of distant vague echoes resonating within me. Photos of me playing in our garden with Miss Jean, the only child of Lord and Lady Glentanar, certainly ring bells and these must have been taken

Lady Grethe Glentanar
née Thorenson.

when I was probably about two years old. This gives me the chance to outline the history of the estate as it affected my family, although it does overlap some of my father's history, which I have referred to from time to time.

The Hon. Miss Jean & Junior.

Before Apartheid.

As previously recorded, my father was engaged in the first year of the First World War (1914 -1918), by the then George Coats, Esq.. He was one of the Coats family which owned the J and P Coats empire. Manufacturers of cotton thread, they had factories spread around the globe from Russia to South America and have been recognised as the first multi-national company in the world. George Coats (1849 -1918), as noted in chapter 1, was a severe asthmatic, latterly requiring frequent oxygen and depending increasingly on my father. My father in turn recalled those early years with nostalgia and felt a really deep affection for his ailing employer. George Coats had bought the Glen Tanar estate in 1905 from the previous owner

Sir Cunliffe Brooks for the princely sum of £155,000. During the war, Lloyd George, the then prime minister, had decided to sell titles to the rich to provide money for the costly war effort and it was understood from my father's accounts that George Coats would probably have paid around £50,000 for the honour. On reading *The Honour's System* by Michael De-la-Noy, I find that a peerage cost £100,000, a baronetcy £40,000 and a knighthood £10,000. It is recorded that the baronetcy was conferred on George Coats in the King's Birthday Honours List of the 3rd June 1916 and the title Lord Glentanar was registered on the 29th June 1916.

His only son was Thomas Coats, born 14th December 1894, died 28th June 1971, who inherited the title on his father's death and my father stayed on to administer to him as valet/courier and later as butler/valet in the thirties. In December 1927, Tom Glentanar married Grethe D Thorenson, of the Norwegian shipping line, born 27th November 1907, died 19th March 1940. They had one child, Jean, born on the 19th October 1928, one month before my birth. In view of the closeness of our birthdays my father asked the laird if he would be my godfather, to which he agreed. For the first few years, I was a fairly frequent companion to Jean and I do vaguely remember Nurse Hetherington, the nanny, with us in the mansion house nursery and taking us out around the Wander Walks. Outside the nursery was the figure of a black minstrel wearing a straw boater while sitting embracing the back of his chair and holding a Charlie Chaplin type walking stick. I have a vivid memory of being repeatedly startled, so realistic did he appear. George Coats' widow, the Dowager Lady Glentanar was still alive then and living with the family. Before her marriage she had been Margaret Lothian Black (1853 -1935) of the prominent Edinburgh publishing house and was considered by my father as a real first generation titled nouveau riche. She thoroughly disapproved of her grandchild having anything to do with a servant's child and so, by the age of four as far as I was concerned, Miss Jean had become the lonely girl who lived in the big house.

An interesting interlude here relates to the life of Professor Joseph Coats (1846 -1899), first Professor of Pathology at Glasgow University (1894). A brilliant student and the first Glasgow graduate to make pathology his main interest, he was also one of the Paisley thread-making dynasty and would have probably been George Coats' second or third cousin. This medical association may go some way to explaining some of Tom Glentanar's subsequent interest in health and in developing his contacts with such people as Professor Sir Stanley Davidson, in the years ahead.

I was relatively unaware that having a titled aristocrat as a godfather could have a possible influence on my life, with the result that I tended to shun the association and, in retrospect, probably did not turn to him for advice as I could justifiably have done. The laird was a large man, both in stature and personality. Loud of voice, he did not fill one with a feeling that one could approach him easily; but, when the chips were down and my university entrance might have been difficult, he gave me an excellent reference.

Lord Glentanar was a talented musician and he had a large organ installed in the ballroom, which when played, would boom out all the way over to our house. This could be very pleasant, except that in later years, after his wife died from an acute respiratory infection and tuberculosis in 1940, he would take to playing during the night when he could not sleep, or when the barley flowed too strongly through his veins.

1927 - Happy Days
before the Intruder.

1928 - First Signs
of the Intruder.

My parents were a rather ill-matched pair and it was never very clear to me, why in their relative middle age, they had decided to marry. My cousin Evelyn, five years older than me, tells me that Auntie Becky was a real stunner as a young woman and hinted that she had been involved in romances which, on occasion, had required the helpful intervention of her two sisters. From her sophisticated life as a lady's maid to the aristocracy in London and the good life, why mother ever chose to come so far north, into an alien environment, I never did find out.

As a result of her life in service, travels abroad, as well as working at Roehampton Hospital in the First World War, Mother had lost any sign of being a miner's daughter from Northumberland and had at times all the airs and graces of the well-bred. Yet she never seemed to have broadened her outlook beyond seeing herself as English and regarding the rest of the world, including the Scots, as second-class citizens.

Calais for her, was where foreigners started and she often questioned how she could ever have come to marry one. "You've made your bed, however, and now you will just have to lie on it" was her own mother's response to the news that her daughter was to marry a Frenchman. In years to come, Mother would occasionally recall her mother's discouragingly ominous prophecy, admitting that perhaps it had been a shrewd assessment of the situation. She also viewed her neighbours with some disdain and was probably regarded in return as a complete snob. Above all, she detested my father being called a butler, and would describe him to strangers in a superior voice as being Lord Glentanar's house steward. How this improved my father's status is uncertain, but in those days, below stairs, it obviously had some meaning. Yet, despite her grand airs, she loved tittle-tattle and liked nothing better than to gossip over the garden wall, although I scarcely remember many neighbours ever coming to visit her.

1930 -
Cousin Evelyn and Junior.
Nappy showing.

1951 -
Evelyn & My God-daughter,
Petrina.

21 Years Later...

She was immensely houseproud, believing in a place for everything and everything in its place. This was the background, admirable in its way, against which I was reared. I was invited happily into other people's houses, but no children were readily welcomed into our abode. She visited the poultry-man's wife, Mrs Livingstone, once a week for eggs. Otherwise her life was spent in a set routine doing house chores in the morning; then after lunch she would change into her tailored coat and skirt. She would then get out her trusty walking stick and walk two miles up the road to Mount Keen as far as the *Black Ship* pool on the Tanar and back again. She certainly did this almost every week-day of her life in the Glen. In final recognition of this, my daughter Nicky and I scattered her ashes all along this road in 1989 - I'm sure she would have been delighted. On Saturdays, with my father driving the Austin 10, she would go down to Aboyne for her messages and to catch up with all the news. Prior to getting the car, the estate ran its own Albion bus to the village for employees, and I have early happy memories of this singular treat.

My mother was undoubtedly bright, listened to classical music, played the piano and had a good singing voice. She read widely and, although she did at times act haughtily, this is understandable when one considers that she would have had relatively little in common with those around her. As a young child, I was read and sung to in the most tender fashion, although she was a very undemonstrative mother - cuddles and kisses were not her style. Could it be, however, that I felt uneasy when it came to showing affection, since I knew from bitter experience that any sign of the more sensitive side of my nature would lead to my being ridiculed by my macho peers? Mother's one real luxury in life over all the years in Glen Tanar was her weekly dabble on the football pools. Strang's Pools were faithfully filled in and sent off every week and on many Saturday nights the excitement climbed to fever pitch as my mother thought she had won a fortune. How these mistaken ideas came about I do not remember, but over all the years I believe twenty pounds was the biggest jackpot she ever achieved. Nevertheless, there is no doubt that this excitement and anticipation greatly raised Mother's morale and provided some relief from the dullness of her life. For one whose mind was forever very sharp, but grossly understretched, this mental stimulus of the flutter on the pools was particularly welcome.

Mother was a very fine seamstress but she must have been a nightmare to Mr Youngston, the tailor in Aboyne Square, when every few years, she decided to have a new coat and skirt. I remember interminable visits to the tailor as she kept finding fault with his fitting and then deciding that she really did not like the suit after all. She was not the most diplomatic of people and seemed to have little insight into how her behaviour might hurt others, although being fairly sensitive to criticism of herself. She was a lioness at bay, if she thought I was being got at as a child and I soon learnt not to make a big deal over small incidents, in case she intervened to make it so much worse. Mrs Archibald, in my presence, told the gardener next door about something I had done and after I had repeated the comments at home, there erupted a war of attrition which lasted for about ten years. But, because this took place in such a small society the matter was blown out of all proportion. I learnt to keep my mouth shut after that, or very nearly. Late at night before going to bed, sitting in front of our warm range with a cup of Horlicks, I would be lulled into giving away some delicate information. While lying in bed one Saturday morning, I heard my mother relaying this highly confidential information to Mrs Dawson over the garden wall. Having sworn her to secrecy the night before, I felt totally betrayed and her bland unapologetic rebuttal of my fury made it certain that never again would I fully trust her.

My father was a completely different type. Very dapper and smart, he had the small man's apparent self-assurance, which blossomed forth into pure swank when we returned to France on holidays. Flourishing a large cigar, he came over as a very suave film director of the old school, whereas his beginnings had been very basic. He was of small stature, probably about five feet five inches tall - a good inch shorter than my mother. He put this down to the amount of heavy manual work he had been involved in from the age of ten when, as the eldest son, he worked the farm with his father. He was totally self-educated and by dint of application and pure perseverance he had succeeded in learning a foreign language and travelling all over the world. Looking back, I feel that he was not as intelligent as my mother was. But dogged determination would ensure that he achieved even more than she did at times. In my senior class at Aboyne, we were regularly given homework to stretch our abilities, particularly in mathematics.

Occasionally my mother and I would be completely defeated by some difficult problem, whereupon my father, coming home from work late in the evening, would settle down to solve it, even if it meant staying up into the small hours. I had a great admiration for what he achieved in life and, being someone who has never really looked up to people as heroes, I make an exception of my father and always felt very proud of him.

He was, however, far from perfect as a husband, being petulant and sulky with my mother at times. He probably had good cause, but his behaviour distressed me all the same. He was also not a pleasant inebriate and became argumentative and querulous with too much alcohol. His day was long and after serving dinner at night, he had all the washing and drying of the silver to supervise, while planning for the next day and seeing that all the laird's clothes and shoes were in pristine condition. He would obviously feel the need to bolster his energy levels with a Johnny Walker or two and on these occasions we could immediately sense the effects as soon as he came into the house at night.

The Glen Tanar Dynasty

The Rt. Hon. Lord Glentanar.
1924 - Travelling in Spain.

December 1927 - Oslo.
A Norwegian Bride for Glen Tanar.

Glen Tanar - 1932.
The Hon. Miss Jean Coats with willing Serf.

Photographs From The Family Album

June 1929 -
Nurse Hetherington with
Junior and Miss Jean.

*Two peas in a pod, yet in
reality a world apart.*

July 1932 -
Lady Glentanar and Donkey,
Miss Jean and Junior.

August 1932 -
Junior and Miss Jean
tidy the Rolls.

1932 -
The Stable Yard, Alfie
admiring the new machine.

*Note the hooter point on the
Estate Office wall.*

July 1932 -
The Tanar at Eitnach.
The Halleys and the Fouins.

Stones in the Tanar.
*Study in
Concentration.*

In the Ballroom -
Miss Jean and Dad.

The Dowager Lady
Glentanar.
*Servants are always
servants.*

1933 -
Cousin Evelyn and Junior on the
Knockie Bridge.

Sport's Day on the
Golf Course - 1934.

*Mrs Archibald in the flower-pot hat,
Junior & Miss Jean in mid-ground
with Willie in romper suit and curls
in the foreground.*

It was an odd sensation, as he was in no way drunk, but his whole demeanour had changed from a pleasant relaxed person to someone on the edge of aggressiveness. He was very friendly with his local bank manager, Adrian Stronach and Mr Sanderson, the owner of the Huntly Arms Hotel in Aboyne, and seemingly quite convivial sessions could result in Mother being on tenterhooks until he got home, especially after he got the car. Then the sparks would fly. Later on the parents became very friendly with the McKays who owned the Birse Lodge Hotel in Aboyne. With Mr Sanderson now long gone, Dad's friendship with Mr and Mrs McKay could still occasionally produce the same reaction in our household as those early days of yore in the old Huntly Arms. However, Mother would often be included in this socialising, so now peace would reign for a time.

My mother was frequently very unhappy both with her marriage and living in such relative isolation. Occasionally, following a spat with my father, she would talk to me about throwing herself into the lake or into the dam, which frightened me immensely until I saw her returning to the house. The spectre of suicide was very real in Glen Tanar and I can remember two drowning incidents up the hill in the black dam. On another occasion one of the gamekeepers shot himself, so I had real cause for concern. I look back with some sympathy for my mother's life style, but feel she failed me by involving a child in such dire threats, when he did not have the experience to distinguish between suicidal feelings and the real thing. I respected many of my mother's strengths, but also detested some of her weaknesses, showing much less patience towards her shortcomings than I did towards those of my father.

My father always treated me fairly, never put me under strain over my schoolwork and was always supportive in whatever I did. He did have a very bad temper at times, which resulted in a huge hiding for me on one occasion. One day when I was coming home from school, aged about six, the Clerk of Works came past and we as little brats, picked up handfuls of leaves and threw them at the car as it passed. That evening my father stormed into the house and said that the Clerk of Works, Mr Smith, had phoned him to say I had thrown stones at his car and that he was extremely angry about it. My father refused to listen to me and I was taken through to the wash-house and given the hiding of my life with a big strap. I was left sobbing my heart out in the cold wash-house for an hour, before being taken inside and sent to bed. Days later, my father learnt from another father that we had indeed only thrown leaves and he was mortified that he hadn't listened to me. He often referred to that incident in later life, as having taught him a real lesson, and never again was I unfairly treated.

The only other time I remember being severely disciplined, was when I got too big for my boots and bought a Diana air rifle from Turner's garage in Aboyne, without really consulting the parents. I was probably eleven years old and the gun cost me seventeen shillings and six pence (87p) - a huge amount at that time. But having saved the money from summer work on the farm and in the forestry, I seemed to think I could spend it as I wished. It was the most exciting thing I had ever bought and my parents grudgingly gave in. However, two weeks after the purchase, some neighbour said that I had been firing across the road with the result that my father confiscated the gun for about six months, much to my displeasure. I have to admit that he was probably quite right to do so on that occasion.

Father would always accompany the laird on his frequent trips abroad. There would be visits to many Coats factories, cruising in the Med on the yacht *Pliosaurus* and much time spent in Cannes and Nice, as well as spells in Norway at Lady Glentanar's parents home. It was on his return from one of these trips that Father presented me with a very fine model Rolls Royce which he had probably bought at Hamleys, that London toyshop mecca for children that I was to visit later in life when on holiday. It was a solidly built little car, which I sat in and pedalled. From studying early photographs of the time, I guess that I must have been about three years old. In those days, such an expensive pedal-car would have been considered a very exotic toy for any child of a working-class family. I had great fun and satisfaction from it however, but I'm sure my chums and their parents considered me a spoilt brat.

The highlight of the Rolls' life came at the Aberdeen Agricultural Show in 1936, when the laird wished to show off his new 'bumper' gates. These gates were divided in two, hinged to outside posts and had sprung metal bars attached to each side in the middle, which slotted into the road surface to hold them shut. A car would go up to the gate and stop with its bumper just touching the bars. When ready you would move forward slowly, but with enough motion to push the gates open and would accelerate through, before the gates shut behind you. It needed a lot of confidence, because if you stalled half way through, the gates would swing back and damage the sides of the car. To sell the idea, the laird had the joiner construct model gates. To demonstrate the method, I was asked to go to the show with my little car and do my stuff on the first day. Alfie and Douglas Young, the factor's son, would take my place in the car as demonstrators on subsequent days. I can well remember that trip as very special. Going the thirty miles to Aberdeen itself was the equivalent today of crossing the Atlantic and to go to the show was an added bonus. I duly went through my paces and two or three of these gates were installed on the estate; but the laird's plans to market them were never realised. They were just too difficult for the average driver, although later in life, I drove our Austin through them frequently without any hitches.

There are many books written about life on Highland estates, which exactly mirror my own experiences. The very feudalism of workers' lives had to be experienced to understand how it really was, for so many. The tied house, the various perks, the paternalism of the lairds, all made for a secure and yet in many ways an insecure existence. Conformity was essential, as was loyalty. If sacked, you found yourself out of your house with no references and penniless. Salaries on estates took into account the free house, coal, etc, so that the wage packet was never over-generous. In those days however few luxuries were available so little was spent unnecessarily other than on the occasional drink at weekends and of course the inevitable

Father always treated me fairly.

cigarettes. Cigarette smoking seemed universal among the men while ladies smoking was looked on as being rather chic if not actually risqué. Both parents smoked although I'm certain my mother never inhaled. In later life however

Rolls Royce and Genuine Basque Beret.

their habit disappeared, except for my father's traditional cigar on important occasions, while the temptation totally passed me by.

My father would have earned under £250 a year for a long time and even up to his retirement in 1955 he would have had only £400 a year. He supplemented his income with tips from the visiting gentry, who seemed to be ever present when the laird was at home pre-war. These tips must have added up to quite a sum over the year, as we went on holiday to France for a month every two years and money seemed no object to my father then. He faithfully gave his month's salary unopened, to my mother and still seemed to have money to invest in stocks and shares, an interest he passed on to me from an early age. Buying a new Austin 10 in 1937 costing probably £175, was a fantastic event and again it seems to have been funded from income outwith his wages. No one, other than the well off, could afford this luxury and to have bought it new rather than second hand seems an amazing feat even today. There is little doubt that he was worth every penny of his tips, as he was a meticulous man in all that he did. He would spend hours polishing the laird's shoes until they looked like patent leather; while the fortune in silver that filled the huge walk-in safe was always in pristine condition.

Father was very highly regarded by all around him, as a true professional in his sphere. His responsibilities were huge, as the laird revelled in holding open house at Glen Tanar. This meant that my father had to supervise the requirements of some of the leading national figures including royalty, industrialists, diplomats, politicians, aristocrats, and foreign dignitaries.

There is no record of Winston Churchill being at Glen Tanar; but my father had attended him, presumably when the Coats's entertained widely in Hill Street in London in the early days. My father found him an unattractive, boorish man in his dealings with servants and was never very enthusiastic about Winnie, even in his days of triumph throughout the war years.

The laird, as an accomplished musician and keen theatre-goer, would invite composers, conductors, actors and actresses to come to stay, many of them performing in the ballroom with its full-size stage and organ. My father appeared to cope with all this without showing any real strain, except in later years, when he was more frequently tired. His flat feet certainly took a heavy toll on him by the end of a long day, but he rarely complained.

For all his undoubted ability, I always felt that my father, in some peculiar way, always remained a Frenchman in a Scottish environment. He had close friends in France from childhood; but in Britain, apart from some, such as his bank manager, he did not seem to have any real friends. Arthur Prior in Edinburgh and Albert Farve in London are names from his past, but in Glen Tanar he would not have regarded anyone as a close friend. His relationship with the new laird, I am sure, never reached the level of satisfaction that he had experienced with the laird's father. I felt my father was perhaps at times a little too much his own man for the young laird, who could be quite peevish on occasions. My father used to say "the laird may own my body, but my mind belongs to myself," a maxim which I always found so reassuring and which seems to be a trait handed down to both my children. Nevertheless, my father would get inordinate pleasure from little signs of kindness or appreciation from the laird, which I felt at the time he should have brushed aside. Yet through all our lives, it is pleasant and comforting to have someone showing us that they care. Throughout the thirties, the estate was kept meticulously by an army of employees. The drives were raked daily and in later years, when cycling to school, my tyre marks were the first to disfigure the perfectly uniform surface. The Wander Walks round the lake were also kept up to the same standard and nowhere was there anything marring the image of a well-managed establishment. The Rolls Royces were washed daily by Mr Gowans and the whole Stable Yard kept spick and span. The big estate gardens were totally free of weeds and borders of flowers existed everywhere.

My father was very keen on both his flower garden in front of our house and also his allotment. He borrowed the hand mower from the big garden to tend lovingly his little lawn while his dahlias always seemed to be in flower. His allotment beside the recreation hall was almost too big for just three of us, but it had to be up to scratch. In later years, digging it became my Easter holiday chore. There always seemed to be an endless area of garden which stretched behind me, still to be dug, and I resented spending so many good playing hours at this tedious job. I can never remember shirking it, however, as I think I always appreciated my father's readiness to help me at all times. The postscript to this chapter relates to the home of my childhood and the many visual images it still evokes. That I grew up very proud of our house needs little emphasising. End house just around the corner from the Stable Yard proper, meant a sense of some superiority.

1938 - Our Garden seemed so large and the
flowers were always in bloom.

Through a child's eyes, a substantial walled garden with lawn and flower borders was simply icing on the cake. Flanked by imposing granite pillars, the entrance gate was of solid wrought iron with a corkscrew-like peak. This was jokingly said by the locals to obviously depict the butler's house. A fine gravel path to the front door all added to the impression that my father must be a man of some substance in this estate hierarchy. The house of solid granite with beautifully dressed granite windowsills and many coloured-glass leaded window panes all added up to a sense of total perfection. There were two public rooms downstairs with a narrow scullery which later on housed a small Aga when the old black-leaded kitchen range was replaced in our living room. Two bedrooms upstairs with a cosy bathroom between them were ample for the three of us. The bathroom must have been a late extension, but before my time, as it was erected on stilts in the backyard. The view from this bathroom window every morning was across the immaculate estate gardens with the tops of the farm buildings peeping through the trees beyond and then the broad sweep upwards across the High Road to the Belrorie wood on the skyline. This was a view to invigorate even the drabbest of my days.

In a closed-in back yard was the toilet closet, the stick shed with the ever necessary large paraffin tank, the coal cellar and a large airy wash-house. Here was the depository for all the junk accumulated by my parents over the years plus all my steadily increasing horde of odds and ends. Here also was the old-fashioned boiler that Mother fired up every Monday morning to do the weekly wash. Running along below ceiling level, were all the lead pipes, with their multiple bulges resulting from solder repairs These would occasionally burst again sometime during those harsh winter months. It seems senseless that no lagging was applied, but burst pipes were just accepted with a shrug of the shoulders and the plumber sent for to apply yet another bulge.

The habit of keeping one room as the rather posh sitting-room, while passing all our lives in the living-room, now appears rather ridiculous. Linoleum was the norm in those early days but we boasted a mainly carpeted living-room, with a solid leather three-piece suite, dining table and chairs, an ample sideboard and the wireless, that real luxury, in pride of place. All year round this is where life existed except for one single day in the year. The sitting-room hosted a fine corduroy suite camouflaged in chintz covers, a writing table, the odd hard chair and side table as well as Mother's pride and joy, her upright Loeb piano and a stool packed to overflowing with sheet music. *Red Sails in the Sunset* and *There is a Green Hill Far Away* surge now into my mind as I hear again Mother's pleasant contralto voice. With almost tearful emotion the strains of that mystical *Green Hill Far Away* holds so many memories and was eventually my salute to her on her way to heaven many years later.

A rather fine pseudo-Indian carpet set off this room to perfection conveying a sense of sophisticated living. The room, holly-decked with a bright cheery fire and Christmas-tree, came to life for one day in the year and the memory of it still sends shivers of nostalgia down my spine. For a couple of weeks beforehand I used to creep into this room and peer down the side of the piano to where the parcels from my aunts would be concealed leaving me with a delicious sense of anticipation. Christmas lunch was always memorable and in the afternoon I would lie in front of this sitting-room fire lost in my own wonderland of toy-town make-believe.

Our sitting-room very occasionally came back into use at other times and you could always tell the importance of the company if Mother ushered guests into this, her inner sanctum. That the house now looks much smaller – the lawn tiny, the leaded windows all replaced apart from one next the front door and now with a back door where the wash-house window used to be, has robbed my old home of much of its enthralment. But above the front door, my old bedroom window looks exactly as it did those seventy years ago when my whole life seemed enshrined in its unforgettable outlook. Life, before going to school, has left me with a sense of endless summer days spent round the lake catching bandy minnows with Alfie Dawson and my mother, or going up the Tanar to have picnics and throwing countless stones into the crystal clear water. However, nothing had prepared me for the cultural shock of life in a rural school, among a tough breed of children such as I had never imagined existed.

The Innocent Years

Around the Lake Catching Bandies.
Alfie & I enjoying carefree days.

On the banks of the Tanar at Eitnach.
Throwing Stones with Aunty Belle and Mother.

Chapter 3
Glen Tanar School

Glen Tanar Public School was about two and a half miles from our house, but over the hill into the main valley of the river Dee. On a spring morning in 1935, my mother accompanied me, along with the head gardener's daughter, Nessie Urquhart, who was also going to school for the first time. The route lay along the main road for half a mile as far as Matane, before climbing up through a birch wood, which was known as the Piggery, for obvious reasons. Then out on to the unsurfaced High Road, which led over the Belrorie hill and down the Fir Mounth Pass into the Dee valley, to a lovely granite-built school with its imposing fountain on the side of the South Deeside Road.

This route was full of history, as it was supposed that the English invaders under Edward I of England had come this way during the invasion of Scotland in the years 1290 and 1303; while in 1645 the army of Montrose had also used this route. To record this event, a stone had been erected at the head of the Fir Mounth by the previous owner of the estate, Sir Cunliffe Brooks. It has to be said that some historians have come to doubt that this was the actual line of march. About fifty yards further on was the Snake's Well, with a stone inscription *"The worm of the still is the deadliest snake on the hill"*. This intrigued us as children as we always anticipated finding real snakes crawling around there; but the inscription obviously refers to the illicit distilling of alcohol, as practised by so many in these parts in the past.

Glen Tanar was a two-teacher school where Miss Pirie was the infant mistress and the head teacher or dominie, Mr Gauld, was in another room teaching the older pupils up to age fourteen. I remember being very self-conscious because of my mother's presence, as all the other children had no accompanying adult and I told her very firmly not to come back for me in the afternoon. The first day inside school is unclear, but the youngest pupils got out early, probably about 3.15pm, as I remember Nessie and myself running off for home on our own.

On reaching the top of the Fir Mounth road, a little Cairn terrier came dashing through the trees towards us and stood barking ferociously at us from the top of a bank. These terriers were used by the gamekeepers to flush foxes out of their dens and were frightening little beasts. On the estate, no employee had dogs, other than those on the farm or for shooting, so we had no experience in dealing with them. Nessie and I were terrified. So, the only way to get past was by climbing into the plantation on the other side of the road and creeping up the fence-side. I remember the plantation was dense and making progress was not only difficult, but also painful - it seemed like hours before we got far enough away to come out and scamper off home. I can still relive the trauma of that episode today: the danger was really non-existent, but in our tiny minds we felt real terror.

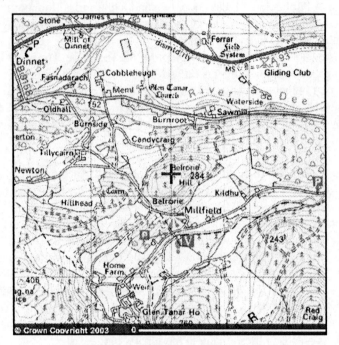

The Route to Glen Tanar School.

Glen Tanar House - up left of Belrorie Hill - down to Meml, site of the old school on the South Deeside Road.

Reproduced by kind permission of Ordnance Survey©
Crown Copyright NC/2003/22323

Glen Tanar School is so full of memories both good and bad. Sir Cunliffe Brooks, who initially owned Glen Tanar estate, built the school around the time of Queen Victoria's jubilee, before 1900. Some landowners at this time were very conscious of their duty to the community and Brooks was to build solid granite houses for employees and improved many farm buildings for his tenant farmers. The interior of the two classrooms had all the well-known sayings of Victorian times engraved into the wooden partition doors between the two rooms and also around the granite sills of the fireplaces.

A resumé of these sayings is worth recalling, as they so typify the work ethic of those far-off days. *"A stitch in time saves nine;" "Spare the rod and spoil the child;" "Work today, you may be hindered tomorrow;" "What is worth doing at all is worth doing well;" "Sloth makes all things difficult; Industry makes all things easy;" "Well begun is half done;" "A place for everything and everything in its place;" "Evil is wrought by want of thought, as much as evil by intent;" "As the twig is bent, so is the tree inclined;" "In the street of the by-and-by, you arrive at the house of never;" "For all the blessed souls in heaven, are both Forgivers and Forgiven;" "Order is heaven's first law."*

GlenTanar School and Queen Victoria's Jubilee Fountain.

With these words engraved on our young minds is it little wonder that I still seem driven by so many of those Victorian directives today? The culture of the whole school was also still strict Victorian, with the strap much in evidence; a ruler across the fingers at any moment and a cuff round the ear not infrequent. I suffered from three drawbacks in this setting - one was being left-handed, another, though not recognised until years later, partial red and total green colour-blindness and, of course, my foreign name.

We used slates with slate pencils for writing and from the very beginning the ruler across my fingers was a painful reminder that life was about being right-handed. Knitting and raffia work also totally undermined my confidence, as I appeared to be unable to differentiate between the reds, greens and browns to Miss Pirie's total exasperation. The confidence-sapping realisation that you are unable to do what seems so easy to your peers must have shaken me to my foundations. My mother was well aware of her own father's colour-blindness but insisted that I was merely unable to attach the correct names to the perceived colours.

From our present-day perspective, it seems unforgivable that Miss Pirie or my mother should have ignored the obvious symptoms of this condition. However, catty's tails presented me with no problems and was one of my delights. Using an old thread reel with four nails in the top, we intertwined wool around the nails, so producing a long rope of wool with which we then went on to make dinner mats etc.

Victorian Values Imprinted on Young Minds.

Miss Pirie, the infant teacher, was a total tyrant in my eyes, yet in retrospect she had all our interests at heart. My name singled me out from the start, not only among my fellows, but also with the adults. "His name is Pierre not Peer". Children are cruel and none more so than rural Aberdeenshire kids from backgrounds of estate workers, farm servants and tenant farmers. Froggy Fouin was a mild nickname, but still made me very sensitive, not to be seen as any weaker and not to be thought a mummy's boy. Coming from a relatively sophisticated home, I was very aware of how basic were the backgrounds of many of those around me. But at that age the need to conform and not stick out like a sore thumb, was essential for a quiet life.

Sadly, from being a rather cocky confident lad, my travails rapidly began to make me doubt myself and this has tended to persist over the years. I am sure some of this may be hereditary, but I feel quite convinced that many of my uncertainties throughout adult life have been aggravated by those early unsettling experiences. Children are very conscious of any aspect that makes one person stand out from the rest and this is particularly true of appearance and clothing. These were extremely poor times when people tended to have large families, so clothes were basic and handed down from one child to the next. Being an only child, of elderly parents, I was always properly dressed. My wearing smart clothes among a bunch of boys in odd assorted jerseys and jackets made me very conscious of the need to conform. Similarly, footwear among the boys was without exception ' tackety beets'. These were heavy-duty boots, heavily studded on the sole and they mirrored the adult footwear, needed in farming and other countryside work. I started school with the equivalent in black boots to my *'Little Dukes'* shoes - very posh. But within weeks I was champing at the bit to get a pair of proper "beets". I remember selecting the heaviest toughest boots I could get from Mosie Gordon's shoe shop in Aboyne and placing them on a chair by my bedside, so that I might experience the thrill of ownership from my first waking moment. I still recall how heavy they were and I took quite a time to get used to dragging these boots two and a half miles to school and back every day - but it was all so satisfying to be as tough as the rest.

If I had all too readily spurned my fancy *'Little Dukes'* footwear as being too sophisticated for this school, the same did not apply to my navy-blue trench coat. Bought at Esslemont & McIntosh, Union Street, Aberdeen, it had a quality gaberdine finish, making it my pride and joy. Over the years, as I grew taller, there were regular expeditions to E & M's to purchase ever-larger coats. The introduction of clothing coupons together with wartime deprivation put a stop to these visits. Nevertheless, I was being trained at an early age to appreciate only the best. However, expensive tastes can have their drawbacks when finances are stretched.

My mother detested the accepted boys' hairstyle, which often consisted of almost shaven heads with a tuft of hair left on the front. So Doshie McPetrie, the local Aboyne hairdresser, had always to give me a shaped cut and none of that two-minute crop, which was the norm. I never fancied this shaven headed appearance; yet, oddly enough, nowadays if I let my hair grow too long I feel uncomfortable; not that I have to worry too much now!

Bullying was a daily affair, and keeping out of trouble was a full-time preoccupation. I was partially shielded in that the factor's son, Douglas Young, came to school a year behind me and at once became the butt of the bullyboys. The factor on an estate is the laird's man - the person who is seen to be always snooping and is the person who hires and fires. To say he is hated, probably exaggerates somewhat, but children quickly picked up the vibes from home conversations that he was not very popular and poor Doug suffered the consequences. Carrot-haired, he just attracted trouble, with the big boys egging on the little ones to give him a hiding. Thus, like a coward, I could keep a low profile. Doug went on to the Aberdeen Grammar School, the year behind me.

But, for a long time he was left with a tic, that nervous twitching of the eyes, possibly a legacy from those difficult early days.

My early buddies at school were John Strang, a son of the head gamekeeper and Jimmy Hepburn, a son of the keeper at Hillhead whose dog had so terrified me on that first day at school. We were known by our teacher as Peter, James and John after the three disciples; but that is where any possible likeness ends. My two associates came from backgrounds of somewhat bleak houses, tough parents and basic living, which made my home seem a haven of cushiness. I shared friendship with them, but with many of my school fellows their view of life was so much at variance with mine, that I look back and wonder at the level of toughness and callousness which existed in those communities.

1936 - Glen Tanar Public School.
Miss Kate Pirie's Classroom.

Back Row	Far right -Doug Espie, Self next with Jimmy Hepburn on my right wearing the class medal.
Second Row	Nessie Urquhart third from right with John Strang on far left.
Third Row	Mary Brand fourth from right with medal & making herself prominent. Her young sister Londie is first on the right.
Front Row	Alfie Dawson second from right with Willie Archibald third from right in the middle.

Cruelty to other children, animals and birds was the norm. While setting fire to hedgerows or smashing anything breakable seemed standard behaviour. The pranks of children are universal, but I always felt that Glen Tanar School had a maliciousness that tested the limits of my tolerance. Some examples still come to mind, such as baiting fishhooks with bread in order to catch the seagulls on the end of a line. The smashing of all bird's eggs was small beer compared with a habit which the big boys had of tormenting the little boys by burning the backs of their hands with the sun's rays, using small magnifying glasses. We lived in terror of the older boys raiding our playground and I made a point of hardly ever using the toilets, as they were often liable to turn the hoses on us or lock us in. There is little doubt that my precious child background had not prepared me too well for this particular school. At the same time I feel it did me no end of good to be toughened up to face the future, which would never again seem so hard by comparison.

Years later, when reading the history of the North-east and the lives of the workers from the early eighteen hundreds, I was made more fully aware of the harshness of the times. Glen Tanar School left me with a feeling not that far away from this period. It reminded me of the 'feein' of the farm servants to work for peanuts for the farmers; the associated drunken times when they escaped from the drudgery at week-ends; and the tales of up to a hundred men in the Tarland district in 1840, fighting pitched battles for no good reason.

The thought of school meals still brings a wave of nausea over me, as we were fed on hare soup - the hares provided by the estate, thick potato soup and the most horrible fatty black mince imaginable. The dining room was a barren place containing long forms and bare well-scrubbed tables at which we sat to eat our meals. The soup was cooked in big boilers similar to those my mother used for washing clothes. The one redeeming factor was that we were allowed to toast our bread in front of the boiler fires - this was a real treat. After a time my stomach just refused to accept the food and my mother took to giving me a "piece" to school instead. I can still see me sitting outside the dining hall, eating my lunch and memories of her lovely pork and egg pies are still vividly with me.

Were there any good features then about those earliest school days? Yes, I believe there were and I believe the educational grounding was fairly good. I seemed to be mostly first or second in class, but I hated mental arithmetic and dreaded the days, when the class was taken out to the front while Miss Pirie fired figures at us, moving us up or down the line, depending on our answers. Looking back, this was a time when my self-confidence was rapidly ebbing away and I hated the pressure which nimbler minds seemed to take in their stride. I was also developing a trait that has at times unsettled me throughout life, in that I hated to lose face among my peers. I did not consider myself clever, but I never liked to appear more stupid than I felt. This is well remembered when the local inspector of schools, old Dominie Walker, made his regular visit, with us all standing out on the floor, doing mental arithmetic. I had been absent from school the previous day and you automatically went to the bottom of the class on your return. Thus when Mr Walker came in, there was I, isolated at the foot of the line. He came over to speak to us and, with a sad shake of his head, told me I would have to buck up. I was left feeling humiliated. Years later he had his impression of me further confirmed when he came to Aboyne School. I was in the qualifying class when he came up unexpectedly behind my chair and asked me out of the blue "What is ten times nothing?" Panic-stricken, I blurted out – "Ten," to the horror of all and sundry, but particularly my poor teacher, who felt totally let down by this idiot child.

There is no doubt that Dominie Walker held some sort of spell over me. He died long before I could ever prove my real worth to him - such is life! My other lasting memory of him relates to his bicycle which he rode regularly between Aboyne and Dalwhing where he lived. When we were cycling home from Aboyne School, we would often come across him walking his bike up the Craigendinnie Brae. Reaching the top of the hill he would mount the bike using a back step which he hopped onto and then swung his leg over the bar. This was probably a regular feature of old bicycles, but to us it looked hilariously antiquated. Yet the image remains with me, as fresh today, as it did all those sixty years ago.

Magical Memories - Wet clothes drying,
then Lessons round this Fire.

Miss Pirie had a cupboard behind her desk, which was to us an Aladdin's cave, holding all sorts of interesting objects. She also had a small library there and, if we did something outstanding, she would present us with a book. I gained one or two, and these seemed almost magical to me and left me ever since with a love of books, no matter what their content. Prizes were presented for all subjects and I still come across some in the loft. Reading, writing, arithmetic, bible studies and, of course, good attendance, received prizes at the year-end. The attendance prize always seemed within reach and I would not miss school under any circumstances. However, I do remember going half way up the Piggery road to the little gate and convincing myself that I didn't feel well and turning back home: perhaps it was a mental arithmetic day. That stands out as the only day in my life that I shirked the school, so I must have really felt under pressure.

The only time we entered the dominie's room was for our singing lesson once a week, gathered around Miss Pirie at the piano. *'Bobby Shafto's gone to sea - he'll come back and marry me'* - whereupon I caught Mary Brand's eye ogling me from across the piano. All the class seemed to see it, and week after week, all the grinning faces turned towards me, as they boisterously bawled out those dreaded lines while Mary smirked fiendishly in triumph. Cowering down into myself, while mouthing the lines without a note being uttered, I felt totally desolate. Bad enough to be Froggy Fouin in the playground, but this foppish Bobby Shafto in class was almost too much for one poor innocent to bear. So, gradually, the outer skin thickens and with my mother's constant adage *"Sticks and stones will break your bones but names will never hurt you,"* ringing in my ears, I somehow survived. But it was a very stressful time for me, not yet knowing how to fight back.

Positive memories relate to walking to school and especially the walk home after the bell rang for the end of the day. The sense of release was wonderful as we ran up the Fir Mounth road, perhaps stopping for a moment to jump into a field and select a small juicy turnip; or climb a nearby gean tree to feed on the wild cherries. The various colours of the hedgerow flowers and the brilliant yellow of the broom seemed to fill our senses. On winter days, as the evenings drew down, we scurried up the road much more quickly, especially with the stags roaring in the forest, seeming in the gloaming to be almost on top of us. Later, at Aboyne School, I was to feel even more anxious and isolated at such times. When cycling home on my own, with the eeriness all around me, or coming upon an old tramp or gypsy plodding along in the gloom, I felt a sudden racing of the heart and a need to pedal ever faster.

We walked in all weathers, and failure to get there for reasons, other than illness, was proof that you were a wimp. The winters were often very severe and trudging through the snowdrifts was exhausting, but thrilling. To reach school and take off our wet clothes and boots to set them before the fire in the schoolroom and then cluster round the fire to do our lessons, produced a magical feeling of wellbeing. Then watching the snow falling silently and stealthily outside our big windows for hours, until we were let out early, gave me a wonderful sense of anticipation and excitement. I cannot remember any of our parents ever coming to the school to meet us no matter how bad the weather. This was just not done. One snowy day when we were halfway to school, big Archie Phillips picked me up and threw me over a wall into a deep snowdrift, leaving me to trail in behind the others. I remember being very sorry for myself and not very pleased with my so-called friends, who seemed to think that it was a big joke. Such experiences would have been common in a big family, whereas I was probably suffering from the 'only-child syndrome.'

Another memory from this period of my life is of us coming down the brae to the school and seeing Miss Kate Pirie, accompanied by three or four schoolgirls, coming along the main road from Dinnet, where she lodged. The mere sight of her carrying her little case and walking so purposefully filled me with apprehension. No boy would be seen walking near her, as this would mark him out as a teacher's pet forever after. Kate Pirr, as we called her, was also a fine wielder of the strap or tawse, as it was known in Scottish schools and she did not hesitate to use it quite freely. I have no lasting memory of being smacked

La Famille Fouin.

A family group that says so much about those early days. Youngster with buck teeth, while Mother is decked out in her tailored suit and Father holds the inevitable cigar.

with it, but I can still feel the ruler across my left knuckles, as the slate pencil strayed once again into my dominant hand. Other recollected events were of hanging on to the little wicker gate at the side of the school to watch a motor rally pass by, while being pushed and jostled by my excited schoolmates. In our early years, games in the playground were girlie-games such as 'Ring a Ring o'Roses' and 'Hide and Seek'. Later, came more rumbustious sports such as 'Statues,' where the object of the game was to capture jackets laid out along a back line. If, however, you were caught crossing into opposition territory, you had to stand still until one of your side could cross and free you by touching. 'Horsies,' which was the game of knocking each other off the backs of our mates, was also very popular; but kicking a football was for the big boys' playground only.

The diving, wheeling pee-wits out on the moor, the raucous oyster-catchers and gulls cavorting around the playground, or the burbling notes of the skylark as he rose higher and higher into a cloudless sky, recall this as a very special time in my life. Acute sadness, even fear for one moment, to be replaced by the ecstasy of just being alive in this wonderful setting. The morning hand bell would summon us back into Victoriana: but in the afternoon the same bell released us once more into the real world, when we would dash joyously homeward to the smells of delicious food and a haven from the harshness of this new life. At the end of the summer term came one of the highlights of the school year. This took the form of the display of model boats on a small pond near the school. The big boys in the Dominie's classroom had made these boats throughout the year and to our eyes they were things to be marvelled at; such was the professionalism produced under the eagle eye of Mr Gauld. I always looked on their artistic achievements as something unsurpassed in any of the other schools that I subsequently attended.

When I was five, my parents bought me a brand new Hercules bicycle, and I struggled for months, trying to learn to ride it. It had very narrow handlebars and was fitted with a carrier at the back. At first my father had the joiner make wooden blocks to fit on the pedals, as I had difficulty sitting in the saddle and reaching the pedals properly. I tried to master this machine for what seemed like an age and I am sure it was put away for a period, because I had become so disheartened. Then one day, pottering about on my own, up and down the Stable Yard, sitting on the carrier instead of the saddle, I was suddenly conscious that I had mastered it. The pleasure and relief was immense and I became a complete cycling fanatic. So it was that in my final summer term at school, my parents allowed me to cycle to school. Going over the hill was not really feasible, so I had to cycle half way to Aboyne, round the Tower of Ess and back up the South Deeside Road to the school, which was probably nearly four miles. My classmate, Nessie Urquhart, and her elder brother, Martin, had been doing it for a term before me, so I joined up with them feeling grown up at last.

Aged eight, the world of sex had never entered my consciousness, but this cycling to school was about to make me discover that life held some unsettling questions that no adult was prepared to answer. Just as I failed to uncover the truth about Father Xmas for a long time, so I found that I was not nearly so well-informed as many of my colleagues, whose ideas on perpetuating the species were crude and rudimentary, but did show glimmers of insight. Asking why Martin aged ten and a girl went off behind the bushes when cycling on our way home, I was told they were away having a f***. Totally bewildered, I related the tale to my mother with the explicit terminology, whereupon she dropped everything and took off like a scalded cat to confront Martin's parents. I never did learn the outcome of her visit, nor did I get any explanation; but thereafter, I gathered that girls and boys were made differently for some unknown and embarrassing purpose. Not very long afterwards, Mr Urquhart and the family left the Glen. So Nessie moved out of my life and I can only hope it was nothing I said that caused this sad parting.

Even before this episode, my parents had obviously become rather unhappy with the school. Whether this was due to my attitude to it, or to a nagging doubt that the education was below par, I cannot remember, but they had approached the headmaster of Aboyne Higher Grade Public School, to see if I could transfer to the village school. I sense that there was a lot of ill-feeling generated over the move, probably because it was felt that my parents thought Glen Tanar School was not good enough for their little boy. So it was that on a lovely summer's day in June 1937 my father picked me up from school in our brand new Austin for us to go off to France on holiday. Turning my back on all those memories and never to return again to the Glen school was a turning-point in my life - never to be regretted.

A postscript to those far off days came about in the mid 1970's. Towing our caravan, I went down memory lane, taking the family up to the old school and parking in the big boy's playground. The school had been closed down a few years beforehand, but the caretaker allowed me in to look around. The years fell away as I sat at one of the little desks and looked again at all the old adages around the doors and fireplaces. Then, to my amazement, in the little teacher's side room, there in a desk were all the attendance registers and progress reports of Miss Pirie's pupils over the years. Unbelievably, my own name came jumping out of the pages at me, with a record in the margin, in Miss Pirie's own handwriting – "graduated Aberdeen University MB ChB 1954." To say that it brought a lump to my throat would be no exaggeration. The woman whom I had feared in my infancy, had still followed my career, as if saying, "there goes one of my boys doing really well". Away from those days of near terror, I have come to see that dedicated spinster in a totally different light. I trust that, having retired to Macduff, her latter years were spent with some of the pleasanter memories, which I too have now come to appreciate far more.

Aboyne School was on the horizon; but before going down that road of never-ending study, let us pause to look at those early days on the estate and enjoy the leisure pursuits that were available to us.

Chapter 4
A Children's Paradise

The era of going to the school over the hill changed everything about my life in the Glen. Gone were the days of playing around the doors in familiar surroundings. The discipline of school life with the new uncertainties within the schoolroom, out in the playground or on the way home, had brought about a total change in perspective. My widened horizon now took in boys and their families who had been outwith my ken earlier on.

The Stable Yard community of neighbouring playmates was still central to my world, but now other children started to encroach. Gradually the Doric dialect loomed up as a bone of contention within our household as Glen Tanar School had hugely expanded my playground vocabulary. My mother had long since lost any trace of her Geordie roots, while my father spoke a French accented Standard English. To talk other than correctly in our household was not only seen as slipshod, but as distinctly vulgar. No one with any breeding spoke the harsh foreign tongue of the North-east, which, in any case, my mother never did come to understand. Being reprimanded very severely by her, I developed a dual personality of talking correctly at home, but outside, vying with my school chums to let them see I was no different from them. Moreover, Miss Pirie would never tolerate slovenly language in class. Thus I came to associate the Doric with being uncouth. So are changes in society brought about, and if voices later on had not

West Lodge, Glen Tanar 2003.
Other than the cars, unchanged since 1934.

been raised to challenge this view, our native dialect would by now be even more eroded. It has seemed to me over the years that Deeside Doric is much more restricted and far less broad than that of the Vale of Alford and further North. Thus the problem of translating Charles Murray's Hamewith at school needed considerable thought and perseverance. I have come to treasure my dialect and to enthusiastically support its retention, while still being that dual person when donning my professional hat and talking 'properly.' Up at the West Lodge lived the Downies with their two children Elsie and Bill. Bill was only a baby but Elsie, who was probably about nine years old, belonged to the older group who seemed very grown-up to us. West Lodge bordered on the edge of the forest and it was up amongst the trees that Elsie had her housie and shop. All sorts of household utensils and bottles were in her domain and she ran it like a little old lady, very fussy and ordered. We were intrigued with this new experience and played for hours without realising that such domestic make-believe was seen by our more macho comrades as being only for cissies. Hours were spent brewing up medicines and other concoctions and putting them into bottles and jars, all to be labelled. Rowans and elderberries etc were faithfully collected and brewed up on an imaginary fire before being bottled to sell in the wee shop. Sadly, this make-believe period came to an end all too soon when Mr Downie moved away to another job nearer town.

My buddy from school, the John of the three disciples, lived up the kennel brae where his father was head keeper. In my eyes the Strangs were a very large and impressive family. The two girls, Margaret and Dolly were older, followed by Donald, who died aged nine in a diphtheria and measles epidemic. Two years ahead of me came Peter and then John, while the youngest Alastair was still a tiny babe. Mrs Strang who, to me, was a hugely formidable lady dominated the Strang's household. Their house had none of the apparent refinement my mother had brought to our home and to me it seemed a cold and austere place. Mrs Strang, wearing her dark working clothes, big boots and with a bonnet on her head, always seemed to be hacking huge sticks whenever I was around. This was probably an exaggerated impression but I was always in awe of her, although she was kind to me in her own undemonstrative way. Staying for tea, I was introduced to Golden Syrup for the very first time and I insisted having it at home; but I'm afraid it was not greatly to my mother's taste. The Strang boys played their games with a much more tough and daring approach. Climbing trees, swinging through the branches or scaling various buildings was all done without fear; while showing any apprehension was to lead to your being branded as a feartie. The Strang's genes however were of the right type, as all, in their own way, prospered, especially Alastair, to whom I shall return later on.

A traditional Norwegian stable was erected by the laird in the field across from the kennels and was a popular place for us to play in. The barn above the stable had a door facing out to the road, which was convenient for filling it with hay directly off a cart. This door was probably ten feet up and one day Peter Strang caught us up there and dared us all to jump from the door across the road and on to the bank on the other side. This was no mean feat. For, in order to avoid injuring ourselves by landing heavily on the hard road, a running jump was required to launch us into space. Under the threat of being hit by flying stones, one by one we plucked up courage to make the leap. It was all very stressful, but no doubt another toughening experience for life ahead. This lovely barn was to meet its fate a few years later when Charlie Garland, the valet's young son, together with a pal were playing there and somehow set the hay alight. They escaped unharmed, but the showpiece barn and stable were reduced to ashes. There is no record of how the laird reacted to the event and only Charlie, now in Australia, knows the answer.

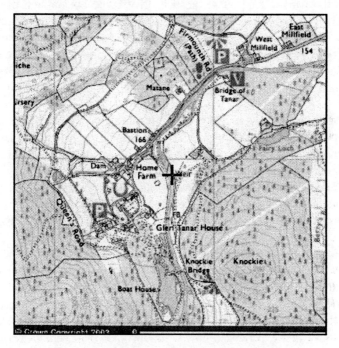

Mansion House, Lake and Policies with
Golf Course and St. Lesmo's Chapel to right
of Cross at "Weir".

Reproduced by kind permission of Ordnance Survey©
Crown Copyright NC/2003/22323

It is difficult to judge whether or not it was the influence of this daredevil element but, from now on, climbing in the Stable Yard came to be a major pastime for Bill, Alfie and me. Every roof in the immediate area was climbed and we took a delight in going right round the Stable Yard along the peaks of the roofs, descending only to cross the odd gap. Nothing daunted, we took on the challenge of every possible roof in the district, including the farm, where we made first ascents all over the place. Having conquered the buildings, we turned to the trees; but unless there was a bird's nest we wished to raid, we were not so enthralled with this hobby. Going straight up gave us less of a thrill, whereas going up and sideways was far more satisfying. Looking back on those days, I am amazed that our parents never interfered or wanted to know what we were doing. They appeared to accept that boys are boys and trusted that we would come to little harm. Later, as a parent I could never have accepted this so easily, as I was so aware that the chance of serious injury was never far away. The sawmill was another of our haunts, whether crawling into the engine shed through the narrow gap where the belt drive came out through the wall, or playing on the heavy bogies on rails which were used to move the timber around the yard. The two bogies gave us probably scores of hours of pleasure when, having been pushed up to the top of the hill, they could gather quite a turn of speed, hurtling down past the creosote tank to the far end, a distance of probably four hundred yards. There is little doubt that this was highly dangerous.

Both bogies going down together, or one coming up while another came down, always produced the possibility of a nasty accident, especially when they jumped the points. As with so many situations where an accident is waiting to happen, we escaped without a scratch, although the powers that be tried to stop us after a time. The pounding of the wheels could be heard from a long way off; so latterly we would try to arrange that our escapades coincided with a time when our elders were less likely to be around. Thus this daredevil hobby persisted for many years.

Another of our favourite haunts was in the joiner's shed with its shute, down which the boards were sent to the joiner at his sawing and planing machines. This was little more than the slides which children play on in the parks today, but for us when very young, it was a place to spend hours, as well as clambering about among the rafters. It was at the back of this shed, where the keepers kept their ferrets, that I first experienced how young people could perhaps come off the straight and narrow. Some of the older boys in the district seemed to hang about this spot at times and one evening I was enticed along to one of their illicit meetings. It was getting dark and they had built a little lean-to and had brought a small paraffin lamp, built a fire and were of all things - smoking. I felt very vulnerable and really wanted to dash off home, as this was something way over my head at age six or seven. Fires were something that nobody lit for fear of risking their parents' jobs and here was I caught up in this heinous crime. Not wanting to lose face, I just stuck it out until I could honourably withdraw. Nothing occurred which involved any real law breaking, but I felt like a criminal and, young as I was, realised how difficult it could be for children to break out of this gang culture if once enticed into it. Thankfully the boys moved off our patch and never again was I called on to make the decision of whether to stay or flee. Over the wall from our house a small burn appeared from its subterranean meandering and was the scene of much activity over the years. Making dams, then making harbours and excavating out more and more earth to get ever-greater development, was a supreme challenge for our imaginations. The next spate, of course, washed everything away so we had to start all over again with now more innovative ideas, only to see them disappear in a boiling torrent of peaty water. Looking at this little dribble of water again a few months ago, I am amazed that my memory of this substantial burn has been so reduced by the march of time.

The various workings of the estate could always be guaranteed to attract us to see what was happening. The game larder was always of interest, whether it was to watch the deer being strung up to be skinned, or gathering round as literally hundreds of grouse were being unloaded from the game cart. A highlight of our year was when the student beaters were around for the grouse season and the area throbbed to all these strangers. Glen Tanar keepers seemed to be in abundance in those days, all kitted out in their special green cloth suits, with dogs leaping about in every direction. This very special atmosphere has lived on with me ever since and brings back many interesting smells and visions. In later years, probably into the '40's, the gamekeepers were supplied with suits made of the Glen Tanar tartan which, for me, somehow detracted from the previous atmosphere of timelessness.

The joiner's shop where Alfie's father ruled is a vivid memory. The smell of new-sawn timber and the marvellous ability of expert craftsmen to produce works of art in no time at all have always made me very envious of the talented carpenter. From *The Glen Tanar Estate Papers* in the Aberdeen Central Library comes the following quotation: "Such being the way of life for hundreds of years, the people of Glen Tanar became known, to a proverb, for their skill as craftsmen in timber working.

"Saw an inch and rive a span,
Is the mark of a good Glen Tanar man"

My little pedal car obviously made others envious of me with the result that Mr Dawson set about levelling the score by producing a lovely little model for Alfie. As a result we were able to play happily together without my being harassed all the time for a 'shottie'.

Always of great interest to us were the comings and goings of all the different vans, baker, grocer, fishman and butcher whose visits made it unnecessary for anyone to go near a shop for supplies in those days. French's big provisions van from Logie Coldstone and Daisy Williams' dad driving the baker's van from Aboyne are well remembered, especially as I got my pet rabbit from Mr Williams. The estate had a number of gates which were always a nuisance for the vanmen to open and we quickly learnt which ones would give us a halfpenny for letting them through without stopping. Vying with one another to reach the gate first was always a serious game, especially when playing up at the Strangs, as John always knew the value of a halfpenny. The memory of postie Souter still remains with me as he came to the estate for years and we clamoured around him for any letters. He used to have to cycle all the six miles further to Eitnach on at least two days in the week just to deliver the odd letter to one house, which seems so ridiculous to us now in this modern age.

In those early days there grew, just outside our garden gate, on top of a grassy bank, a huge fir tree which literally towered over the house. When I was about five it was deemed necessary to have it cut down as it was becoming a hazard, as well as cutting out the natural light from our small windows. It proved to be a tricky job, but eventually it was dropped away from our house into undergrowth. Often after that I would wake at night with the vision of that tree dropping down on top of me. Round about the same time a new flagpole was erected on a site about a hundred yards beyond that of the old tree and it rose up to a hundred feet. When the laird was in residence Mr Silver would bring the flag down from the recreation hall and hoist it before eight o'clock every morning and then take it down at sunset. I feel the flag was probably the St Andrew's cross, but I can also see another yellow flag in my mind, with a stag on it, which must have been Glentanar's own ensign. This was always flown on special occasions. Roused from sleep in the morning, I can still hear the tell-tale metal click of that little wicker gate, as Mr Silver punctually warned me that it was time to get up and face another new day.

The Recreation Hall and our
beloved football pitch.

A Children's Paradise

Early morning was also the time for John the Piper to go through the little wicker gate down to play the pipes around the mansion house at about seven-thirty, whenever the laird was in residence. This was a routine that never seemed to vary, until one-day poor John decided to blow his brains out and that finished the piping for good.

The real centre of our universe in the Glen, however, was the ample strip of grass in front of the recreation hall. I believe I must have played there for hundreds, if not thousands of hours from early childhood until the 1940's. Football was the most important game, but over the years we played hockey, shinty and cricket, so that at times the pitch was reduced to mud, especially around the goals. From time-to-time goalposts were replaced with improvements and repaired after having been vandalised by other marauding kids. Usually, it was my football that was used for our games. In later years, medical colleagues sometimes used the analogy of the selfish child going off home with his ball to describe difficult big-headed doctors. I know exactly what they meant. Alfie kept his pet rabbit in a hutch at the side of the grass and I would let my rabbit come from behind our house to run up there and exercise on most days. Blackie knew exactly where he was going whenever I opened the hutch door. Off he went up the little road, up the steps and on to the grass, all of three hundred yards from his home. Getting him back was of course a different story; but owning a pet was a wonderful experience and instilled in me a love and attachment to our one cat and to the many wonderful Labrador retrievers that I owned during later years.

The view from my bedroom window, and a recurring theme in these memoirs, will remain with me forever - out across to the flagpole, with the mansion house roofs peeping above the tall rhododendron bushes and the Knockie Hill forming a fitting background beyond. In later years, probably at the end of the Second World War (1939 -1946), the Knockie was being thinned of its dense brushwood. One night I was awakened to find my bedroom irradiated by a strange light. Looking out, I was amazed to see the whole hillside enveloped in a mass of flames. Then for the only time in my life, I was permitted to press that tempting red button on the hooter outside to summon the fire brigade. That window also brings back the memory of my incarceration in bed for over a week with German Measles. It was springtime and Alfie, Willie and I had been across to the Tanar River, assembling individual rafts from lengths of logs left lying by the foresters. We had nearly finished when I was struck down with measles. Dismayed and frustrated, I watched from my bedroom window as the other two went off on a lovely warm day to launch their rafts, leaving me stuck in bed. There was some consolation on their return however, when it turned out that we had underestimated the number of logs required to support our weights with the result that, on launching their craft, both bold heroes got rather wet.

One or two characters from those far off days still stand out. Mr Gowans was an early chauffeur and I well recall being taken to Aboyne in the old square-type Rolls Royce on a snowy day with the big car slithering all over the road and feeling sure my end was near. Jock Begrie used to drive the Albion bus on the regular trip to Aboyne as well as transporting all the shooters and beaters during the grouse season. In those early days Aboyne could be reached by any of three ways, namely on foot, by bicycle or on the Albion bus on a Saturday. As my parents never cycled anywhere, the bus was their main means of escaping the Glen. However, Mr Gowans would occasionally drive them in the Rolls: and when neither of these options was available, I remember sometimes being forced to walk all the way to Aboyne and back. In 1937 my father bought a car; moreover, I was by this time becoming an experienced and enthusiastic cyclist. Consequently we, as a family, felt liberated and revelled in our new-found independence. Mr Dawson next door also bought a second-hand Singer but the Archibalds never came to own their own motorised transport. Mr Archibald however fitted a solid large leather seat to the bar of his bicycle and over the years used to carry one of his four children regularly to Aboyne on a Saturday, until each became old enough to ride his own bicycle.

The Dawson Family - Mother, Evelyn & Alfie,
proud owners of a 1934 Singer.

Mr Peter Strang, the head gamekeeper, tall and thin with a marked stoop, never seemed to be far away. Also well-remembered were the keepers Charlie Milne and Willie Robertson, (father of Mrs Betty Scace in "Acknowledgements"). Willie Robertson, who was the gamekeeper up the Fungle and later at Headinch started work on the estate as an under keeper in 1903 for the princely salary of £49 a year. On Mr Strang's retirement Jock McLean took his place and was still there when I had long gone from the estate. The burly figure of Mr

A Children's Paradise

Smith the Clerk of Works was ever present to be followed in later years by Mr Duguid. But best recalled was Alec Benzie, working at his forge; the smiddy always attracting us boys like a magnet. An expression, coined I believe by the evacuees, to describe a smith's job that was very rough and very strong, was a 'Benzie weld'. Mr and Mrs Benzie had a small sideline selling sweets and cigarettes to the locals, as there were no shops nearer than Aboyne. One day I had gone to them for some small luxury and must have said something to irritate

Mr Benzie who could be very short-tempered. He took off, chasing me all the way back to the top of the 'Ca Canny' brae and I clearly remember running like the wind, being utterly terrified of this big uncouth man.

In the forestry, Willie Ewen is still fresh in my memory. Living just up the road from Glen Tanar School, he was a constant in our lives with his horse and cart. Willie was a bit glaikit, a very expressive Doric word for being a wee bit simple and soft. However, both in the woods and removing the rubbish around the Glen, he was a cheery integral part of our lives for nearly the whole of my Glen Tanar days. Later on Jock Gray, a Clerk of Works employee, refereed our football matches and I remember him well for his ambivalent attitude to my footballing prowess. When he coached the Dinnet team, I could scarcely ever touch a ball without him blowing up for a foul on the grounds that I was using my arms unfairly in elbowing opponents. Changing over to coach the Glen Tanar team, he never once blew his whistle when I fouled, which I found very baffling.

Glen Tanar House seen from the Wander Walks.
*Pond in foreground scene of confrontation
between the laird and naughty boys.*

Others of note were old Mr Ogston, who replaced Mr Silver as the hall caretaker, and George Allan, the estate electrician. Mr Allan was in charge of the electrician's powerhouse, which held all the batteries used for storing the electricity generated down on the Tanar. This storage depot was another area which intrigued us in the early days as we hung about with Mr Allan and the smell of the battery acid is still in my nostrils. Now, with power supplied via the national grid, this neat little power station, only one hundred yards from our old house, has been converted into very trim domestic accommodation.

Eitnach with the Shepherd's Hut
on the ridge to the Right.

As boys, we also frequently explored the precincts of the generator plant down on the Tanar but, as it was situated in the private policies round the Wander Walks, it was advisable to go there only when the laird was away. Miss Jean's playhouse had been built on top of the generator plant, and we never tired of peering in through the windows to see the doll's house and other toys of great interest. The water flowing from the generator formed quite a deep pool and large trout were always to be seen if one crept up very carefully and peeped over the railings. We never got round to poaching them, however, as the fish were far too wary in the clear water and the slightest movement resulted in their dashing back up the tunnel.

The footnote to this electrical experience comes from my golfing companion in retirement, Fred Masson*. As an apprentice aged nineteen around 1939, he was sent by his firm to Glen Tanar when the mansion house was still dependent on its own generated power. He remembers clearly the ordered life of those days in the Glen just before he was called up into the RAF. This small world of the North-east never seems to allow me to get away from my past but at least Fred's pawky sense of humour keeps it all almost bearable.

A Children's Paradise

Around 1940 a new gamekeeper was appointed to the lonely outpost at Eitnach six miles up the valley from our homes. As time went on he proved to be a great character and many were the tales told of Jock McHardy. His refined wife had been a ladies' maid in the past and seemed to live the life of a partial recluse as she was seldom seen by any of us. They had one child, Marigold, who would have been about the same age as me. For all the years I knew him, Jock owned an ancient car which was probably a 1934-35 Morris 8 - square and unstable looking, which Jock frequently proved it to be. Came the weekend and Jock's first stop would be the Boat Bar in Aboyne.

Over the years the tales of his drinking sessions became legendary and the times he came to grief on the lonely road home to Eitnach, late on Saturdays, filled us with much amusement. He was a true character of old - pleasant when sober while hilarious and noisy when inebriated. In later years with Marigold playing piano in a local dance band, two rather merry individuals would wend their way homeward from Dinnet and other dance venues. What was said from behind closed doors at Eitnach after these exploits never filtered down the valley, but it takes little imagination to believe that Mount Keen would have some stormy tales to tell.

Mr Duncan Ross, the head forester, was a cheery well-kent figure. In later years, Dugald Brand, father of my Bobby Shafto friend Mary Brand, who lived in *The Bungalow,* was always referred to as being a communist, although the title meant little to us at the time. Quiet Ronnie McKay, at school some years ahead of me, went to work in the Estate Office and became a part of the estate management for many years. In my mind he is associated with the large gean tree which stood close by his house and had produced wonderful big cherries which always seemed just out of our reach as we passed by on our way home from school.

One of the red-letter days in any Glen Tanar year was the opening of the gardens on a Sunday in summer. Hordes of visitors invaded our tranquil world and we all revelled in it. As small boys, we took the opportunity to steal as many tomatoes and as much fruit as we could lay our hands on safely. The yellow tomatoes were particular favourites for plundering, as they looked and tasted so different. Later, as cubs and scouts, we were drafted in to control car parking and to be on hand in the recreation hall for teas, as well as directing visitors around the grounds. Plunder was much more difficult to achieve in our uniforms, but no doubt we still managed to pluck some booty from the bushes. Mr Skene was now head gardener and he seemed to view a few stolen products as no big deal and was always the perfect gentleman.

When I return to Glen Tanar now after sixty years, I cannot help but compare the present day condition of the estate with the way it was in my childhood.

Good management, meticulous attention to detail with a plentiful supply of cheap labour is in stark contrast with what can be achieved under present day conditions. Mr Urquhart's and later Mr Skene's gardeners were out at first light to ensure that not a footprint marred the beautifully raked paths and drives around the mansion house. A sense of order of the highest degree permeated this whole micro-society and no one accepted second-best standards of workmanship. My father was exacting, not only in his own department, but also where the work of those around him was concerned. On reflection, it seems to me that every other department expected the same high standards. George Cruickshank was one of the gardeners who lived in West Lodge after the Downies left. George was to give me a telling-off once or twice over the years for stealing apples over our wall: but little did either of us think that I was to look after him and Mrs Cruickshank medically in their retirement. They were a delightful couple and never a word was ever said about stolen apples!

These musings on past times lead me to digress briefly, while I consider my attitude to the vexed question of privilege. I have always regarded the possession of privilege, through either titles or money - especially huge amounts of inherited wealth - as being essentially at odds with my belief in the inherent equality of human beings. Inherited titles and wealth, combined, in many people, with a sense of absolute superiority, exhibits a vain and shallow attitude: yet so many of the less privileged among us will today still happily accept this state of affairs, or at least pay lip service to it. It also seems to me that the twice-yearly routine of the Queen's Honours satisfies the feelings of so many who are little more than children at heart. Tiered into layers of pseudo-importance, the awards' system pays lip service to fair play by recognising some of the humble, so justifying and perpetuating the really notable awards and titles for the status-seeking rich and privileged - what a way to run a country! Chastised at times by colleagues that I would be no different in accepting such an award, I reply that 21st century British society should be mature enough not to expose me to such temptation. Few of us are free from some self-conceit not to get satisfaction from being lauded by our peers and although most seem to see the honours system as a harmless convention I remain a sceptic in this class-ridden land of ours. Awards presented from our own related organisations whether in academia, work or recreation are, I feel, totally different whereas national awards, other than for gallantry, are a vestige from the days of unashamed patronage.

It is no small wonder that the Americans stipulated in their Constitution that no foreign titles were to be accepted by anyone involved in state service. Looking around the UK today, it seems that knighthoods and peerages are doled out routinely often as a reward for financial contributions to a political party - a state of affairs, which strikes me as totally degrading. As the renowned sociologist Professor A H Halsey says, having himself turned down countless honours and titles, "No proud cat would deign to tie such noisy tin-cans to his tail". I deplore the fact that neither state nor citizenry appear to have the moral courage nor pride to throw out a custom which is a complete anachronism in this twenty-first century.

It is easy to see how all these ideas and attitudes originated and developed in me as a result of living in this tight little society. That we, as children of the Glen, had a wonderful life in our admittedly feudal environment, has always given me great satisfaction. But, at the same time, I would not wish this way of life on my children or grandchildren, as it requires real determination to break out of the mode of deferential behaviour which is at the heart of the class system.

On the one hand, there is my childhood image of the ordered structure of the Glen Tanar microcosm, with the staff at all levels working hard and conscientiously, proud of a job well done. On the other hand I cannot help comparing this picture with what I see today around me, namely, a general laxness, a result partially due to the narrowing of the gap between rich and poor. Perhaps this is the price we have to pay for the material improvements and benefits most workers now enjoy.

The early childhood days drifted past in a seemingly never-ending routine of school for five days and the carefree pleasure of the weekends, while holidays never seemed to come quickly enough. I was blissfully unaware that time was passing and that we were getting older and more senior among our fellows. Before embarking on my days at school in Aboyne, let me step back in time in order to describe to you an unusual experience, which turned out to have an unforeseen influence on me during a significant period of my life.

*My friend Fred Masson, referred to in this chapter, died of a heart attack on his eighty first birthday - the 17th April 2003, prior to these memoirs appearing. So I lose yet another wonderful companion who has brightened many a day for me in retirement with his positive outlook, scintillating repartee and above all, good fellowship.

Chapter 5
Crawfie

As an interlude, let me conjure up this vignette from my childhood. Three little girls in a donkey-cart are laughing and talking among themselves. One of these is Miss Jean, daughter of the laird, while her companions are none other than the two princesses, Elizabeth and Margaret Rose, presently on holiday at Balmoral. They, as occasional visitors to Glen Tanar, are accompanied by their governess, Miss Marion Crawford. Watching the little procession drive past are two small boys lounging casually on the Estate Office wall. I was one of those urchins and, had I been gifted with prophetic powers, and approached the lady, declaring "I am destined to look after you in your old age", I wonder what her response would have been?

Marion Crawford had come from an impoverished childhood after her father was killed in New Zealand and her mother had to return to Scotland to live in Dunfermline. Educated in Edinburgh and becoming well qualified as a teacher, she obtained a post as temporary governess to the Elgins in the early 1930's at the age of twenty-two. Lord Elgin's younger brother, James Bruce, would, by a strange twist in this involved story, come to marry Miss Jean Coats in 1950. But who could have foreseen the most unlikely course of events, which would result in one of those little estate boys on the wall becoming caught up in this web.

In 1932, Miss Crawford joined the royal household as governess to Elizabeth and Margaret, at a time when their father, the Duke of York, appeared unlikely ever to become king. However on the abdication of his brother Edward VIII, the Duke of York, somewhat against his will, became King George VI. Crawfie, as the family had now dubbed her, found herself elevated overnight to a position of greater importance, with the future Queen's upbringing and development in her hands.

Throughout my childhood and adolescence, I, along with the rest of the nation, was very aware of the Royal family and their lives were a constant source of interest to the national press and to magazines throughout the world. Women, in particular, still seemed to romanticise the Royal family and shrewd business men made sure that their interest was sustained by every means possible. The existence of Balmoral Castle on Royal Deeside as their summer residence, gave us a certain sense of ownership of our King and Queen. Equally, however, we applaud the fact that our local populace took it in their stride to allow the family their privacy to enjoy the environment as much as we did as natives.

Trog's Cartoon of the Two Princesses and their Governess.
(By kind permission of Trog)

Fine depiction of the princesses but Crawfie would have seen cheery laughter as unseemly while this exaggerated smile would have been grossly undignified.

In the late 1940's, once the princesses had grown up, Crawfie retired and married a divorcee, Major George Buthlay who, after his army service, had become a banker. He was sixteen years older than his bride. Two months later Princess Elizabeth married Prince Philip, by which time Major and Mrs Buthlay were cosily settled into their Grace and Favour house behind Kensington Palace.

Life should now have been idyllic for the thirty-eight years old retired governess; but events were about to disrupt her life forever. A furore arose in 1950 with the appearance of Crawfie's book, *The Little Princesses*, describing life with the Royal family. From our present perspective, the ensuing fuss has all the appearance of a storm in a very small teacup. For those born after this period, however, it may be helpful to outline the events leading up to this traumatic saga.

Following the end of the Second World War, Britain was to all intents and purposes bankrupt, owing massive debts to the USA. Despite this, the British Royal Family was hugely popular with the American public and a shrewd Foreign Office wondered if somehow this might be exploited to benefit our ailing economy and to stimulate trade with the US. Some bright spark came up with the idea of a book about the princesses, targeted at the vast feminine readership always eager for more details of life with the English Royalty. But who could have the insight to write such a book? Crawfie's name was raised and the Palace was approached to approve the idea in principle. There seemed to be no problem, and, although initially doubtful about the project, Crawfie agreed to do it with the help of a ghostwriter. It was further agreed that the Royal Family would vet the book before publication to ensure that it followed protocol. Crawfie was warned by the Queen to keep in the background and to keep "oyster", presumably meaning that nothing too personal was to be revealed.

Now enter the shrewd wheeler-dealers of the business world to exploit the situation to the full. An American publishing company got wind of the project and, directly involving George Buthlay, arranged for the serialisation and publication of the book in the States and drew up the necessary contract. Meanwhile, back at the Palace, Crawfie depended on her friendship with either the King's private secretary or his equerry, as her trusted go-between, to liaise with the King and Queen to ensure that all went smoothly. The book now under way, there were signs that the Queen was still having doubts and voicing her concern lest Crawfie's name became too closely associated with the book. Anticipating the possible collapse of the whole enterprise, the sharp business people were already a jump ahead. Tucked down at the foot of Crawfie's contract and obviously well understood by George Buthlay, was the right to proceed with the publication even without royal consent. The bland book, at first serialised, was a massive success in America and later in Britain, but at a tragic cost to its author. Overnight, Crawfie had become a top box-office attraction with the public on both sides of the Atlantic. But behind her, the gates of Buckingham Palace clanged shut with a terrible finality, never to open again to the surrogate mother of the two little princesses.

George Buthlay rode out the storm with a belligerent defence of his wife and, in truth, was certainly the one who saved her from herself. He made money out of the deal, but at least he never for one moment was other than her champion through thick and thin. As far as she was concerned, the money now seemed relatively unimportant, although in some perverse way she got a kick out of being famous and having the press chase after her. She kept all the press cuttings and continued to take a delight in press references to her in later years, while shutting herself away like a recluse to evade the very people who had given her the publicity in which she quietly revelled.

In retrospect however, I feel she would have willingly foregone the transient pleasure of being front page news, just to blot the whole episode out and continue to live in her Grace and Favour house and receive her Xmas cards from the Royals as usual.

Everything she had done and achieved in life was centred in the Royal Household. That was her real home - her real family, and now she was cast out as a leper without a sign of recognition from any family member. A life given over to the two most prestigious girls in the land counted for nothing, once she was perceived to have breached royal protocol.

Once it became clear to the media that the serialisations and the book on both sides of the Atlantic had become taboo in royal circles, with the ex-governess now persona non grata, the scandal fed the frenzied interest. Book sales further rocketed. But for Crawfie to continue living in a Grace and Favour residence was unthinkable and she crept into virtual isolation from the outside world, back into the Buthlay home territory of Aberdeen.

One day around 1970, my secretary handed me a summons to call in at 5 Hillhead Road, Bieldside to visit a new patient called Mrs Marion Buthlay. At this point Glen Tanar's association with the little princesses and their governess would never have crossed my mind had it not been that, after making a few discreet enquiries, I discovered that Mrs Marion Buthlay was none other than Miss Marion Crawford.

A date and time having been arranged, I duly drove up to the house which was surrounded by high wooden fencing to exclude any prying eyes. As I approached the gate, a lady's brusque voice said but one word – "Yes?" Having introduced myself, her attitude mellowed somewhat to a sort of reserved acceptance, but with little warmth. Marion Buthlay, tall and well-built, was dressed in a tweed skirt and bulky woollen jumper topped off with a shapeless soft hat giving her a rather bizarre appearance.

An imperious aura about her however sent out a clear message that one should tread very warily here. Having been ushered into the house, I was introduced to the Major. Thus began my association with the couple that lasted for nearly twenty years, during which time I was to come to know a complex and unforgettable personality.

Crawfie's Bieldside Retreat.
*The Royals passed along this road annually
on their way to Balmoral.*

In 2001, having agreed with Blakeway Productions to take part in their presentation of "Crawfie" for Channel 4, I had to do a lot of soul searching to decide what should be said and what left out. I was very conscious that not only might I breach my ethical code, but that the producers might take my remarks out of context. I should not have worried as Blakeway lived up to their promise of not abusing my trust in them and I feel they made a very creditable programme.

Over the years I visited the couple regularly each month on a Wednesday. Arriving promptly at 12.30 pm I would be handed a large sherry, meanwhile trying to evaluate if they had any medical needs. The greeting at the door was always the same, the proffered back of the hand as if to be kissed, and the exaggerated haughty greeting of "How nice to see you". After the first few sentences, the atmosphere thawed a little and by the time George had greeted me like a long lost brother, the formality fell away. The departure also never varied. Rain or shine Crawfie would accompany me to the gate proffering a cheek to be pecked, as I closed the gate. Like a little boy being sent home for his lunch, was a feeling that never left me over all those years.

Good General Practice in the past was recognised as the ability to blend science with the art of inter-personal relationship, so producing the most satisfying outcome for those in need. This was most effectively achieved through continuity of care where patient and doctor knew and understood one another through all manner of family illnesses and problems. Trust became the watchword. But the doctor could never allow himself to take it for granted. In this way many of us, unconsciously, became experts in managing such relationships.

George and Marion, however, were a combination of personalities the management of whom would have defeated most of us. George was a simmering volcano while Crawfie would wave away any objection with an imperious gesture of her hand, so I soon learnt to adopt a very gentle role in their lives. Their need was simply to have the reassuring interest of the doctor and I found them undemanding as patients as long as I did not give them any advice which they might consider to be unwarranted. Home visiting in those days, in West-end practices like mine, was gauged on either need or privilege. Visiting the Buthlays certainly came under the second heading, but in such circumstances it is often preferable to acquiesce rather than stand on one's dignity. While some doctors get the thrill of reflected glory attending the rich or famous, my background made me totally dismissive of this attitude, making me initially a somewhat grudging carer of the royal governess.

Time smoothes out many problems and so it turned out that the Buthlays became an integral part of my working life and the Wednesday sherry once a month became a pleasant interlude. George with his crude barrack-room jokes, with Crawfie sitting primly on the edge of her seat, legs tucked decorously under the high backed chair and hands folded in her lap, was a recurring picture. George guffawing loudly, with me politely joining in, while Crawfie's deadpan expression gave no indication as to how she viewed these two stupid men, never ceased to surprise me. That a lady who had taught Royalty the elements of etiquette could tolerate such behaviour could only be explained by her appreciation of her husband as her treasured saviour, warts and all.

George Buthlay's temper was well known to their cost among the business fraternity. Punctuality and efficiency were bywords with George and God help those who failed to live up to his standards. Only once was I on the receiving end of one of his outbursts. In 1975 George had complained of some aches and pains, and as Crawfie was becoming quite concerned, I arranged for a consultant colleague to visit them. An examination was promptly carried out which yielded a clean bill of health. Accordingly I called in the next day simply to add my reassurance. Relaxed and unsuspecting, I was ushered into the entrance hall to hear a bellow of fury from the lounge. George Buthlay in a foul temper was not a pretty sight and now, red-faced, he was almost apoplectic with rage. It transpired that my colleague had not only examined my patient but topped it off with some sort of blessing which George felt totally inappropriate. Crawfie confirmed the impression and I discovered only then that they subscribed to no faith and had felt grossly insulted. The episode blew over as quickly as it had started; but subsequent events showed that they both held strong views on this subject that would be fully confirmed in their attitude to death.

Crawfie.
(By Kind Permission of Paull and Williamsons, Solicitors).
A picture that cleverly captures that sense of elegance and seriousness.

The years passed until the emptiness that Crawfie dreaded finally arrived with the death of George Buthlay in 1977. That, for her, was the end of any vestige of happiness. Following a private cremation, Crawfie chartered a trawler to take his ashes out to the North Sea. Standing in the stern, she committed them to the waves, as George had requested, followed by a solitary wreath. Just as with her own funeral years later, religion played absolutely no part.

In her loneliness, Crawfie gathered around her those on whom she most depended – the lawyer, the banker, the gardener and of course, the doctor. I continued to visit her as before, but the light had gone out and she felt she was a lost soul in an unfriendly world.

George had done all her fighting, had dealt with intrusive pressmen when needed, and ran the house like a military operation. Her attempted suicide, which formed the introduction to Channel 4's programme, was something I missed, being away on holiday at the time. That she had seen this as the only way out did not surprise me. In many ways the question has to be posed, whether a successful suicide would have been preferable to the increasing loneliness, suffering and eventual death from the cancer she so dreaded.

I often wondered, whether this stern somewhat authoritarian spinster would have aroused much tenderness or love in the two young girls, as I would not have chosen Crawfie to bring up my children. Did the royal princesses have any lingering affection for their governess or did the severing of relations with their stand-in mother figure, not greatly concern them? Perhaps, of course, lack of emotion and distant reticent behaviour were qualities expected of both governess and employers in those days, with love and affection being a relatively modern concept in such a relationship. Yet so many titled families have appeared to worship their old nannies and governesses that such love must have been present somewhere.

The full reasons for Crawfie's banishment from the Royal Family have never been satisfactorily explained or understood, but I have come to believe they all hinged around George Buthlay's tremendous influence over her. There was never, in my time, any question who was boss in the household. Crawfie could treat those around her with regal disdain, but what George said was law, and I never heard a murmur of dissent from her over all the years I knew them. George bowed the knee to no one and the fact that the Queen was disapproving made not one iota of difference to him.

Crawfie, a wise old owl in Court circles, was just a naïve little girl in the cruel outside world, but George proved her Sir Galahad. That it all ended up in tears was almost inevitable with such powerful personalities as the Queen and Major Buthlay pulling in opposite directions. Despite a deep sense of grievance over her treatment, never once, even in her declining years, did she ever betray the trust placed in her by criticising any member of the Royal Family. She had a deep affection for her two girls, each so different, and she thought very highly of the King. Of the Queen, she made no mention, even when allowing herself an occasional tear towards the end.

One hundred yards from the front of her house in Bieldside, the Royals always passed by on their annual pilgrimage up Deeside to Balmoral Castle. I felt Crawfie cherished the hope that one of her girls might drop in unofficially just to say that they did remember her with some affection. I believe that would have healed much of the hurt that she continued to carry throughout the rest of her life.

Crawfie

The happy laughter of the three little girls gradually fades away into the distance while the tall upright figure of their companion has totally disappeared. The two little boys still occasionally sit on the Estate Office wall, but now their youth has passed them by and they have become grey-haired old men. No one remembers much about the tall lady, but if we believe in ghosts, I'm absolutely certain that some time in the future she will turn up to haunt me with that outstretched hand and the regal "How nice to see you again".

Chapter 6
The Big House

It was customary for us living in Glen Tanar, to refer to 'The Glen' as if it were the only glen in existence. At school, years later at Aboyne, we were all known as the kids from 'The Glen', by both pupils and teachers alike, and this seemed to confer on us some elevated status, of which we were very aware. However, all over Scotland in the valleys and glens, others were treasuring that same sense of belonging to a community in exactly similar terms. In the same way, 'The Big House' could only mean one thing and that was the laird's mansion, where all our elders' hopes and fears rested and which to us, as small children living near by, was the centre of our universe.

The original Glen Tanar House appears to date back to the early nineteenth century when the estate formed part of the lands of the Marquis of Huntly's family. In 1890 the estate was bought by Sir William Cunliffe Brooks, a Manchester banker and MP, who quickly set about transforming the house into a substantial mansion. George Coats was then to buy the estate in 1905 and during the 1930's his son Thomas, Lord Glentanar, extended the house with modern bedrooms on the south-facing aspect. To me as a child the house always seemed huge, with as many obscure servants' bedrooms in the back quarters, as there were sumptuous rooms occupied by the gentry.

Bob Smith in the *Leopard* magazine of December 2001 has recorded that Brooks in his time in the 1890's kept a regular staff of 240 workmen to rebuild Glen Tanar House, as well as farm buildings and workers' houses throughout the estate. He erected Glen Tanar School and the imposing Tower of Ess, which still stands today as evidence of his imagination and his masons' skills. The size of the workforce seems remarkable by today's standards. But even in the 1930's the Glen had a substantial population, including some masons, who were kept ever busy, dressing granite for the mansion house and its extension. Rummaging in my garage, I come across three chisels from those days when I would have been given my own piece of granite to dress and to work alongside the masons in the sawmill yard. I must have been about four or five at the time, but still recall with pleasure, the patience and kindliness of those grime-faced men in their dusty bonnets and overalls.

Over the years, their job at an end, they seemed to fade away in my memory and certainly by the outbreak of war this trade had totally disappeared from the Glen. The organisation of an estate with literally dozens and, in earlier days, hundreds of employees, brought its own particular structure of pecking order, of which no one was in any doubt. Heads of departments would have consisted of the Clerk of Works, the head forester, the head gamekeeper, the farm manager and the butler, as the mansion house major-domo. All these people would be seen as being below the status of the factor, who would have been directly responsible to the owner for the overall efficiency of the estate. No doubt tensions existed in this arrangement and it seemed to me, in childhood, that the factor was at the root of all evil.

My father never seemed to have anyone interfering in his domain; but my pals were always full of what their parents were complaining about within their four walls, and the factor was always the one to blame, of course. In my time, Mr Gillies and later Mr R D Young were factors and Mr Young was still in post after my father retired in 1955. As a young child I probably did view him with some uneasiness, but as the years passed and he became our scoutmaster, I came to understand what a thankless job he had. I never found him other than helpful and fair; but he always seemed a remote man, not being able to relate too closely with anyone immediately around him. On a Sunday morning he would regularly pass our window accompanied by his son, Douglas, in what appeared a lonely vigil to see that no one had run off with the estate during that day of rest.

The Glen Tanar House of My Childhood.
Modern Windows to the South.

There was one employee at this time who made no attempt to integrate with the estate community. He was Mr Norman Dain, Lord Glentanar's private secretary, someone we passed every day on our way to school, as he walked briskly from his attractive rather superior looking house, to his office in the mansion house. He and his family seemed to exist on some lofty plane beyond our ken and took no part in any of our lives. The two daughters, Margaret and Hilda, were a few years older than me; but having been sent off to private schools, they were scarcely known to us other than when they joined in the occasional sledging session in the early days. If the Dains had disappeared from the estate one night, I am sure few of us would have noticed, so unrelated did they feel. Despite his being in the big house alongside my father over countless years, I can scarcely ever remember Father referring to him, although his greeting to us every day was always a very cheery "Good morning."

The mansion house itself meant different things to me depending on whether the laird was away or in residence. No flag fluttering in the breeze, meant that I could meander my way to visit my father via the little wooden gate in front of our house, down the narrow well-kept path, then through the tall rhododendrons, boldly approaching the big house down the wooden steps. I would walk straight up to the front door or wander past all the public rooms without fear of discovery. However, a flag tugging at the masthead, meant that a careful walk round the back road was indicated, keeping out of sight of the dining-room across the lawns, and stealing quietly into the tradesman's entrance. The bleakness of the covered cobbled forecourt leading up three steps into the servants' tiled entrance hall, used to fill me with an acute sense of belonging to the peasant class. Past the little boot hole where my

Mr R D Young - The Glen Tanar Factor.

Aboyne Games Committee Member.

father spent hundreds of hours making the laird's shoes glisten and gleam, to pause for a moment at the pressing-room door, where the iron so often hissed and steamed under my father's expert hands. Watching my father, I would sometimes make my exit from this room through a back door into the gun-room, to stand and gape at the array of Purdeys and Stephen Grants in their glass cases and just marvel at what wealth could bring to some.

The clattering of my feet on the hallway's red clay tiles made me self-conscious so that I would painfully try to tiptoe the rest of the way lest I bring others to see who was coming. I would go past the servants' hall, with one wall completely lined with leather-bound volumes of *Punch*, and then on past the maid's room and the housekeeper's room, until I turned into my father's own quarters. Here, in a rather dark work area, was where all the food came via a hatch from the kitchen on its way through to the dining room. It was here that all the crystal and silver was washed after use before being stored away in the walk-in safe that was my father's pride and joy. The meticulous way in which Father would supervise the washing of the silver remains with me still. Handled ever so gently through the foaming suds, the pieces were placed on the draining board and then carefully sluiced down with fresh clean water to remove all traces of soap. This was a routine that never varied. To scratch the silver was a heinous crime in my father's eyes as probably many well-meaning footmen learnt to their cost. Across the room, the startling mass of gleaming silver in the spacious walk-in safe was something I never tired of admiring, whenever the door was ajar.

Out in the passageway from the work area stood an anonymous-looking door which might have been a cupboard, but which held a great attraction for small boys. On opening the door, one came upon a stone stair which led steeply down into the bowels of the earth and which was lit only dimly by a couple of cobweb-covered bulbs. Here were rows of dusty bottles containing priceless maturing wines that my father had purchased over the years in order to keep the laird in the forefront of wine connoisseurs. I would stand marvelling at the hundreds of bottles and wonder how anyone was ever going to drink them all. My father never made any reference to his expertise in this field, just as he never boasted about his prowess in any other area of his life. Only when he was on holiday back in France did he ever show any hint of cockiness; otherwise he was always the same self-effacing individual. In the years to come he would always let me judge the wine we were drinking first and never give any indication of how he rated it. Only after I had committed myself to a firm opinion would he then offer an assessment. Sad to say, my palate has never been fully educated to rival my father's; but at least I know what I like and it was not for the lack of sampling the best that I have remained a relative novice.

My father's own little room was adjacent to the work area and here I spent many tedious minutes waiting for him to return from being summoned to attend to his employer's needs. That room has left a scar on me from the earliest days. It was so small, so inconsequential, that my heart bled for my father. To think that his employer had so little apparent appreciation of his position, as to expect him to exist in these surroundings. The room contained his desk, a bed in the corner, a small dressing table, a washstand and a large wardrobe that seemed to fill the entire room. In the corner was the smallest and smokiest fireplace you could imagine. Did the room reflect how their employers viewed butlers when the house was built; or was this one of Cunliffe Brook's own perspectives? My father's predecessors had obviously just accepted it; and never did I hear him complain, other than when he was smoked out by a wind in the wrong airt. On the other hand, life below stairs found the butler, valet and lady's maid taking afternoon tea in the housekeeper's room, with the housekeeper in the role of hostess and very conscious of her standing in the order of things. No doubt her room was used by senior staff at other times and my father would only retreat to his own bolt-hole when putting his feet up or restoring his energies with a spot of Johnnie Walker or White Horse from the large wardrobe.

Even as a boy, the internal workings of the mansion house intrigued me. My mother, having spent much of her working life in this environment, knew exactly where everyone slotted in and it was unheard of for anyone to step out of line. The housekeeper's room was the meeting place for senior staff and I remember Nellie Strachan (later to be Mrs Begg) being the dominant figure there. Her name was taboo in our house for as long as I can remember and although I never really discovered the reason, my mother often hinted that Nellie had had designs on my father in the early days. I am uncertain as to whether there was any basis for this suspicion, especially since Mrs Begg was a large buxom lady, scarcely someone my dapper little father would have coped with, though stranger things have happened.

Nellie Begg may not have exactly put a curse on our family, but her memory was kept alive for me throughout my career as if she was somewhere out there in the shadows. Her nephew, a month older than me, used to come to visit her at the Glen and I met him there on one or two occasions. Thereafter I found him ahead of me at the Grammar School.

Later, who was awarded the post of medical general practitioner at Udny Station instead of me but Nellie's large nephew. In due course Dr Ken Sutherland and I became quite good friends, yet who was still in post when I had long retired, but Nellie's boy. My mother, with her vivid imagination and half belief in the supernatural, would have been shaking her head now, convinced that her sixth sense had been right all along. Obviously the spirit of Mrs Begg still lived on through her nephew, out of sheer jealousy.

Prior to Nelly Begg's appointment to the prestigious post of housekeeper, her predecessor, was Mrs Irvine whom I remember visiting before the war. She was well regarded by my father from his early days in the Glen and we drove to see her on a number of occasions when she was living with her family in Dyce. For me, however, she was but a figure from the past, along with names like Mr James Cameron, the old head gamekeeper, whose picture still hangs in the ballroom. Those names along with many others kept constantly recurring during my parents' tales of their own 'good old days'.

The other person wielding power in the household in those 'good old days' was the chef, whose name Blande also kept recurring through my early youth, although I cannot picture him. It appears that he was a brilliant chef but, in true temperamental French style, not the easiest man to work with, and he obviously kept everyone, including the laird and Lady Glentanar, on their toes. Later, Mrs Smith, one of the most obese but kindliest of people I knew, took on the role of head cook. Unmarried, she was always addressed as Mrs Smith or to my parents later on as Lena, which was an unusual breach of etiquette in those days. In marked contrast to my father's room, Mrs Smith had a very pleasant little room off the grand airy kitchen. As I grew older I would often pop in to see her so that I could sample some tasty morsel. To be presented with a succulent piece of home-cured ham, was in those early days, a real luxury. These hams hanging up in the back cold room had a flavour which I have never come across since; or is it that time dulls our sensitivity to such flavours?

In those times, the use of Christian names by children to their elders was never even contemplated. Even our parents rarely called their neighbours by their first names. My mother knew our neighbours as Mrs Dawson or Mrs Archibald, but addressed Mr Archibald as George as he worked in my father's department. The laird himself was generally referred to on the estate as "Lordy", especially in our household, and to me as a child this always sounded rather threatening. My father was always Mr Fouin to everyone and only the laird and his family ever addressed my father by the Christian name of Francis, instead of Francois: while my mother always referred to him as Lou instead of Louis. He would in turn call my mother Beck or Peg instead of Rebecca or 'Becky' as she was known to my aunts and cousin. Very confusing to a child, as neither name seemed to fit either of them. For me, addressing my father it was always "Dad", while my mother always referred to him as "your father". My own term to my mother as far back as I can remember was just that - "Mother" and probably had much to do with my never wanting to be thought of as a mummy's boy by using a more endearing term.

One of my earliest images of the pecking order below stairs was acquired when I arrived at the big house, just as the servants' lunch hour was beginning. On opening the door of the servants' hall I was confronted by the long table packed with people, with my father sitting at the head and the housekeeper at the far end. Peter, the hall-boy, was serving out the soup and I beat a hasty retreat through to my father's room to await the end of the meal. Staff in those days would have consisted of three footmen, a hall-boy, the odd-job man, housemaids, assistant cooks, and stillroom maids and possibly, at times the servants of the laird's guests.

The names Robert, Henry and John are plucked out of the air as names of footmen of the past, with Peter as hall-boy. No surnames were ever attached and only when John Ritchie left to become a butler in his own right to Wallace of Candacraig in Strathdon was I aware of his full name. My father was fond of John and rated him very highly. I recall two or three occasions when my father and I drove over to Strathdon to visit the Ritchies in their new venture.

My trip to the mansion house often stopped outside the back door where Mr Archibald, as the odd-job man, had his little workshop-cum-store. There with Willie his son, we used to spend much time just poking around the contents or watching his father carry out some intricate repair to a piece of household equipment. The huge coke fired boiler to centrally heat the mansion house was down some steep steps just here and in cold weather we delighted in watching Mr Archibald feverishly stoking the fire like any locomotive fireman.

The ability of many workers in those days seemed to go far beyond what we would expect today; but then that ability now would have seen them in skilled occupations. If Mr Archibald was not to be found, Willie and I might then go out through the mansion house side door and down the path which led on to the Chapel of St Lesmo, until we came to the little wooden bridge over the Tanar. There on the bridge, leaning on the handrail and with eyes fixed intently on the water below, like a solitary heron, would be Willie's father, patiently watching for the run of sea trout through the pool. He could spend hours in this pursuit after a decent shower of rain. Then in the evening with a cleverly attached brambling worm he would reap the rewards for his infinite patience. He was a gifted fisherman and I always held him in the highest regard, from his ability to grow the best carrots in the district to the hooking of fish in a pool that I had been thrashing unsuccessfully for ages beforehand.

The Spartan surroundings of the servants' wing of the house contrasted quite dramatically with the luxury and plushy comfort beyond the padded door. Out of my father's work-area a passageway led directly into the dining room. A large spacious room of great character, you could well imagine all the important personalities of the time enjoying the experience of the best French cuisine and of a wine cellar second to none.

For me, however, the most memorable moment came when I pushed open the very large padded door to the left of the dining room and passed into another world. Padded, presumably to cut out the mundane clatter of servants washing up, this door and beyond is where the world of luxury commenced. One moved on into an imposing hallway and open lounge, with the dinner-gong prominent at the foot of a broad majestic stairway. The stair swept round on to an upper landing with the nursery figure of the black minstrel sitting there awaiting me in those very early days.

Glen Tanar Exile

When the Cat's away the Mice will play.

*The parents pictured at Miss Jean's swing and monkey
rope with the Mansion House in the background.*

Yes, the padded door into that other world always came to signify for me the epitome of the class structure into which I had been born. I never felt any animosity or real envy for those who inhabited those elegant quarters; only wonder at the pure chance of being born into such contrasting circumstances. Never, even as a small child, did I feel intellectually inferior; nor did I hold such people in great reverence - indeed my father made sure I realised that their beginnings had been just as humble as our own; so no need to bend the knee unnecessarily. Their accents and bearing of course could be intimidating, but from early on I refused to address the laird as 'milord', but simply called him 'sir'. His daughter was always referred to as 'Miss Jean' and we never in those days failed to recognise that the 'Miss' proclaimed a status that the rest of us should always remember. The seeds of dislike and disdain for the British class structure were already fermenting away in my tiny brain and nothing since then has led me to change my views. Happily, I am free from the bitterness that often accompanies this controversial subject. I have always felt privileged to have been brought up in that particular setting and if there was always a degree of feudalism present, I believe that it was administered in as fair a way as circumstances permitted.

Across the open-plan lounge and bearing away to my left, I would come upon the laird's study. It was an intimate pleasant book-lined room with a large desk at which the laird would be seated. When summoned to speak to my godfather - a very dominant character - I was usually conscious of a rising anxiety that culminated in my making my escape as soon as possible. On looking back, I realise that I failed to make full use of the opportunity which was available to me to develop my interest in reading and discussion. Only in the latter years did I appreciate that the laird genuinely had my interests at heart.

On now to my favourite room. Turn right out past the padded door, down a long broad carpeted corridor, past Mr Dain's room on the right, past the morning room on the left and in through the double glass doors to the magnificent ballroom. This today is about all that remains of the original Glentanar House. Now used as a revenue producer, it is available to the public for weddings and charitable functions, so that it retains much of its old glory. With the organ now gone, no longer can I look down into that pit and marvel at the multiple keyboards.

Yet I can still imagine the laird on the organ trying his best to lift the roof off the mansion house at three in the morning. The wonderful antlered ceiling is still there to highlight the priorities of the Victorian era. The raised annex where the grand piano stood and where Miss Jean's electric Hornby trains sped round a circular double track, is unchanged. The trains of course are long gone. But when the laird and family were away, it was here that my father would allow me to play for hours with the ultimate luxury in my little world.

Then close to the fireplace, one came upon the impressive portrait of Lady Glentanar with Miss Jean and Slenta, their old golden retriever. Painted by Cowan Dobson RBA (1893-1980) about 1938, it still hangs exactly where it was first positioned some sixty five years ago. The huge open fireplace that took massive logs is unchanged and here again the memories flood back. Xmas on the estate saw the laird invite all the children to a party in the ballroom where we played games, sang carols, ate prodigiously and then each received a worthwhile present from Santa. The ballroom would be fully decorated and what with the Xmas lights and a roaring fire in the grate, it exuded a magical atmosphere.

In my bird-nesting, egg-collecting years, we tried desperately to discover the nests of the swifts which whirled, screaming endlessly, around the house on those balmy summer evenings. We could see where they got in under the eaves and with the help of George Archibald's very long ladders, which he used to clean the upper windows above the dining room, we stretched precariously ever higher.

Finally, running our hands under the eaves, we could never quite squirm them in far enough and so my extensive egg collection never did come to boast those longish white eggs we knew were only inches away. Those swifts remain for me a favourite bird as they always appeared in the Glen on exactly the same day every year after their long migration flight - the 12th May, my father's birthday. Their unerring appearance in Deeside around that day ever since, never fails to remind me of a very special parent.

Out in front of the mansion house, the lawns swept away down towards the little lake with its water lilies and bulrushes. Down there was to be found the attractive rotating summerhouse that we so loved in those early days. My mother especially liked to sit in it while we wild lads tried to turn the summerhouse ever faster and faster. In the springtime the whole area was profusely carpeted with exotic daffodils and this spot remains for me the pinnacle of my memories.

This area by the small lake held a special enchantment for my father and it was so much to his liking that I always intended to scatter his ashes there. When the time came, however, I momentarily forgot my pledge and spread them amongst the flowers of Aberdeen's Hazlehead Crematorium. In my mind I can still see my parents, happy in their middle age, enjoying the wonderful ambience, at a time when the world around them seemed to have found a true peace at last.

To many, Glentanar House must have seemed large and rambling with little corridors here and there leading to God knows where. I, myself, was never quite certain at times where I was among those corridors and back stairs; but, to me it had an atmosphere all of its own. That it had outlived its period and came to be largely demolished in the 1970's, was a brave but realistic decision by the Coats/Bruce family. Its demise however destroyed much of the character of the Glen for me and I am sure had much the same effect on my old father. Now a modern dwelling abuts the back of what was known as the bachelor's wing and on into the rear of the stage and the ballroom, but that sense of grandeur and timelessness is gone forever.

Wishing to renew his nostalgia for the Glen for one last time, my father, now in his early nineties, asked me to take him back to where he had spent so many happy years. Leaving him to wander about at his leisure, I returned to find him staring with a wistful look at a patch of grass.

Turning to me, he indicated that down there had lain the fortune he had amassed over the decades. Now however, no longer was it the steep stone stairway down to his treasured cellar; just a patch of featureless lawn to emphasise that nothing is forever.

The Big House

At least one other flavour of the past does remain, as out in front of the ballroom, across the lawn and up one of the overgrown pathways, there is the resting-place of so many of those four-legged friends from that age gone by.

The clearing is unkempt; the headstones are askew, with algae and moss obscuring many inscriptions; but it is still a nostalgic place where the past floats back like a haunting tune. And yes, among all the headstones there is one to old Slenta, whose image stares out at us from that memorable portrait by Cowan Dobson on the ballroom wall.

Chapter 7
Aboyne Higher Grade Public School

Aboyne School stood in the centre of the village on the north-west side of the impressive Charleston Green. Directly facing it across the green was the Free Church, with its characteristic spire. Next was the Masonic Hall, alongside Dinnie the butcher's shop, with the Post Office and Knowles the jeweller further along. Afraid that my bicycle might be vandalised, my father approached Mr Dinnie to ask if I could leave the bike in one of his back sheds during the school day. Thus, on the first day of the autumn term of 1937, I parked my bike in the little shed and walked apprehensively across the green, to stand in line at the lower school entrance, a stranger among strangers.

I was eventually allocated to Miss Reid's primary class three, after it being ascertained that although I could have been in Primary Four, I would be better off in three, considering the work I had covered. From that very first day I felt I had come into a civilised society. Bullying was minimal and the big boys tended to break up fights rather than to promote them. Although my school chums were ordinary village children, all the harshness of Glen Tanar was absent and the school radiated a sense of purpose and tranquillity.Miss Rosa Evelyn Reid was the perfect teacher to settle a child who had lost confidence and any real zest for school life. Steadily, I came to look forward to school, especially interval-times when we joined up with the big boys, playing endless games of football on a proper pitch.

The cycle-run of four and a half miles to school and back at night often became tiring, especially pedalling into a head wind going home. Also, the treacherous icy roads in winter required great care; but it never seemed to faze us and missing school for the weather was unthinkable. In rain, we put on our black capes which draped over the handlebars and kept us completely dry, while our head gear of leather helmets had us mimicking the First World War Royal Flying Corps. I remember some really nasty spills on the icy roads, but we just picked ourselves up and got on with it.

Skinned knees had a hastily tied handkerchief applied to them but were otherwise ignored.The other areas threatening skinned knees were the ice slides down the steep bank behind the school and next to the Presbyterian Church. Winter saw dozens of us making these slides, with the bigger boys at the steepest end. Smaller and shorter slides were created for the girls and the younger children. Big boots came into their own again in this pastime and gave us a great thrill.

The pre-war days of Empire still inspired in us a very special feeling. It was regularly pointed out that over a quarter of the world was coloured red, to depict our huge empire and how important we all were as a nation. I still recall Empire Day, which I think was held in May, when we all paraded on the green, wearing our Empire daisies very proudly. It left me at that time with a feeling of security and timelessness that nothing would ever change. Little did we know.

The old Aboyne Higher Grade Public School.
The Junior School entrance was below the flat roof on the right and this is where I stood on that first day in 1937.

Primary Four turned out to be a complete change from the quiet teaching of Miss Reid, for we were now in the hands of the terror of the school, Miss Thrasher Milne. Miss Jane Milne was quite small and, in our eyes seemed much older than Miss Reid. Brooking no slacking by her pupils, she had a fearsome reputation for being a slave driver. Looking back, she was probably the real driving force in my life, outside of my mother's influence. She kept spurring me on to achieve better and better results, especially against Ernest Sim, who was by far the cleverest in the class. Ernest, 'Sonny,' as his father had called him - but 'Sunny' as we thought of him, because it summed up his nature - had lost his father from the effects of gas in the First World War and his mother eked out a living by looking after the Masonic Hall. The genes must have been excellent, as an eldest sister went on to reach the heights of the Civil Service, in the Foreign Office.

Sunny was a natural. He did little or no work yet could easily surpass the rest of the class academically. From an early age he had a job delivering the early morning rolls for the baker in the village. As a result, he was often in need of copying my homework, which he had not had time to prepare. Exam time came around and who would effortlessly be first yet again? Miss Milne used his success to urge me to ever-greater effort until gradually I began to overhaul him, so that by the end of the year, I had outstripped him in one or two subjects. As for Sunny, he couldn't have cared less. Miss Milne, intent on developing my ability as best she could, was so delighted with my progress that I forgave the slave driving. Years later, when I was at University, I revisited the school. My old teacher showed me off to her class as an example of what could be achieved by sheer hard work. She was so proud that it makes me almost tearful to write this now. Those dedicated teachers deserved so much more

Len Halsey and his massive Igloo.

than any of us at that time realised and I have nothing but praise for so many of them, who tirelessly worked to batter the elements of education into our thoughtless minds.

I now moved on to Miss Clubb's qualifying class where, unfortunately, the momentum of the previous year faded away. It was as if we were on a yacht under full sail, but with no breeze to propel us forward. I believe we all idled and Miss Clubb's assessment of my progress to my mother at this time, was that if he was as keen on his lessons as he is on getting on to the football pitch, then he would be doing very well. It was true that football had become very important, in that I was now playing for the school team, which was an honour indeed.

Leonard Halsey was one of the big boys, whose mother provided me with lunch during all my years at Aboyne School. Len's mother had been a cook at Glen Tanar when her husband had been the chauffeur. Unfortunately he drank himself out of the job and later died. Mrs Halsey now lived with her old mother and sister in 'The Cottage', a pleasant house on the Ballater Road.

For much of the year she made a living by having as lodgers, the Halls, who were a moneyed family of three - a father, mother and daughter from Aberdeen. Len was her only child, the apple of his mother's eye and even as a youngster he was a wonderful harmonica player. He looked after me like an elder brother and his influence as a very good footballer ensured that I was considered for the team.

Boys from lower school did not normally play for the school team, but Sandy Philip in my class was such a good player that he was promoted into the team early. This set a precedent with the result that I found myself called in to play at left back. My first game was against our bitter rivals, Banchory, and I found myself up against a huge boy on their right wing. He simply bulldozed his way through the opposition and his supporters obviously expected him to mow down this little guy at left back. I well remember with satisfaction, standing up to this big ox and surprising him and myself by coming out of the tackles with the ball. I learnt then never to be overawed in such situations and my need to appear equal to the challenge outweighed any concern about possible injury.

I never did suffer any injuries at sport; but my bird-nesting caught up with me one day in 1938 when I was returning from school. Ian Mann, who lived in the Tower of Ess, was the almost midget-sized son of one of the estate employees. One day, we were just half a mile from the Tower, when we spied a pigeon sitting on a nest in a fir tree beside the road. I elected to climb the tree, but when about twenty feet up, the branches snapped and I fell heavily to the ground. I must have been knocked unconscious, because when I came round, some of the roadmen, who had been cycling home from work, were now standing over me and I felt a dreadful pain in my right arm. As I was unable to stand, they carried me to the Tower and I can still remember pleading with them to put me down because of the pain. My parents were called and I was taken to Dr Willie's house, where he must have manipulated my broken wrist. Uncertain as to whether it was properly set, he arranged for me to go to Aberdeen Sick Children's Hospital the next day for X-ray. The picture was obviously unsatisfactory, as I was given a general anaesthetic and, in due course, came round to find the arm encased in plaster. The unforgettable smell of ether and the overpowering choking sensation with the facemask remains with me still. For six weeks I had to become left-handed - an almost incongruous situation when one considers how much time had been spent converting to right-handedness. Convalescence was straightforward and I was left with no disability, but with a much greater respect for trees in future.

A major highlight of our year of course was the Aboyne Games. Watching, enthralled as the wagons arrived after all the stands had been erected had us buzzing with excitement. The actual day of the games passed in a haze of memories; but, oddly enough, one of our greatest thrills would occur on the Monday morning after all had departed. Scouring the ground where the shooting galleries had stood, we scrabbled for the little feathered darts that had been dropped and I proudly bore home my cache to fire out of my own airgun. I still come across the odd dart even now among all the bolts, screws and nails stored in the garage.

The Michaelmas Fair or, to the locals, the Michel Fair was one of the old traditional cattle markets which had served the purpose of the community through the ages and which was an annual highlight of Aboyne's agricultural scene. It is recorded that there were three old statutory cattle fairs selling horses, cattle and sheep. These were the Candlemas, Michaelmas and Hallowmass Fairs, but only the Michel Fair is remembered by me. Occurring in the autumn, the week-long fair meant for us roads packed with sheep and attendant dogs. When going to school, those of us who had left everything to the last minute would frequently find ourselves delayed by these dense flocks of sheep. This resulted in late arrival at school and a sharp reprimand. Day after day we were presented with this hurdle, both coming and going. This has left me with a sense of the gentle pace of life in those far-off times. With traffic minimal, the collie dogs would quietly move a flock along a main road that was undisturbed by impatient motorists. What a picture of tranquil country life when compared with present-day driving conditions.

The qualifying class led up to what was later to be called the Eleven-Plus Examination, and passing this exam ensured your progress through school to the Lower Leaving Certificate. In due course, we were all mightily relieved to get this hurdle behind us. Then we were qualified to become upper school pupils and people now of some importance.

1935 - Lord Glentanar and Miss Jean enjoying the Aboyne Games.

The year was 1939 and this was when all our lives were turned upside down with the outbreak of war with Germany. I do not recall much change initially. But then the evacuees from Glasgow's East End descended on us, producing an enormous culture shock. In order to cope with the large number of children now at the school, we attended half days, as did the Glasgow kids in order that they could share the school facilities. Later, there was a steady drift of evacuees back to Glasgow, leaving a much-reduced number behind. Thus after a time we returned to full-time attendance. The influence on our lives in Glen Tanar was immense, with a whole school of evacuees being established there. But at Aboyne, my memory of their presence is much scantier. As the war progressed, life gradually became harder, especially on our football, which became irreplaceable through wear and tear. We spent hours after school, down at Peter Murdoch's tiny saddler's shop in the Square, encouraging him to put yet another patch on top of his previous ones.

My lasting memories from this time are the harvest months when it seemed that all the farmers had left thoughts of overhauling their machinery to the very last moment. Imagine our frustration when, day after day, Mr Murdoch had failed to apply one small patch to our football, while the binder sheets piled up outside his wee door. It is little wonder then, that our harassing the poor man about a trivial football repair produced short-tempered outbursts of exasperation from him at our seeming unreasonable impatience.

I can also remember the need for metal for the war effort and the collection point at the Fountain at the end of the green. Here were left, not only all sorts of metal rails, pots and pans, but also luxury items such as roller and ice skates, which none of us had ever seen before. The rich folk of Aboyne were to us a race apart and, of course, never associated with the locals; so we felt that despite the needs of the war, we could not bear to let such luxuries be melted down to make Spitfires and Hurricanes. Consequently, many a prize object was spirited out of that collection. So much for our patriotic spirit.

Our headmaster at this time was Mr David Richards, who had been instrumental in allowing my change of schools. By the time I reached upper school he was nearing retirement age and his commitment to the school and teaching was diminishing. 'Auld Rickie,' taught us Latin. The lesson was time-tabled for the period following the mid-morning interval and by the time he had returned from his tea-break at his house across the green, it was almost time for the next period. Whether this accounted for my abominable ability at Latin I do not know, but I never did make much of it. Grappling with Latin unseens had painful echoes of Miss Pirie at Glen Tanar School, when she used to line us up for mental arithmetic.

Mr David Richards was followed by Mr John A P Mair, who had been head of the English Department at Banchory Academy. Suddenly, the school had to sit up and the pupils soon became aware that a new regime had arrived. If Miss Milne was my pusher, so Mr Mair was the person who made English come alive for me; and although I can never really say I warmed to him, any proficiency I may have developed in this department, I attribute to his influence. Thus, when I came to Aberdeen Grammar School, the fact that I was placed in top streams, especially in English, was undoubtedly the result of Mr

Mair's teaching and approach. Seniority in school just seems to creep up on you. First you become a class prefect, then captain of this and that, until, before you know it, you are placed in a position of responsibility, becoming a role model for the youngsters below you who look up to the older boys for leadership. The experience was both pleasant and, at the same time, humbling. I believe that we continued and even improved the civilised culture of Aboyne, which had so impressed me as a new boy. I never saw Mr Mair again after I left school. This is something I now regret, as, despite my often being out of sympathy with his attitude, I feel we owed him a huge debt of gratitude for all he did for us. To him, we must have appeared to be yet another bunch of thankless, self-interested kids. I now realise that a kind word of thanks would have been really appreciated.

Headmasters of Aboyne Higher Grade Public School

Mr David Richards.
Failed to inspire me at Latin.

Mr John A P Mair.
A Guiding Star.

As we grow up, we become aware that our attitude towards girls has changed in a disturbing, yet pleasant way. I remember having a crush on a girl who was a year ahead of me in Miss Milne's class. Annie Henderson seemed to me, wonderful as a nine-year-old and I remember the excitement of suppressed giggles as we passed notes to one another in class. Her pal was a dark-haired beauty called Lottie Forrest, who was then being pursued by two pals of mine, Bob Rose and Sandy Philip. Puppy-love it may have been, but it was obviously the first stirrings of the hormones.

This episode must have died out fairly quickly, as it wasn't until a stunning new pupil was being introduced into our first year class, on our first day in upper school, that I really was star-struck. Marigold McHardy was the only child of the new gamekeeper at the head of the Glen Tanar valley at Eitnach. If our house was some distance from the school, then Eitnach was a further six miles up the valley. The prospect of such a long journey to school made me blanch. During our three years at school together, Marigold scarcely missed a day's attendance and she was held up to the rest of us as a paragon of punctuality. She was really a super girl and, what was more, scholastically she easily outstripped both me and my bright buddy Sunny.

Marigold McHardy.

Halfway Hut on the
road to Eitnach.

The Half Way Hut was not even half way to our house for Marigold. But I never remember her ever being late or complaining about that tedious journey.

She was good at everything and her sparkling eyes and tinkling laugh completely won me over. She constantly teased me about other girls and I was far too shy to tell her the truth. Over the years, my footballing maestro, Sandy Philip, jealously guarded her as his own: but a tough Glasgow evacuee called Michael Savage muscled in for a time. It is amazing that I can recall these facts after all these years; but it all seemed important then and rather heart-rending. After school, on my way home, I would at times hang about in the hope that she might not yet be already ahead of me and occasionally my hopes were realised. But my shyness prevented me from doing more than bask in her company. She went on to Banchory Academy, but it seems that the good life seduced her, with the result that she never really developed her early promise. Moreover, being an accomplished pianist, she joined a local dance-band which, with its associated riotous lifestyle, probably had a further detrimental affect on her. She worked in the laboratory at Bridge of Earn Hospital before marrying a local hotel owner Tommy Gray and they had two daughters. She returned to live in the Glen for some time when her husband left the hotel business and her father retired from the foot of Mount Keen to be housed in the Stable Yard. There, with his usual expressive turn of phrase, she was to be described as the fading Eitnach flower by my old compatriot and then head gamekeeper, Jimmy Oswald. In later life, on the death of her husband, I believe she trained as a teacher in Glasgow and taught there for a number of years. But her father's weakness came to afflict her in the end. For me, however, she always remains that enchanting fourteen-year-old.

Having danced the last waltz with her at the Ghillie's Ball in 1948, Marigold invited me to see her up to the head-keeper's house. Taking the car there to pick up her father, who was already very merry, we had a few treasured moments together when all the shyness of the past years evaporated. As her father was keen to get home quickly, our time alone was cut short. Thus I was unable to tell her how I had felt about her over those early years, though I believe that the confession might have found an amused listener. Sadly, this proved to be our final goodbye and I was never to see her again.

An even sadder post-script to this little tale arose many years later when I had her band-playing boyfriend of those early days, as a patient. He consulted me with the story that he was sure he had a cancer of the oesophagus, which was a rare diagnosis for anyone to make. On being questioned, he said that he had just come from visiting a pal of his, who was dying with such a growth. My initial response would have been to tell him that, as medical students, we all imagined we had some of the diseases we read about in our textbooks. Unfortunately, his history was convincing enough to seek specialist advice. Sure

Entrance Gates to the Estate at the Tower of Ess.
*Distances to Aboyne, Dinnet
and Ballater inscribed.*

enough, it turned out that he had advanced cancer and, despite treatment, he died some months later, a very tragic ending to a bittersweet episode from my schooldays.

Despite my infatuation with my classmate, my knowledge of the mysteries of sex had scarcely progressed very far from that first encounter aged eight, cycling home from Glen Tanar School. Now in my early teens, very conscious of the opposite sex, I was to experience that odd sensation of becoming attracted to certain girls without ever having spoken to them. This is something which is hard to explain, as it seems not only related to attractiveness, but to a certain aura surrounding the desired person, which one can find so alluring. I was greatly attracted to a regular summer visitor to the village. She would have been three years older than I was, but the experience of just cycling past her would make my day. This enthralment persisted over about three years and her name remains vivid in my memory: but the realities of life were to shake me out of the blissfulness and sweet innocence of early adolescence.

As fishing fanatics, Bill Archibald and I were not much attracted to the lower Tanar, from the Swan's Neck to where it flowed into the Dee. However, on this particular summer's evening we decided to cycle to the Tower of Ess. No sooner had we set up our rods than another local boy, fishing below us, came running up excitedly telling us to come and see this spectacle. Crawling through the heather we came upon two lovers on the opposite bank in the process of demonstrating what had never before been fully explained to me. The Canadian soldier and his companion left nothing to the imagination. After a time, my pals, having seen enough, gave full voice to what they thought of such practices. Feeling totally ashamed of my buddies, I watched the startled couple disengage hurriedly. But my surprise was as great as theirs when I recognised the girl to be none other than my holiday stranger. Life can disturb one in a cruel way at times. I felt guilty of being a Peeping -Tom, but at the same time, I was stimulated, yet bewildered by what I had seen. I also felt a deep anger that my boyish dream had been shattered and that nothing would ever have quite that sweet innocence again.

Progressing up the school, we steadily shed those who would not make it academically or whose circumstances were against them. Thus our class gradually thinned out to a handful of boys and the rest were girls. The earliest leaving age at that time was fourteen and such was the relative poverty, that most village youngsters left at the first opportunity to pick up a grocer's or a butcher's message-bike and start earning money for their families. Many would go on to apprenticeships as joiners, plumbers, electricians etc. Many with good brains, who would now be considered university material, were never even allowed to think such thoughts by their parents. The boys, with their eyes to the future, really only numbered three by our third year. My friend Sunny Sim was still there too, but firmly maintaining that he was going to have nothing to do with further education.

Henry Alistair Taylor was the only child of the stationmaster at the little railway station at Dess, down the line from Aboyne. He had been a close buddy of mine from my earliest years at Aboyne. He appeared as a huge boy to us in lower school, as I think he had spent some time in bed convalescing from an illness. This enforced bed-rest had caused him to shoot up in height. In the early days it took three of us to knock him over and hold him down. He stopped growing at about five feet ten inches, while I moved on to be over six feet. Alistair looms large in my mind in upper school as his essays contained words, the meaning of which I had not

Alistair Taylor.
As a Rover Scout in 1948

the faintest idea about. While we toiled to use our limited vocabulary to impress Mr Mair, Alistair was being admonished to restrict his flow of words to reasonable proportions. We always felt that if anyone was to earn the final upper school prize in English, Alistair was out on his own. But Mr Mair had other ideas to prevent him, I think, from becoming too bigheaded. Surprise, surprise, when I shared the prize with Marigold. Yet I always felt Alistair was the one who really deserved it. He went on to take his MA degree at Aberdeen University in 1950 - richly deserved, I am certain.

Alan Simpson.
Hated being Photographed.

Alan Walter Simpson came to Aboyne School in 1939, having come north from London, when his father, a doctor, had volunteered for the RAF at the outbreak of war. Alan was small, with a London accent and as an only child, having been to a private school, was a total alien in our village school culture. He probably had a hard time of it from one or two of his classmates in those early years and I found myself befriended by his mother, in the hope that I might try to acclimatise and protect him. He was a year younger than I was and he seemed to struggle academically at first; but he had an excellent brain and was to blossom forth as the years progressed. He made the grade in our pecking order, when he ascended one of the highest trees, probably a Norwegian spruce, well over one hundred feet, in Aboyne Castle grounds. This he achieved in order to reach a heron's nest. We had dared him to do it, as we well knew that it was not only frighteningly high, but the branches were dangerously slender in places. However, our egg-collecting craze meant that it was imperative that somebody would have to risk the ascent and our little London evacuee rose to the challenge, depositing three eggs safely into our hands. Nobody ever doubted his determination or bravery after that. In those days, Aboyne Castle was derelict, but Alan and his pal Innes Wright would guide us up the rotting stairway on to the roof to gather jackdaw's eggs from nests in the chimneys. Innes, now golf professional at Aboyne Golf Course, readily reminds me of those days whenever I visit in an attempt to master Aboyne's eighteen holes.

Alan was awarded the prize for the most improved pupil over the three years in upper school and he would go on to ever-greater achievement. He will appear frequently in later chapters, as he led the way to a medical degree, a full year ahead of me.

Ernest "Sunny" Sim.

Ernest (Sunny) Sim has been highlighted before. He was a constant presence in class and in my life. Almost white-haired and of a very independent nature, he and I were never really close friends. Yet I always held him in high regard, both for his academic ability and his bloody-minded attitude to a life, which had been pretty hard on him and his family. With Russia battling bravely against the all-conquering Germans, sympathy for the Russian cause had changed many people's attitude from the pre-war fear of the Red menace, to one of total support. No greater enthusiast for the Russian cause was there than Sunny and the more the Russians suffered, so his admiration grew. He was a complete Red and this revolutionary zeal affected all his attitudes. As the poor and under-privileged were his cause, he argued that by going on to further education, he would betray the working classes. He was an expert at bayoneting Germans and I remember that we used to sit in the science classroom, under his tuition, hitting the edge of our hands on the desktop. The idea was that this would harden them up so that we could despatch the hated Germans with one Karate-type swipe. At the end of the day Mr Mair's persuasive arguments prevailed and Sunny grudgingly agreed to go on to Banchory Academy, where I believe some other fine brains overshadowed the Aboyne contingent. He joined the Royal Marines, gaining a commission and served long term, before retiring to Purbrook in Hampshire. Speaking to him recently, I discover that he was now known as Jock to his English family and friends. Moreover, I was amazed that my old Bolshevik had been transformed into a Royalist. Both his daughters had apparently worked as grooms for Prince Charles when they were younger and he was now a changed man. Is there to be nothing permanent in this life of ours? There were two other boys in our year who were not academically inclined. These were Doug McIntosh and Jock Louden. Doug was made head prefect by Mr Mair, I think as an example to the rest of us, that those with presence and good common sense should not be denied a position of authority. He was a very shrewd assessor of human nature was our Mr Mair. Doug and I were both useful athletes, but at the school sports we could never quite get the better of Doug Espie who had been a year behind me at Glen Tanar School and is seen in that school photograph.

Among the girls, I remember particularly Joyce Martin, another war-time bird of passage who had come from Edinburgh. One sensed initially that she was somewhat a cut above us village pupils. However, she was a great character who strutted and stormed her way through her years in Aboyne: but I was very fond of her because she was so way-out and unusual. After Aboyne she went to Mary Erskine's School in Edinburgh before taking an MA at Edinburgh University. She subsequently joined the teaching profession. There was Mary Knowles, the jeweller's daughter, who became a nurse. Our paths crossed during her training. Also well recalled is light-hearted Millicent (Misty) Bell from Ballogie who was our lovable giggler of that period. Dark-haired Betty Coutts, whom I still recall sitting beside in my first day as the new boy; and quiet, shy Margaret Murray from Burnroot Farm, who was the butt of Marigold's teasing over me. Looking back, we were a very happy homogeneous class and I really missed them all when the day came to go on to greater things out in the wider world.

"Misty" Bell.

Joyce Martin, Terry Milne,
Self and Alistair Taylor.

Betty Coutts.

When cycling to school across the Aboyne bridge in the early morning I used to pass a pretty tubby young girl with long hair, also on her way to school. Terry Milne was a friend of Joyce Martin and always seemed so cheery and smiling; but of course much too junior for a senior pupil to talk to. My young friends Ian Watt and Alastair Strang were to pay homage to her. But on coming to Aberdeen, lo-and-behold I found that she was now on the arm of my rumbustious rugby-playing medical classmate, Douglas Robbie. I took great delight in telling her she should have stuck with the civilised young men of Aboyne, but of course she ignored my advice and married Doug. They went to live in London, where he became a consultant at the Royal Marsden Hospital. I am still in contact with both of them after all this time.

Mr Robbie Still.
Good Master but mirthless to us as boys.

Robert (Robbie) Still deserves a special mention, as our science and maths master for those upper three years. Grey-haired, he always seemed old, but it was only a few years ago in the mid-1990's, that he died in Aboyne in his nineties. He was severe and mirthless to us as boys, but all sweetness and light to the girls. He was a competent teacher and I believe did his best for us all. I seemed destined to break things in horseplay, and smashing Mr Still's fancy wall barometer was pure disaster. What I threw is now unclear, but just as the glass smashed, he entered the room to find a spreading lake of mercury coming to meet him across the floor. I must have had some form of punishment, yet Robbie never seemed to bear me any particular grudge after that.

In First Year, six of the best with the strap administered by Mr Richards ensued, when I threw Alan Simpson's hardback jotter through a cabinet window in the woodwork room. I was a poor liar and never could sit and not own up to my misdemeanours, especially if the whole class was set to suffer. Owning up was something I found not all my colleagues would do and many a time we all got a hundred lines because the culprits just sat tight. My final assessment from school fell to Mr Still. When meeting my mother on the bus one day, just after we had all left school, he hazarded that with a good average brain, I should probably do all right in the world. I do not know if that was a rating just ahead of what my mother was expecting. However, it did leave me with the sense that, despite sharing the final mathematics prize with Sunny, I shouldn't get too excited about my prospects.

One of the highlights of any academic year was the prize-giving, which took place before we broke up for summer holidays. Over the years I remember the presentation tables groaning with prizes for the whole school and the many tempting objects on view. I took my fair share of the spoils, but in addition to all the books I gained, my most memorable prize was a set of hair brushes in a leather case, which I went on to use for decades. The other major prize on offer was the Glentanar Essay Award donated annually by the laird. If I remember correctly, it was some sort of gift token. The essay subject was known for a week beforehand and my mother and I would sit for hours perfecting my offering, before committing it to memory to be produced, as if by magic, in the examination room.

For a number of years I seemed to have won it by right; but in our final year Marigold took it from under my nose. Writing under a nom de plume, so that the laird, judging the essays, was unaware of the identity of the writers, I found out that Marigold, under pressure, had disclosed her identity. Belonging to the Girl Guides, run principally for the benefit of Jean Coats and her fellow schoolmates in Glentanar House during the war, Jean and her buddies had bantered with Marigold until she revealed her nom de plume, after which they all went off to read her essay. I remember feeling very upset at this unethical behaviour and was certain that the laird had been cajoled into awarding the prize to her. In truth, this was probably quite false, as Marigold was well able to win in her own right; but the outcome still rankled with me for some time - not that I begrudged my favourite classmate the prize, but I resented a system that I felt was flawed. No thought however that my own prepared approach could perhaps be seen as somewhat outwith the spirit of the competition.

I cannot end this romance with Aboyne without mentioning the stirrings of adult life through our school dances and Alan Simpson's parties. It is difficult to remember when we were first taught to dance, but it was probably in Upper School during our PT sessions and towards the end of term. The normal PT for school was held in the Masonic Hall across the green. However, the dancing lessons took place in the church hall where, years before, we had been taught in Miss Clubb's qualifying class. The first dance we learnt was the *Haymaker's Jig*, proceeding from there to *Strip the Willow* and the *Eightsome Reel*. Dances, such as the waltz, were probably also taught, but it was mainly the Scottish dances that dominated.

The school dance was an end-of-term highlight for us and in our final year I remember my mother making the large posters to pin on the walls listing the order of dances. She was very good at printing, which, being a big head, I probably passed off as my work. The boys sat on one side of the hall, with the girls seated opposite and you needed to look sharp if you wanted to dance with your favourite. Regrettably it used to come to an end all too soon, after all the work we had put into it.

The other party scene was organised by Alan's mother. I clearly recall my first mixed party in Golf Road, where the Simpsons were renting rooms. Alistair Taylor and I stayed overnight, sharing one bed, which meant we had little sleep and a night of hilarious euphoric laughter. Alistair had very strict God-fearing parents and I remember that he went home the next day post-haste. I am sure his mother thought of Mrs Simpson as the proverbial scarlet woman. The second party took place in our last year and was held in Auchtertool Cottage, which the Simpsons now rented. We emerged from our childhood by playing Postman's Knock and Spin the Bottle, which were the party games that made up most of the evening. No one seemed to object to them at all.

A postscript to those happy days at Aboyne came in the form of a book which I read recently. *'On the Lonely Shore'* was written by Don Whyte, the son of Sir Ian Whyte, late conductor of the Scottish National Orchestra. Lord Glentanar had been a patron of Ian Whyte and probably smoothed his way to the top and Ian was a very frequent visitor to the big house in the thirties. Married, he had one son Don, who unhappily contracted polio in his late teens, but overcame his disability to become a reporter with the Daily Express in Glasgow where he was highly rated. Jack Webster, also making his name with the Daily Express at that time, was a colleague of Don's and brought this little book to my attention, as it mirrored so many of my own reminiscences from those years of the '30's.

During his early life, the Whytes took a house in Aboyne and Don went to the school, probably about four years ahead of me. In his book he outlines the culture shock which hit him on coming to school in this rough, tough environment with the occasional bullying that went with it. The picture he paints is so much at odds with my memories that I wonder whether we are talking about the same place. Admittedly, some of us did suffer bullying at the hands of a playfully belligerent Hamish Grant, until having learned to attack first, we found that the problem behaviour disappeared. It just goes to show, however, that different times throw up different experiences and of course my hard baptism at Glen Tanar School might have given me a totally different perspective and expectancy.

It is with great sadness that I now record the fact that, while I was writing these early pages, Alistair Taylor, who was to be my proof reader for these memoirs, developed jaundice and required an operation for presumably carcinoma of the pancreas. Before leaving for South Africa on holiday in March 2001, I spoke briefly to him, finding him feeling weak and not quite up to embarking on this project. On my return from holiday his phone number was unattainable and from the local minister I learnt that my old friend had quietly slipped away.

He had never married and had retired to Torphins after a career in teaching, which all sounded pretty lonely. I was looking forward to resuming our close friendship of past years by working on the memoirs together; but fate cruelly intervened. Sadly, another old friend, Innes Wright, has also passed away. Those days around Aboyne Castle and the loch, which were the source of such delightful reminiscences for us both, are gone forever.

Chapter 8
Boyhood Pastimes

Sport has always taken up a large part of my life since the time that I was given my first football. There is little doubt that I had more of life's luxuries than most of my fellows because, as the only child of older parents with more disposable income, I never experienced poverty. My mother was an excellent controller of the family purse, with so much every month going into the Halifax Building Society. She would not buy bananas this week if they were a halfpenny dearer than they had been the week before. I also had a maiden aunt called Molly who loved to indulge both my cousin Evelyn and myself, as we were her only two young relatives.

For as long as I can remember, we used to play football with my ball on the green in front of the recreation hall. Consequently, when I was called in for my tea, that heralded the end of the game. No one used to complain, although regular knocks at the door asking me to come out and play were prompted more by the desire to regain the ball rather than the pleasure of my company. School football occurred on the Aboyne green at interval times, lunchtime and, occasionally, for an hour after school; while, from time-to-time inter-school matches were arranged. Unfortunately, the war intruded to cut these activities to the minimum, as replacement footballs were non-existent. We were crazy about our soccer and, although never a star, I was always a useful left winger.

My aunt, Molly Watson, was a wonderful Santa Claus to me, and Xmas morning had an expectancy about it that made sleep that night impossible. Over the years toy lead soldiers in their scarlet and blue uniforms, field guns, Hornby trains with carriages, the stations, books and games contributed to some memorable Christmases. Looking back, I realised that I was truly indulged and, as the years went by, my aunt used to buy nearly every new book on birds that came on the market. Even while I was at University she continued to give me a few shillings a week to see me through these impecunious times. I look back with such regret to think that I took all these generous gifts so much for granted and returned so little to her in her declining years. A lament, often repeated throughout this journal, of failing to show my sincere gratitude before it was too late.

The Tanar is more than a brook, but scarcely a sizeable river. Nevertheless, it is big enough for large salmon to gain the upper reaches to spawn. With the river situated so close to our house, it is no wonder that Alfie, Willie and I pinched garden canes, painted them and set off to find the elusive trout with

115

the proverbial bent pin and a box of worms. Of course there is no record of any fish having been caught, but it was great fun.

Budding Fishermen.

*Willie and the Author
in the Bent Pin Era.*

Later with proper fishing tackle Willie and I scoured the river and its tributaries in search of trout and sea trout. Up and down we went for miles catching an occasional salmon taken, no doubt, by anything but fair means. The little brambling worms taken from the dung heap behind the stables did the damage. Having been toughened up for a couple of days in a box of sphagnum moss they were less likely to come off the hook at every cast. Individual pools became associated in our minds with the really large fish taken from them over the years. Spates, or floods, brought up runs of sea trout which gave us amazing fights, the fish weighing between one and two pounds.

I enjoyed the traditional boyhood pastime of guddling trout at my first cub camp at Corntulloch Farm at Dinnet, probably in 1939. The stream alongside the field seemed too small to hold any worthwhile fish, but I was amazed at the number that we actually did snaffle under the tutelage of the gamekeeper's son. What a thrill it was to feel the firm back of a fish under the bank and gently to slip my finger into its gills to bring forth a lovely speckled brown trout weighing about half a pound. This was really amazing, as no one could believe that any fish weighing more than a few ounces could exist in such a small stream.

Guddling salmon later on in the Tanar was a completely different experience. One lovely summer's day, just beyond the Halfway Hut, Willie and I decided that worming the river was producing no results with the sun so high in the sky. So we decided to strip off and take a dip in one of the big pools. We had noted half a dozen salmon lying in the headwaters and were astonished to see them dash up into the rapids above as soon as we started splashing about. The hunter's instinct immediately alerted, we followed, and came upon the fish lying half-exposed in the shallows. Believing that all we had to do was firmly to grasp a tail, I got the shock of my life, when a salmon I caught hold of, leapt away and was off like lightning. In so doing, I skinned my knuckles on the stones as I tried to hang on to it. Attempting to run our hands into the gills of the next fish produced a similar result. So on finding the final salmon, I threw sophistication to the winds and delivered the coup de grâce with a firm well-aimed boulder. Quietly hiding the prize on the bank under a pile of bracken, I persuaded my father and mother to drive the Austin towards Eitnach on the Sunday where I made a swift retrieval. The salmon, none the worse for having lain in the heather for a couple of days, went down a treat with my mother's wonderful home-made mayonnaise.

The Bridge of Feugh at Banchory is a favourite place for viewing salmon ascending the falls and, ten years later, I took my new girl-friend there on the back of my motor-bike. This was the scene of a public exhibition of my guddling prowess also known as the art of 'tickling' fish. Having descended on to the rocks, I knelt down beside one of the narrow water channels above the falls and proceeded to flick out a ten-pound salmon as it passed by. It is debatable whether it was the salmon or I who got the greatest surprise. With a beautiful silvery fresh-run fish flopping about on the rocks, while being observed by an enthralled gallery on the bridge, I found myself in an embarrassing situation. Having to return the ten-pounder to its environment broke my heart, but eventually discretion demanded that, while poaching in private was one thing, to walk away brazenly with such a trophy in these circumstances was quite another.

Too many fishing memories come to mind to recall them all; but some will suffice to paint the picture. The overflow from the lake makes its way down a waterfall into a pleasant pool where the dipper often nests beneath the bank. One Sunday afternoon after church, I decided to spend an hour on the river. Starting in this pool and then fishing on down-river, I made the first cast. The line stopped invitingly half way down and I tightened it firmly, expecting a small trout of less than four ounces to emerge. The sudden rush of the line through and out of the pool took me completely by surprise and, before I could steady myself, the fish was already twenty yards away and not responding to any pressure. I ran along the bank trying to keep up with it until the fish decided to turn and come back upstream. It took me a full twenty minutes to tire that fish out. Having finally beached it on the shingle, I then realised that I had hooked a seatrout of two-and-a-half pounds in the tail, which explained my inability to control its headlong dashes.

A Satisfying Evening
Catch from the Dee.

Amazed by the pure chance of it all, I hared off home as proud as punch, while keeping an eagle eye out for the laird or any keeper. It should be remembered that seatrout were strictly not to be taken at any time and certainly not on the Sabbath. Seatrout belong to the salmon family and, as such, were considered too special for estate workers or their offspring to catch.

My father had always promised me a kilt when I reached my teens. So he took me to Edinburgh to have the kilt made by Andersons of George Street, one of the top kilt makers in the country. I was extremely proud of it, but the occasions to wear it were not too frequent. On this occasion, we may have been visiting my aunt Isobel's family-in-laws at Dunecht estate, where Bill Smith was head gardener to Lord Cowdray and a person of some considerable standing in those days. I must have been about fifteen years old, and was wearing my very expensive Buchanan tartan kilt on this day. Having an hour to spend before my father was ready to go, I decided to dash down to Dain's pool, as the river was just at the right height for catching a seatrout. Sure enough, within ten minutes I had a lovely silvery fresh-run fish of about a pound and three-quarters and set off home in exuberant mood. Too exuberant, as it turned out. For, instead of going round to the gate out of the field, I decided to vault the fence. There was a horrible tearing sound as the barbed wire caught my billowing kilt and I turned round to find a foot long strip of tartan hanging from the barbs. Imagine my utter despair at the prospect of facing my father with such a disaster. Mercifully, he took it in his stride, admonished me appropriately, and the next week sent it to Andersons for repair. That was another lesson learned the hard way; never to let one's enthusiasm bound ahead of common sense.

A Cunliffe-Brooks' Stone encouraging his
Ghillies to keep fishing the Lorne Pool.
*Dry Lines were unknown to us in those
days of fabulous Fishing.*

Willie's father was an excellent fisherman, catching fish when no one else was touching anything, and he encouraged Willie and me to go to the river Dee to fish correctly with fly. Over the years, we had tremendous sport with seatrout and the occasional salmon, caught legitimately now, but still considered technically as poaching by the powers-that-be. Ghillies would turn a blind eye as long as no toffs were fishing and in the evenings the river was always deserted, as the laird's guests, bedecked in their evening finery, were expected for dinner at 7.30pm.

Glen Tanar Exile

In 1950, on the day of the Aboyne Games we had our greatest bonanza. With heavy overnight rain swelling the river, Bill Archibald and I decided to try our luck on the Dee behind Dalwhing. Knowing that the ghillies would all be away at the Games, we prepared to fish for the whole day. No sooner had Bill started fishing than he was into a large sea-trout and by the time I had netted it and picked up my rod he was into another one. Twice more this occurred so I left him to land his own catch as I had not even started fishing. The day was one long miracle and by mid-afternoon we had had enough, with four salmon and thirty-four sea- trout on the bank. I do not remember how we disposed of them all, but a massacre like that is a once-in-a-life-time experience.

Fishing in the gloaming provided the greatest opportunities and many an evening we would be delighted with half a dozen sea-trout each. There was a popular belief at that time that the white grub found at the base of the tansy was irresistible to sea-trout. The problem was that digging up tansies and finding these grubs among the roots was often hard and fruitless work. However, there was no doubt that this lure was an absolute killer in the evening light and the sea-trout were desperate to get them. Our only problem was that the grub tended to come off the hook too easily with the result that we used up our precious stock all too soon. My father also enjoyed fishing and we had one or two memorable evenings with him and Mr Archibald. Taken by car to the Deskrie Burn at Boltenstone, we enjoyed these trips tremendously. After one fabulous night with the worm on a swollen burn above Tarland, Willie and I cycled the eight miles there a few weeks later only to find the burn now a trickle and not a trout to be seen. Such are the highs and lows of fishing.

Bird nesting in the spring was an annual sport, stimulated initially by the desire to collect eggs. Over the years I amassed an impressive collection, going to all sorts of extremes to climb trees, cliffs and buildings to add the rarer eggs and gather extra ones to swap with other collectors. After a time we had all the common species. Each year we would still poke in all the hedgerows, trees and fields just to say we had found the nests but then left without disturbing them. Many birds' nests were extremely hard to find and I have lain out on the moor for hours with field glasses watching and listening to the golden plover, without ever finding a nest. Curlews and of course green plovers (the peewit) were somewhat easier; but the wheatears' nests in burrows also took many hours of watching and waiting to find. One year we heard that the keepers had shot a hen sparrow-hawk off her nest in the Belrorie wood so we "borrowed" a set of climbing irons and, driving them into the tree, as we ascended, we managed to reach the almost inaccessible nest. Great was our rejoicing when we retrieved a full clutch of eggs before the hoody-crows found them. These irons were borrowed at other times to reach the spotted woodpecker's nesting holes, but a lot of hard work was needed after that before we enlarged the hole enough to reach the eggs. The greater the difficulty however the greater the satisfaction.

The Lorne Pool – Craigendinnie, Aboyne.
*Morven in the Background and the mouth
of the Tanar just off to the Left.*

These experiences gave me an interest in birds and, with the help of my Aunt Molly's books, I became really addicted to the hobby. The moor and hills became another playground for us, Alfie and I walking miles across the hills for the sheer pleasure of it all.

Walter E. Higham was a leading bird photographer of the time, with many publications to his name, and I had communicated with him about one of his books. As a result he came to see me, being keen that I should show him some eagles' eyries. Mr R D Young, the factor, did not really approve of my initiative, as eagles were protected and not to be exhibited to strangers. However, he did grudgingly agree to let me take him to the eyrie at the Forfary Bridge and I spent an interesting day in the company of this celebrated specialist in the field. The quartz cliff at the head of the valley on the side of Mount Keen was home, not only to eagles, but also to that master of the skies, the peregrine falcon. Alfie, Bill and I made two excursions there, carrying a great thick rope which we had 'borrowed' from the sawmill yard. This we used to try to lower ourselves down to the nest. Looking back, it was all extremely hazardous, but to us the goal of peregrine's eggs was worth all the danger. We never did get down to the nest, but did eventually manage the ascent to the eagle's eyrie, only to find it empty. However, a couple of years later, on a lone autumn hike to the Allachy eyrie, I was able to ascend the tree just to obtain a view. To my amazement and delight, lying there was a solitary egg. Its presence there, so late on in the season, meant that either it was addled or the female had deserted the nest. I felt no guilt, therefore, in removing it and adding it as the crowning glory to my collection. To be found in possession of such an egg nowadays would result in a very stiff fine.

Still in the hills, winter brought a special fascination induced by trudging through the snow, while marvelling at the spectacle of frosted trees glistening in the sun and the line of a white horizon blending with a winter's sky. Being a Norwegian, Lady Glentanar was naturally a ski enthusiast, so the family were often seen out on their skis around the estate. Children being great imitators, we eagerly sought out planks of wood and, with a couple of walking sticks, tried to emulate the gentry. Not satisfied with this, we then took to shaping our planks and steaming them to have turned-up tips, with only moderate success. The next problem concerned the strapping of our feet firmly enough to the rudimentary skis - something we really never mastered. The laird, seeing our keenness, lent me a set of very long skis that were used for pulling people behind sleighs in Norway. They were cumbersome and difficult to control on any but the easiest of hills and, to my regret, I never became a very proficient skier.

When I must have been only six or seven, my father bought me an air gun. It was a muzzle-type loader and you unscrewed the end in order to insert the pellet into the long tube. It killed little birds, such as sparrows, if you could get close enough. But it wasn't until I purchased the Diana that my proficiency at shooting birds improved. In youth the cruelty of it all was overlooked. However, one day I shot a beautifully coloured bullfinch on a fence, only to find I had also shot his mate, sitting right behind him. This made me pause and think that this destruction of such gorgeous birds was somehow wrong. From that time onwards I lost much of my enthusiasm.

In order to offset the cost of buying the Diana, I sold the old airgun to John Strang, the head keeper's son. About a year later, when playing in the Strang's house, I came out of a bedroom and was struck in the stomach by a blow that totally winded me. Gasping for breath, I was helped downstairs by Mrs Strang; but it was quite some time before I could breathe properly again. It turned out that I had been struck by a pea which had been fired from my old gun by the elder brother, Peter Strang. But more of him later. Fired from very close range, it had a powerful effect for all its size, and I carried the pigmented bruise for years afterwards. Not long after this incident a similar effect was experienced when I fell from the ladder leading into the hayloft at the end of the Stable Yard. Coming down heavily from some nine feet, I was completely winded and felt unable to breathe for about ten minutes. That a pea could have caused exactly the same effect seems unbelievable, but to experience is to believe.

A hobby that was to remain with me well into adolescence and beyond, was building model aeroplanes and gliders. The gliders gave us the biggest thrill when, having been towed up into a windless sky, they would take off and fly away out on to the Knockie Hill. If, as sometimes happened, a glider became lodged in some high branches, it would require much patience and care to extricate it without causing too much damage. Later on, when confined to bed with pleurisy, I found that the building of a bigger model kept me from dwelling on my misfortune. Later still, when suffering the trauma of university exams, building models helped me to keep life in perspective.

We were always building huts in the woods or excavating trenches and covering them with brushwood, either up the hillsides or in plantations. Up on the hill from the West Lodge, where, as five-year-olds, we had played with Elsie Downie, we now used this area to play soldiers, with one group trying to crawl through the heather and surprise those holding the fort at the top. For me, this game lost all its enjoyment when, while crawling across a patch of grass among the heather, I came face to face with an adder. This narrow escape taught me never to crawl in heather again. A laughable postscript to all this construction-work was reported to me many years later. While thinning out the wood behind West Lodge, above the sawmill, the foresters came upon a well-excavated pit covered over by a wooden frame. Puzzled, they came to the conclusion that it had been constructed as an air-raid shelter by Fred Silver, the occupant of West Lodge during the war. How they ever came up with such an explanation is beyond me. But, having built this secret hideout, I can assure them that Fred and his family would have got precious little protection from our flimsy construction. In addition, they would all have developed early rheumatism, as it was so damp that we quickly decided that it had been one of our poorer concepts and deserted it within a week. Nevertheless, it really tickled my fancy to visualise people scratching their heads over it a decade later.

Parked in a loading bay outside the joiner's shop, was an old float that had been used for moving cattle. As it appeared to have outlived its usefulness, we decided, without permission, that this would convert into an ideal gang hut. Roofing it with wood from the sawmill, we put it together with nails acquired by the simple method of climbing in by the skylight of the joiner's shop and taking all we required. This hut was re-erected on many occasions, always with more improvements and even a second storey added. Why no one questioned us as to where we got the wood or how we obtained so many nails, I shall never understand. This den became our pride and joy, with a secret access door and locks that were put in place to make it really secure. We had years of fun in it and when I eventually left the Glen, I think it was still standing there. The bigger boys used to raid us and on one occasion when Peter Strang evicted us, we started stoning him from the outside. I still remember his hand grasping the edge of the glassless window, when all my animosity for him over the years made me take careful aim and strike the bulls-eye. When Peter emerged nursing a badly fractured thumb, I surprised myself by feeling absolutely no remorse and, instead, satisfaction that justice had been achieved at last. He seemed to bear me no ill-will afterwards and just accepted it as one of the hazards of growing up. Little did he know that it was not quite the lucky shot he presumed it to be.

Primitive Rafts on the Golf Course Pool.
*No need for sophisticated toys here - these rafts
gave us hundreds of hours of pleasure.*

The raft pool was a long quiet stretch of the Tanar bordering the edge of the golf course, with a depth of two to three feet of water for most of the year. It was perfect for our home made rafts which were constructed from large oil barrels fixed into a frame of wooden beams. The enjoyment of hours spent punting or rowing these unwieldy craft up and down the river over the years, was rivalled only by our football addiction. With the river in flood, we would don our swimming trunks and take a delight in entering the water at the top of this pool to be swept in the raging torrent down to the weir, which was probably a distance of about five hundred yards. No one seemed to consider this to be a dangerous pursuit, although our parents were quite unaware of what we were up to and would have been horrified to see the height of the river. The Fairy Lake had been drained a few years earlier and some large pike had found their way into our pool. So we had great fun stalking them from the raft and throwing a wire trace baited with a minnow which they seemed unable to resist. We totally eliminated the incomers eventually, but justified our massacre by seeing them as predators of the trout which, of course, we were also quite happy to catch.

The big lake had a boathouse which nestled along the north bank. It could be accessed by clambering out along the roughcast wall above the water and easing ourselves around the entrance to get a footing on the walkway inside. The reason for this precarious method of entry was due to the fact that the door was always locked to keep the likes of us firmly outside. There were always two very trim, beautifully varnished rowing boats housed here and it gave us great pleasure to sit in them imagining ourselves rowing out across the lake. The chance of being caught on the lake was far too likely for even seasoned brigands like us to risk.

Firstly we would have had to face the wrath of the laird and then that of our parents. However, Bill and I did discover a lovely canoe which Miss Jean and her friends had been using on one of the smaller lakes close to the mansion house. Every evening for a week, we went skimming around this lake with great enthusiasm. The enjoyment came to a sudden end one evening, when a very loud imperious voice demanded what we thought we were up to and, in due course, we were escorted firmly out of the policies by a rather irate laird. Estates being little less than feudal kingdoms, our behaviour could have had serious consequences for our parents. Instant dismissal could occur for certain trespasses and as we grew older we began to realise that all our freebooting could bring our parents into conflict with the factor and thence with the laird.

Alfie and the Pike.

Despite our visible presence they could not resist the Bait.

Poaching of any sort was a hazardous pursuit, but this still did not totally deter us. In the autumn the salmon came up in their hundreds to spawn in the head waters of the Tanar and some pools were alive with them. Such a pool was *The Black Ship* where, on one memorable day, we found the salmon present in abundance. There and then Alfie and I decided that a few for the pot would be appreciated. Fetching some large boulders from the shore, we dropped them off the bridge into the milling throng. In this way we killed about four fair-sized salmon. The problem now was how to get them home undetected.

As we were no longer children, there would have been a lot of trouble if we had been seen. Keeping off the beaten track and sticking to the woods, we eventually reached the sawmill that was within sight of our homes, but across open country. Undaunted, Alfie fetched his father's barrow and we loaded it with firewood to which his father had access. Then, with the salmon hidden below the logs, we gained the safety of our houses and could sigh with relief. The fact that the salmon were red and really past their best for eating, certainly did not stop our parents making full use of the windfall; but fingers were wagged warning us against any further escapades.

My father was a very keen shot and got a great thrill when he had the chance to go out with the keepers to shoot grouse, blackcock and greyhen, pheasant, partridge, woodcock, snipe, hares or rabbits. On a memorable day before the war, I accompanied Father with the rest of the keepers around the Fairy Lake, on a capercaillie shoot. These birds are almost extinct now, but at that time they seemed to be very common. I was probably nine at the time and I clearly remember standing in the ride, a firebreak through the wood, with guns lined up on either side and having these huge birds driven to us by the other keepers. The cock capers came across the trees like zeppelins, seeming to blot out the sky and looking all too easy to shoot. Because of their size, their speed of flight was deceptive and it therefore amazed me how few were brought down. Nevertheless, this has remained a red-letter day in my memory.

Occasionally my father would borrow one of the laird's very expensive shotguns, such as a *Stephen Grant*, and taking one of the keeper's dogs, we would walk up towards *The Black Ship*, where on the hillside were numerous blackgame and greyhen. Walking home one evening from a foray, my father handed me the gun and told me to fire at some branches. Apprehension gripped me as the tales of bruised shoulders and faces were common; but I gritted my teeth and fired off a couple of cartridges. So was born the love for a new sport.

The collecting of cigarette cards was a total addiction for us and we would hassle every available smoker in our eagerness to complete a full set. Certain cards were in short supply, so that while we had plenty of the common cards to swop, we owned very few of the rarer ones. We would have gone to almost any lengths, beg, borrow or steal, to be the first boy to complete a set.

Boyhood Pastimes

I ended up with dozens of cigarette card albums, lovingly collected over many years. Ownership of certain cards produced an almost magical sensation and I remember the collection of English cricketers with the emblems of their counties awakening an interest in cricket, which blossomed forth during my teens. The set of steam engines was probably my favourite album; but I was to use doubtful methods to complete the set. That, however, is a story for another chapter.

We tended to collect anything and everything – match-box tops, milk bottle tops and, of course, stamps, the collecting of which was pursued with the same intensity as the cigarette cards. We all seemed to be obsessive acquirers, as nails, bolts, screws, bits of wire and anything that might remotely come in useful were put into pockets. In my garage, I can still rummage through jars of odds and ends to find some odd screw that I probably picked up as a ten-year-old. The blacksmith's shop, with Alec Benzie at the forge, was also a place where we stocked up on horse nails or bits of iron, while we watched him making the shoes and then fitting them to the Clydesdales. The smell of the smiddy is something that stays with you for life. Likewise, the pumping of the bellows and the hissing of a horseshoe in the water-barrel are noises that I can vividly recall.

If this picture gives an impression of eternal action and interest on the estate, it would be quite misleading. I can remember often trudging despondently into the house and complaining to my mother that we had nothing to do. She had very little time for this attitude and I would be promptly directed towards some chore that awaited me. This usually had the effect of galvanising me into remembering something that needed my immediate attention, such as damming the burn below our house.

Perhaps because we sometimes ran out of ideas for play, we found employment from quite an early age in the forestry nursery, weeding the young trees up at Belrorie. This was a tedious job, but for two shillings a day (10p) it seemed to be worth it. There was a certain camaraderie that developed among us workers and I suppose, in retrospect, that the discipline and attention to detail were attributes that did us no harm in the years to come. Later, we were also employed on the farm, but I always hated this. Hoeing turnips must be one of the most boring jobs in life and working in a line with the farm grieve and farm labourers, who set out to make it difficult for the children, was always soul-destroying. I used to arrive home exhausted, not so much by the work as from desperately trying to keep up with people who took a delight in making it hard for us. Potato-gathering, on the other hand, was always fun with a good group of people around you to make light of the work. In those days two shillings and six pence a day (12.5p) seemed to us to be the ultimate in pay and we all worked very hard to earn it. Much later on, the tedium of weeding trees in the nursery was alleviated by the Italian prisoners of war that were enlisted to help, and their happy-go-lucky presence made the days simply fly past.

A game that seems to have died out among our children is marbles. We played this at a certain time of the year and fierce were the competitions to get your boolies into the kypie. Those who were very good could win so many marbles that they cleaned out their opponents who would have to do deals to continue playing or go off and buy some more. I still have a tin-full of these multi-coloured glass marbles but who would want them now? The recreation hall boasted a very fine billiard table and, when we became older, this used to provide hours of entertainment, especially on rainy days. I am sad to say that this was one game that I was never really able to master and I feel that the Scout Show we once put on, using the billiard table as the stage, was by far my greatest success on it. The hall also acted as the public library and books were regularly changed from the central library. I got into the habit of taking out books, but what I read is mostly forgotten, apart from innumerable Westerns. The hall was used also for regular whist drives and dances, but neither of my parents ever attended. My mother was certainly anti-social in such company and my father never seemed to be free.

They both enjoyed card games, however, and often on a Sunday night both of them got a great kick out of the three of us spending many hours in serious combat. I never inherited this love and I consequently was always the one who needed to be persuaded to give up some favourite pastime and to join in the game. My father in his early bachelor days would have spent many hours a week in his Piccadilly club where his card game of choice was piquet; but for us at home it was always either nap or whist.

In those early days, although the mansion house had its own electricity supply generated from the Tanar, no other houses had it and we were dependent on Aladdin lamps. Our Aladdin was hung from mid-ceiling in the living room and was fitted with a very sensitive mantle. Often, while totally absorbed in a card game, no one would notice the flame flaring up, until the mantle turned black and the flame was smoking up the glass funnel and blackening the ceiling. Later we had a pressurised Tilley lamp and the days of the flaring mantle passed, although little hand-held oil lamps were required wherever else we went upstairs, out into the kitchen or out to the toilet.

The wireless came into its own during the thirties, replacing the crystal set. We originally had a tall cabinet that was full of batteries that had to be taken regularly to Walter Wright in Aboyne to be recharged. Just before the war my father bought a shiny new Murphy - the latest fashion in radio receivers - and we really thought we had arrived. We had two low-tension batteries so that we could always have one in use. Thus, a regular weekly chore was to go to Aboyne with the flat battery and collect the fresh one. Children's hour was of course my initial love, with Auntie Kathleen, its ever-faithful presenter in those pre-war days. This, coupled with my early introduction to the comic, *Mickey Mouse*, delivered every Tuesday, was the favourite indoor entertainment of the week; but I shall leave that for another chapter when I shall discuss my reading preferences.

Our cycles gave us a marked degree of freedom. I am amazed at the trusting nature of our parents in that they never once enquired where we were going. As the journey to school in Aboyne, four and a half miles away, was our regular weekday chore, we did not often go there except during the holidays. However, just before the war we became obsessed with the affairs of Aberdeen Football Club. Thus, our eagerness to obtain the results on a Saturday night meant that every week we had to cycle to Aboyne Station to buy our Green Finals. The memory of standing on that chilly platform and experiencing the thrill of watching the steam engine coming into sight, half a mile away still sends a shiver of excitement done my spine. Next stop would be the chip shop at the top of the brae out of the Square; and we were then haring off home to capture news of the Dons' latest glories. Piles of these Green finals were kept so that we would not forget all those triumphs.

A day came in the autumn of 1955 when my father decided to retire. Mother in desperation took the bull by the horns and all my lovely collections, comics and memorabilia, all gathered with so much dedication over the years, along with not a few of my children's books, were consigned to the waste paper depot. Only now, in retrospect, do I realise what treasures were discarded then as of no importance or possible value.

Chapter 9
Holidays And Black Beauty

Let me now cast my mind back to the 1930's when my father took his holidays and we travelled where most boys from my background would only have dreamed about. The first great adventure has unfortunately almost totally disappeared from my memory, as it occurred when I was four. That must have been in 1933 at the time of the great slump that was affecting the Western world, but obviously having no effect on my family.

Hitler had come to power but had not yet set out on his dream to rule the world and the British aristocracy continued to live in the lap of luxury. My father would have benefited from the constant house parties at Glentanar House, with the resultant gratuities from well-satisfied guests. Father took his holiday every two years. By amalgamating his fortnight's annual holiday leave, we were thus able to go abroad for a month-long visit to France.

The first of my trips was to Paris, but I have only the haziest recollections of running around a hotel corridor. I was told I was in my element with absolutely no shyness and making friends with all and sundry. From there we would have gone to my father's old home outside St Julien de Vouvantes. In my album there is a very poignant photo of a small fair-haired boy standing with his grandmother Fouin and

1933 - Granny Fouin, Aunt and Cousins with a very shy Grandson.

La Riviere Besnier, Grugé l'Hopital.

his Aunt Josephine, both dressed in black, together with two small cousins outside their farmhouse at Gruge l'Hopital. This would appear to be the only record of Dad's mother and I have no record at all of my French grandfather other than a very faded family group from around 1919.

131

By 1935 when I was now six years old, holiday memories are becoming clearer, although the details of the rail journey to Southampton have gone. Sailing down Southampton Water with the sun setting is still a wonderful memory. Living at the Corvesier's hotel in Combrée, has left vivid memories of fantastic food. Having eaten too much of the first three courses, I learned to control myself in order to appreciate the usual ten course dinner. I do not think I ever again got so much pleasure from food as at Dad's friend's hotel here and I remember the staff of pretty girls thoroughly complementing this effect.

The other memory is of the haunting sound of the church bells, something we scarcely ever heard at home. In Combrée they rang out almost continuously during the Sunday morning. Moving on, we stayed with my Uncle Henry at St Martin Brionne, where he was stationmaster at this tiny station. Aunt Juliette was a large lady of imposing appearance, while Uncle Henry was a small jack-in-the-box of a man of great energy and jollity. My cousin Denise was a few years older than me, but a pleasant companion. This was a very happy holiday. I believe this was the first time we went to stay at La Baule sur Mer. Staying in a hotel overlooking the sea, the memory is again about the quality of the food and of playing on a lovely white beach, making huge sandcastles.

St Martin Brione Railway Station – 1935.

Dad, Aunt Juliette, Uncle Henry and
Cousin Denise on the busy platform.

Around this time, my mother and I had a holiday in Morpeth, staying with my grandparents at 5 Bennetts Walk. Hazy recollections of that elderly couple remain with me and I can still hear my mother tut-tutting over my critical remarks about her father's manners. Watching grandfather dunking his biscuit into his tea and then pouring the tea into a saucer and noisily slurping between pursed lips had me all agog. Never allowed such a breach of good manners at home, I couldn't let this pass without much audible comment, much to my mother's great embarrassment. The other lasting memory was of the dry privy in a row of little sheds at the side of the garden. Used only to a flush toilet, I found this thunder-box a barbaric method for my regular ten minutes after breakfast routine and rapidly became constipated as I tried to dodge this degrading experience.

1937 saw the end of my schooling at Glen Tanar School and I clearly remember the thrill of my father coming to collect me in the new Austin10. Next day we set off for France in AV 9442, the car that was my father's pride and joy. Buying the car had represented a real achievement in his life, all the more so because few people could afford anything more than a bicycle or a very ancient car. This shiny black beauty had mounted on the boot an oval white disc on which were displayed the letters 'GB' in black. This car thus became one of the most distinctive in the district.

Grandfather Watson.
5 Bennett's Walk, Morpeth.
The Thunderbox caused Problems.

My father had driven the laird when he was away travelling with him; but as a chauffeur was usually in attendance as well, Father probably didn't have many opportunities to drive. In any case, he was only a moderately skilled driver and I am glad that in those days I didn't have my advanced driver's insight into his driving, as I would probably have refused to ride with him. Our first stop was Edinburgh where Father took us to the North British Hotel to start the holiday off in the right spirit. He may only have been a butler/valet, but his tastes were those of the highborn. His whole demeanour changed when he went on holiday. Out would come the large cigar and he would become as expansive as any wealthy businessman, with lobster in the best hotel in Edinburgh as the starting point. He never grudged any expense and I have never been able to adopt this attitude over the years, despite being almost in the millionaire class compared to my dad.

Mother's youngest sister was Auntie Isobel or Auntie Belle as I always called her. She had the best brains in the Watson family, obtaining a teaching degree

Balmaha - 1933.

Uncle Will Halley, Aunty Molly,
Cousin Evelyn and Aunty Belle.

from Moray House, Edinburgh where she emerged as the top graduate. She had married Will Halley, who was then circulation manager for Scotland for the Daily Mail and who, as a sideline, ran a fleet of delivery vans under the name Halley's Deliveries. My maiden-aunt Molly, who lived with the Halleys, ran this business. They lived in a lovely big bungalow at 67 Greenbank Crescent, looking out over the Braid Hills, which seemed to me to be the lap of luxury. Evelyn, their only child, was six years older than me and is someone I have always been extremely fond of. Educated at George Watson's Ladies' College, she had had a good start in life.

Sadly, just when Uncle Will was beginning to prosper, he died suddenly just before the war, leaving my aunt and cousin in reduced circumstances. Aunt Molly was then destined to become deputy superintendent of the Soldier's, Sailor's, and Airmen's Institute in Edinburgh.

Leaving Edinburgh, we had travelled about ten miles south where, at a wet corner, my father managed to skid the car in a really alarming manner. Though we came to no harm, it was a warning that motoring could be a dangerous form of travel even in those days of light traffic conditions. I can remember the car being hoisted on board the ferryboat at Southampton, but the trip across the Channel remains a hazy memory. Small fragments of the journey remain, such as the thrill of standing on the front seat and waving to other GB cars from out of the sunroof; and the sight of the AA men on their yellow motorcycles saluting our AA badge whenever they passed us.

My father was in his element on this holiday, as owning a car signified that he had arrived and his big cigars just confirmed the impression. I never felt like deflating his ego as, although he was like a puffed-up peacock, I always felt he fully deserved his moments of triumph. In addition, he was never obnoxious and the relatives' obvious delight in his success benefited everyone. My mother remained the perfect stylish English gentlewoman among the dark drab dresses of these peasant folk and she made no real attempt to try and come to terms with the language. A few words of greeting and farewell were as much as she could muster. However, she did at least seem to enjoy the company and never ducked the round of visiting relatives, knowing that it meant a great deal to Father.

A Breton Country Wedding. The year 1919 and my Uncle John
marries Germaine Bossard in St Julien de Vouvantes.

*Behind the young girl and on Uncle John's right, sits my Grandfather
whom I never knew, as he died before my visits to France. Eighteen
years later, as I recall, nothing much had changed on the farms from
the sombre scene above.*

The beach at La Baule was a great escape from the family visits in the summer
heat and was on the whole a relaxing experience. One episode spoils the idyllic
picture. It happened when I was left in the town with a family who were
acquaintances of my father. The children were about my own age and when
my parents decided to leave me to play with them, I suddenly felt lost, a fish
out of water. After a time the four children went indoors and I took off into the
town to seek out my folks. On the previous day, we had gone to a hair-dressing
salon to make an appointment for my mother for the next day; so I knew that
at some time they were likely to be there. I remember retracing our steps
through the town until I came close to the salon. Being too shy to go in and see
if they were there, I stood on the street corner for what seemed like an hour. I
felt terribly alone and a bit apprehensive in this large town and in addition my
bladder was almost bursting. When I had almost totally lost heart, both parents
suddenly appeared and I was told off for being so stupid. Their main concern
was that the family would be worrying about me. Sure enough, there were a
lot of frowns and shaking of heads when we got back and I think I embarrassed
my parents quite badly. I didn't feel very proud of myself either; but this

language barrier has held me back throughout my life and prevented me from maintaining proper contact with my cousins after my father's death.

1937 - St. Julien de Vouvante's magnificent
Roman Catholic Church.

Father was christened here in 1881 – the wealth of the church surrounded by so much poverty in the village affected his attitude from an early age.

The trip home went very well until we came to Chatham where we stopped to spend the night. My mother was very excited as Tyrone Guthrie, the eminent theatrical director, was staying in the hotel and, as he was a celebrity, I asked him for his autograph. On the following day, while motoring north, we came up behind a slow-moving army lorry full of soldiers. The soldiers in the back waved my father to pass, although they obviously could not see what was coming. My father pulled out and was almost past when the lorry swung across the road to go down a side road on the right.

The lorry struck us on the back wing, tipping the car over on to two wheels and we seemed to go along like this for ages before the car righted again. The driver turned out to be a learner who had never seen us coming. As a result, our back wing was severely dented. We managed to go back to Chatham to get some quick repairs done before proceeding on our way the next day. The accident gave my mother and me quite a fright, although Father never showed any emotion.

In 1939 the storm clouds were gathering over Europe and I think my father

1935 - St. Martin
Brionne Station.

decided that despite Mr Chamberlain's Munich Treaty, we would be better advised to stay at home. As it turned out we were but a couple of months from the outbreak of war. It was not until the 1960's that my father would return to France.

In those pre-war days, at the end of the summer term, the school would visit exotic places of interest, such as the Aberdeen beach, Girdleness Lighthouse; or, perhaps, go as far afield as Montrose. These were highlights of the children's year, when a distance of ten miles from home was a major event. Most pupils still did not own bicycles personally. However, the County Council provided bikes for children living some distance from the school. All my friends were given Council bicycles, but my father did not believe in charity, so would not accept one on my behalf. In any case, I had had a bicycle from an early age and it seemed unfair of me to have claimed yet another one. My first bicycle was the Hercules, which was sold on to the Strangs when I got a bigger one at age nine or ten. This was a Vindec, which my father bought from Turner's garage. I was very disappointed, as I had really wanted a Raleigh. The Raleigh was top of the range and obviously more expensive. Despite using it until I was seventeen, I never really liked my Vindec. I learned from Mr Turner, the supplier, who was a friend of my father, that it was constructed from parts supplied by various manufacturers so was really a hybrid which did not endear it to me. In a severe head wind I would feel that my lack of progress was due to its being a rotten bike and would kick it in frustration at times. Doing this once too often one night on the way home, I kicked the front wheel and went over the handlebars when my foot was trapped in the spokes. Having buckled the front wheel, I had to walk home, but never admitted what had really happened.

1937 - La Baule Beach.

The bus trip or, better still, the train journey to Aberdeen, was a pleasant and exciting experience. Once there, a visit to the beach was heaven itself in those days. Later, being the owners of a car enabled us to go to Aberdeen more frequently. However, the enjoyment of the occasion was marred by the fact that I had usually to go to the dentist first of all. Although old Mr Soper in Golden Square was a nice quiet man, dentistry was a most trying experience for me. I can still relive the sensation of severe apprehension as this white-coated figure operated the belt-driven drill that made a characteristic whirring sound, while I looked out on a bleak granite wall. Lunch in the old Palace Hotel at the top of Bridge Street went a long way towards retrieving the day, as I was eating in one of the grandest of Aberdeen establishments at that time. My father always seemed to know the right person to find us a good table, and the luxury of the food and the general ambience were in keeping with the North British Hotel in Edinburgh.

A visit to Collies, the quality grocers in Union Street, was another unforgettable experience. Outside, as you approached the shop, the wonderful aroma of freshly ground coffee welcomed you as it wafted up into the fresh air from the basement grille. Old Mr Buchanan in his traditional tail-coat and high starched collar, was always on hand to take us into his office and refresh my father with an appetiser and me with a ginger beer from one of those old clay bottles. My father called in once a year to re-stock the cellar of Glentanar House, and so was a really important client for Mr Buchanan the owner.

His manager, Mr John McDonald, a very pleasant good-looking man, would then take my father to the wine cellars to sample the various vintages before placing his order. I was left to kick my heels for another half-hour while the ritual was performed. Life takes many odd turns and in the 1960's I was called out by the police to attend a fatal traffic accident near Tor-na-Dee Hospital outside Aberdeen. It eventually turned out, on post mortem evidence, that the driver had suffered a heart attack, causing him to veer into a lamp-post. Having certified the unknown driver as being dead on the spot, I was therefore astounded to find out later that it was the very same John McDonald of those never-to-be-forgotten days in Collies' wonderful shop.

Aberdeen seemed a different city then, when Union Street boasted real quality shops such as Gordon and Smith, Galloway and Sykes, Ogilvies, and let us not forget Kennaways Tea Rooms. Another treat on these occasions came when my mother would take me to 'the pictures' in a real cinema house. This seemed luxury indeed compared with watching the primitive lantern shows and later the school films shown by means of a temperamental projector.

1937 was a memorable year, not only because of the new Austin, but because buying it had involved Alec Prior who, in addition to being a car salesman, also played right back for Hibernian Football Club. His father, Arthur, was a friend of my aunt Molly and my parents, so that whenever Dad went to Edinburgh, he and Arthur Prior would go off to Mr Prior's private club from which they usually returned in more than good spirits. These men's clubs were an essential part of life in those days and were bastions of male chauvinism that are now vanishing from our lives. During his years in London my father looked on his club as his second home, as so many of the rich and powerful still do in order to keep them exclusive.

Following our purchase of the new car, Alec Prior and his wife Rose were invited to come and stay with us for a couple of days when Hibs were due to play Aberdeen at Pittodrie. As a bonus we were given complimentary tickets to attend the match on the Saturday. Such a luxurious experience was almost unknown to rural communities at that time. In our minds Pittodrie appeared as far away as New York does to the modern-day youngsters. On entering the stadium, I was to experience for the very first time in my life a level of excitement that was unimaginable. I found myself literally trembling for the full ninety minutes and nothing I could do would control it. The match result has been obliterated in the intervening years; but I have still in my possession a treasured autograph book with the signatures of all the Hibs players. For months afterwards I dined out on the kudos of this with my mates, revelling in the reflected glory of that occasion. Infrequent visits to Pittodrie over the years have never again recreated that sensation. By now I recognise it to be pure commercial entertainment, dependent on club-based sentimentality and the need for so many of us to desperately brighten up our humdrum lives.

My first venture into Aberdeen, accompanied by Alfie Dawson, probably took place in 1942 when we saw the film *El Alamein*. This dramatised the battle of El Alamein when General Montgomery's army broke through General Rommel's lines in North Africa and gave Britain the first glimmer of hope in the Second World War. This trip was indeed an adventure, as neither of us had ever ventured so far afield on our own. Strachan's bus to Bon Accord Square, then on to Union Street, turn right and go along on the same side past two side streets, Crown Street and Dee Street, until you come to The Picture House - these were our instructions.

All went well and we were thrilled by the film. But when coming out on to the street, I felt totally disorientated. Under the impression that I was on the opposite side of the street, I set off by turning right. Coming quickly to the traffic lights at Bridge Street, I realised our mistake. It was a totally disconcerting experience to find how a city could so upset my countryman's sense of direction. Over the years, I have often experienced this sensation and have never got used to the irritation it causes. This trip was followed by our taking the bus to Ballater occasionally on a Saturday afternoon. Going to the cinema there seemed much more of a thrill compared with cycling to Aboyne to see the pictures in the Victory Hall, which after all was not a real cinema. The cinema was a staple entertainment, especially throughout the war, when there was so little opportunity for people to escape from the gloom and hardship of living in wartime Britain.

During the bleak war years, holidays were never even contemplated. Thus a holiday in London at the end of my secondary education in 1947 was to be the start of a new era. However, just prior to this, a working holiday on the West Coast was offered to me. I accepted the opportunity with some grave misgivings. The proposed job was that of cook/handyman on Lord Glentanar's luxury yacht *Pamela*, moored just off the island of Kerrara in Oban Bay. Not being much of a cook, I was going to find providing food for the skipper and the two crew a most trying experience - in both senses of the word! However, they were very patient with me. The episode that caused them far more stress was caused by my absolute stupidity as a crewman.

As we were a full mile away from Oban across the bay, we had to go ashore for provisions every day. On one or two occasions the sea was very rough but on this particular morning it was dead calm, with a brilliant sun and life felt good. While returning in our small launch from our morning ashore, we were halfway home when our engine spluttered to a halt. This was a regular occurrence and was due to dirt in the tank that kept fouling the carburettor. The skipper told me to follow the usual procedure and unscrew the main jet, blowing through it to clear the blockage. Unthinkingly I held the jet over the side of the boat and proceeded to blow it right out of my fingers; as I watched, mesmerised, it went spinning and twisting in the sunlight, until it sank ever so slowly out of sight.

The boat was not spotless, so why I should have felt it necessary to blow the dirt over the side remains a mystery. Perhaps it was a natural response produced as a result of my training regarding cleanliness. Whatever the reason, the oars had to come out and it was a disgruntled skipper and a very red-faced boy that struggled back to *Pamela*. To make matters worse, we found out that a new jet was only available from Glasgow, which meant that we had to wait for three days before it was delivered to us. I had become a pretty good oarsman by the time the launch's motor fired again, as my shipmates made sure I appreciated my folly. They were all really decent to me, but the shiver of disbelief at my crass stupidity lives with me still.

Pamela at Kerrara off Oban.
Scene of a Crew Member's Stupidity.

The postscript to this chapter concerns my father's greatest toy, the Austin 10 Saloon. It arrived one day at our door in 1937, black, and sparkling new. It remained in his possession until its eventual demise in 1968. While AV 9442 gave my father much pleasure, it gave the whole family some anxious times. Apart from our accident with the army lorry outside Chatham back in 1937, my father had managed to crash his car on a number of occasions. Skidding on icy roads and hitting lampposts occurred at least twice; while he managed to overturn it near the entrance to Aboyne from the east. At that time the road rose up to cross the railway and somehow he hit the fence on the approach to the bridge and rolled the car right down the banking. Unhurt, he just sent it off once more for repairs.

My history with the car is yet another embarrassing tale of incompetence. In the winter, draining off the water from the radiator was my father's preferred method in case of frost. This was such a routine procedure that I never thought twice about it. But on this occasion, in about 1950, I must have had other more interesting things on my mind and as a result I failed to drain it. Next time my father came to start the engine he found that the engine block was split, the water having been frozen solid. I was mortified, but my patient father simply regretted my carelessness and put the car in to be repaired once more.

Our most serious accident happened probably about 1952, when Dad and I went off for a few days' trip round the West Coast. Driving into Fort William, we were struck by a Swedish tourist driving a Volvo. He had mistaken the Glen

Nevis branch road for the main road just as I was passing the side road junction. The Volvo struck us head-on into the side of our car and his bonnet pushed the driver's door into my lap. Although cut slightly around the face with flying glass, neither of us was really hurt; but this was my first experience of post-traumatic stress. Being driven to a hotel where we were to spend the night before catching a train home, I experienced the dreadful sensation of expecting the taxi to crash at any moment. It wore off after a day but subsequently during my career, I could well understand what people meant when they described their reactions to me in similar situations.

The sequel to this tale occurred about one week later. My father had been lamenting the fact that in the heat of the moment we were so relieved to have escaped with our lives, that we had both failed to get the Swedish driver's particulars. The following week, while filling up my motorcycle, at the garage in Aboyne, I watched a red Volvo passing. At that time Volvo's were non-existent on UK roads and, as I watched, I noticed that his bonnet and wing were badly damaged. Unbelievably, this was the self-same car on its way up Deeside. Catching up with him and waving him down a couple of miles further on, I obtained all the necessary details which enabled my father to get a substantial settlement from his insurance company some months later. People talk about a Higher Being looking after our interests – in reality the chance of me being at that one spot as the Volvo passed by must have been at least a thousand to one against.

September 1952 - A Postscript Picture.
My French Cousins, Josette and René Caron.
Who said there was nothing left to shoot in France?

Over the years, I tried hard to persuade Dad to change the car for a newer and better make, such as the laird's 1938 Rover 12 which was for sale; or later still a Sunbeam Talbot 90, which I really coveted. He would show interest, but could never bring himself to part with what he regarded as a symbol of his own achievement. Learning to drive it from the age of sixteen until I became a locum GP in Aberdeen in 1958 was very much part of my growing-up.

However, the Austin never came to mean the same to me as it was to my proud father. Patched and serviced, the old car still looked in pristine condition until that day in 1968 when fate delivered the coup de grâce. Twisted and torn in an accident two miles west of Peterculter, its time had come. It had served the family well; but for this fine old machine the end had now finally arrived and both my parents were very fortunate to be stretchered away from it alive.

Chapter 10
Glen Tanar At War

The unruffled pace of life on a well-ordered private estate had me firmly believing that nothing could ever possibly disturb our futures. Little did I understand that far off in Berlin Adolf Hitler had very different plans that were about to shatter all this narrow complacency. Suddenly the halcyon unchanging days at Glentanar evaporated on 3rd September 1939 when Neville Chamberlain announced to the world that Great Britain was at war with Germany.

A month earlier on the 23rd August when my mother opened the door for me returning as usual from school, I was suddenly jolted into realising that all was not well. My return after cycling the four and a half miles was usually heralded by my mother greeting me on the doorstep, either with a kind word or a mild rebuke for playing football too long after school. I had to wheel the bicycle in through the front door and park it in the passageway, as we had no back door. The smell that greeted me was always highly appetising - spotted dick, chocolate or marmalade pudding, rice or bread pudding, jam roly-poly, apple dumpling: my mother was an expert at them all.

On this particular day she was very sombre and told me immediately that Germany and Russia had signed a non-aggression pact. I was aware that this seemed to her to be very bad news. The significance, to a ten-year-old could not have been very great, but the memory is still so vivid that something about it obviously conveyed the feeling of crisis in the air. While the actual declaration of war on the 3rd of September has been forgotten, the coming of the Glasgow evacuees to the Glen certainly has not.

The belief that air raids were imminent, prompted the government to act in good time, evacuating children from possible vulnerable areas. And very soon, one Saturday, our quota arrived by bus at the Stable Yard at Glen Tanar. The stables had been converted into dormitories upstairs with kitchens and a big dining room down-stairs. I can see them still, a motley crowd of ill-assorted children, mostly shabbily dressed, their gas masks slung around their shoulders and talking in this totally foreign tongue. All the estate employees had assembled to be allocated one or two children per household, while the remainder were accommodated in the converted stables.

My mother, being so house-proud and independent, was not too keen to have anyone billeted on her. However, the authorities decided that, in our two-bedroom house, we should take in one evacuee to share my bedroom. Despite having two children of their own, the Dawsons in a two-bedroom house next door, were allocated the two brothers McDiarmid. So how the allocation was decided remains obscure.

A little waif called Robert Burns was allocated to us and he certainly broadened my vision of life. The children came from the Parkhead district of Glasgow, and were all pupils of St Mungo's School. Their teachers were mostly religious Brothers or Fathers of the Catholic faith. They came with their headmaster, a rather off-putting and unpleasant man called Mr Macdonald. Rabbie Burns, as of course our evacuee was known, came from the tough background of a father who was a boxing booth pugilist and a mother with a large brood of children.

Rabbie presented with a face spotted with impetigo and a head full of lice. My mother promptly popped him in a hot bath, which intrigued him, as he had never experienced such a thing before. Apparently, in his part of the world, baths, when infrequently provided, were for keeping coal in. As he sat on a large white towel in front of our living room fire, while my mother combed his hair for nits, it must have seemed to our little vagabond that he had entered another world.

The culture shock for both sides must have been extreme. This was aggravated by the discovery that Rabbie was a regular bed-wetter. Although only a year younger than me, he seemed like a small child until he started talking about his life in Glasgow. Tales of the razor and chain gangs inhabiting the back streets sounded unbelievable. Even my mother used to sit agog listening to the experiences that had been packed into this tiny nine-year-old's life. Poor Rabbie was really like a duck out of water in our household and he escaped to his roots among the rabble at the end of the yard at the first opportunity. Whether this was engineered by my mother, or whether Rabbie had asked to return there, is unclear; but I believe both parties were heartily relieved to see the back of one another.

Many evacuees found the shock of country life and the separation from their families so traumatic that they fled back to Glasgow at the first opportunity, making it possible for more of the billeted-out children to join their mates in the converted stables. The Dawsons next door held on to their two brothers for a long time and I put this down to Mrs Dawson's couthiness and kindness, in contrast to my mother's sense of superiority and correctness. I must say that I never felt any animosity towards Rabbie, but neither did I feel any kinship. In my own admittedly selfish way, however, I was glad to get my own bedroom to myself again.

Glen Tanar At War

The Bleak Days of War.
A greyness had descended
over our little world.

The chief characteristics of the incomers were their speed of thought and action, their toughness, aggressiveness and their stealing abilities. On that first day, when I was walking through the stables to the back area, I found four boys absolutely absorbed in a game of what turned out to be pitch and toss. Halfpennies were at stake, and the fact that they were openly gambling made us realise that these kids were in a totally different league. They also appeared without fear or shyness and we very soon began to feel rather vulnerable in their presence. To them we were "the locals" and this was said with a distinct tone of disparagement.

They had a marked pecking order. A boy named Mick Tully was the gang-leader. Tully was obviously of a higher social standing than the rest. He had more material possessions, including a Monopoly set. But, whereas in other circumstances this would have led to his being ridiculed by the toughies, he seemed to exert an influence over the rest by the power of his personality. I liked Tully and could feel some affinity with him, but I was always surprised at the way in which the others asked his permission or did his bidding.

The shopkeepers of Aboyne knew to their cost that something had changed. No local child that I was aware of ever stole from shops, but 'knocking' was second nature to these Gorbals kids. They stole anything and everything they could lay their hands on, especially sweets and cigarettes. As the months passed, we became acclimatised to these strangers from 'outer space' and began to make tentative friendships with a few of them. One large redheaded lad was called Big Garrity - I think his Christian name was Robert. I got on well with him and he used me as his fence, usually for cigarettes and sometimes sweets. Years later, when clearing out our shed, I found three packs of sealed Craven A mild blend, which I had kept for Garrity, forgetting to return them. He had probably returned to the East End having forgotten about them - such was the amount of plunder that passed through their hands. I missed Garrity as he was a formidable character who, nevertheless, protected his friends from bullying of any kind. Years later, word filtered back from Glasgow that he was serving a life sentence for murder. I wondered what had happened, as he was really a decent chap at heart. Inevitably, he must have been caught up in this harsh culture of dog-eat-dog.

The evacuees used the recreation hall as their schoolroom and the Stable Yard was alive with their presence. Gone were the days when Alfie and I could enjoy a quiet game of football on the small green. No sooner had the ball appeared than a squad of howling youngsters would descend on us, hustling and hassling to get into the game Their desire was to play for their beloved Celtic and to leave the locals to represent Rangers. No game was ever placid again, as these vigorous sons of the Gorbals brought all the fire and emotion of the back streets to enliven even the simplest of games.

They were tough, but seldom do I remember much in the way of fisticuffs, as they seemed to have developed a very structured pecking order into which each fitted naturally. I believe they regarded us as an inferior lot, just as the conquering Spanish Conquistadors would have viewed the Maya natives of South America – there, but of little significance. We, in turn, viewed them with some concern mixed with a grudging admiration for their city experience, their obvious confidence, wit and aggressiveness. Added to that, they were all Roman Catholics, a religion that still raised eyebrows and had the same social stigma as saying someone had consumption. Apart from their headmaster, Mr McDonald, the holy brothers, who acted as the supervisors and masters of the tribe, were delightful people. Used to dealing with these tough kids, they exuded a presence of effortless ability in all situations, and I really came to appreciate their friendliness and help, especially in two areas of my life at that time.

I had just started first year and was finding algebra particularly difficult to fathom. My mother had gone to Aberdeen to buy a textbook in order that I might learn to grasp the subject more easily; but this seemed to further increase my confusion. Fortunately, Father had found a soulmate in Mr Travers, the assistant head, who suggested I could go for a few lessons to Brother Robert who was their maths master. I went down to their bothy billet in the old groom's quarters for my first lesson and came away with the cloud having been miraculously lifted. After just one lesson, Algebra never again appeared to be difficult - in fact it became one of my favourite subjects. To this day I do not know how this was achieved, such is the art of a born teacher.

My second blessing from the fraternity related to my inability to swim. Swimming was something that, in country districts, few had mastered, mainly due to the climate, poor facilities and a culture of work before play that still existed. The Glaswegians, without exception, all swam from the day they could first toddle down to their local swimming pool and they took it for granted that everybody else could swim. Together with Alfie and Willie, I had regularly gone down to what we called our raft pool on the Tanar. There we would splash about, vainly trying to conquer that sinking feeling.

Some hope came in the shapely form of four students from Dunfermline College of Physical Education. These girls were working in the 'forestry' during their holidays, measuring trees for subsequent felling. The girth of the tree had to be measured some ten feet from ground level, so Alfie and I were employed to carry the long ladder for them. These effervescent young ladies were delightful company and we were very sad when the job was finished. They were, of course, all excellent swimmers, and my favourite student, Margaret Deans, left me her swimming manual to guide me.

The Bridge and Pool at the Black Ship –1939.
Eight feet of water made this a perfect little
swimming pool.

Each week the brothers used to take their flock to swim in a big deep pool on the Tanar known as *The Black Ship*. Come rain or shine, they swam in the summer months and I was encouraged to join them to have lessons from one of the brothers. *The Black Ship*, some say, was so called from the days logs were floated down the Tanar into the Dee and so on to Aberdeen. Logs were first floated in this particular pool, as it was both large and deep, and had a wooden footbridge spanning it. My introduction to the swimming lesson was an invitation to launch myself from the bank into this eight feet deep pool. This was an act that I would normally have considered unthinkable. However, with the group of toughies all around me, the prospect of losing face overcame my fear and so in I plunged. Again, the hand of the Lord must have been present through the agency of these good brothers, as I found myself being able to stay afloat and to doggie-paddle to the side. I wondered what all the fuss had been about. As with cycling, swimming holds no mystery once one has acquired the knack and overcome one's fear.

At first I was absolutely ecstatic, as this seemed to be the ultimate achievement. But then, stern reality stepped in. Prior to this, so desperate was I to learn to swim that I had readily agreed to my mother's proposition which stated that, if I broke the swimming barrier, I would fulfil her hopes for me by promising to take piano lessons. I think at that time I would have happily promised to do anything. But now came the day of reckoning when I had to fulfil my part of the bargain. Sad to say, after half a dozen lessons from my mother, the drudgery of the piano seemed scarcely worth the thrill of those moments when I found I could float. Thus it was that piano study became a lost cause, much to my subsequent regret.

Lord Glentanar was Chief Scout for Scotland and, as such, had encouraged Lady Glentanar to form a cub pack. This was started around 1937and her secretary had the responsibility of running the pack. We met in the ballroom of the big house every Friday night and under our akela we went dib-dib-dobbing with great enthusiasm. I remember having my nose put out of joint as we progressed, when Doug Young was promoted to a sixer ahead of me. This came about on the recommendation of our senior sixer, Peter Strang, who was now too old for the cubs.

Doug was a year younger than I was and I did not see him as deserving promotion because I considered myself to be next in line. This episode, however, taught me that all in life is far from fair. Personal feelings, as well as who you are, can have unlooked-for results. As Doug was the factor's son, this could have influenced the decision. Furthermore, I did not exactly feel at one with the senior sixer. Justice was done a few months later when someone else moved on and I became a sixer; but it still irked me over the years that I was never the senior. Peter Strang did pay a price eventually, as previously recorded, so that in later years, I felt I had so evened the score that thereafter I got on reasonably well with him.

The coming of the evacuees marked the start of a Scout Troop, with my bête noir, Mr McDonald, as scoutmaster. Within months, I had become too old for cubs and so moved up to the troop which, of course, was dominated by my Glasgow renegades. I do not think I enjoyed it too much, but I still remember scout camp at the Swan's Neck - a site on the road to Aboyne, where we slept in Bell tents. One afternoon Willie and I went off fishing in the Tanar and, having lost track of time, we missed tea; whereupon my friend Mr McDonald took a delight in making life tough for the two of us after that. He was a man who always made you feel that, because you did not belong to the faith, not only was there no place for you in heaven, but also little place for you here on earth.

Although I am unclear where we met regularly for our scouting evenings, a night in the ballroom is still vivid in my memory. A popular game consisted of the scouts sitting round in a large circle with one of them blindfolded and seated cross-legged in the centre. The object of the game was for one member at a time to try and creep forward to touch the seated scout, without being detected. When my turn came, my apparent acuteness of hearing left me unbeaten after countless attempts. This was in spite of the scouters and the laird himself checking my blindfold repeatedly to make sure that I wasn't cheating. There was a certain amount of disbelief from those around me, but I felt very pleased with myself that night, which is probably why I remember it so well. I only wish my hearing was as acute now, in my advanced years, as it was then.

An abiding memory for me from those wartime days is the bubbling enthusiasm of the Glasgow boys and their tremendous ability when it came to singing and performing without embarrassment. Every weekend they would watch a film show, such as a Laurel and Hardy movie, to be followed by a singsong.

Their repertoire of tunes was endless, with traditional as well as the modern songs rendered with huge gusto. Three songs from those days still remain firmly with me – 'South of the border-down Mexico way', a hit tune of those early days, 'She'll be coming round the mountain' and 'The Quartermaster's Store', all of them abiding favourites. We, who would hardly open our mouths to utter a note because of shyness and fear of being thought a bit effeminate, were simply swept along in this pulsating atmosphere.

Winter brought its own particular delight to us in Glen Tanar in the form of sledging down the 'Ca Canny' Brae when it was covered in snow and, even more hazardous, in ice. The brae is a steep hill on the public road coming up behind the Stable Yard to loop round to our houses and is about three hundred yards long. The brae is called 'Ca Canny' as it has a sign at the top telling people *'Ca canny doon the Brae'* or, in plain English – 'Go carefully down the hill.' In the early days there was so little traffic that sledging was relatively safe. Cars could be heard approaching and no one seemed to mind our making the hill ever more treacherous with our steel runners.

My first sledge was made for me by Gordon Bruce - a forgotten face from the past, who must have been the blacksmith at that time. The sledge was really made to be sat on in comfort and was set on two high runners. It was quite short, so that lying on it was difficult. However, it was highly dangerous to use on the brae as, when sitting upright, you couldn't control the sledge at speed; and because it was so high, it tipped over very easily, depositing you in the nearest snowdrift. After a few years my bitter complaints were heeded, and I

Target Stone on the Factor's Wall.
Wall now demolished & Stone discarded.

graduated to a very low, sturdy machine with broad heavy runners. This sledge was impossible to tip and, in icy conditions, it went like a train. I remember that my father had the runners made and fitted by Fletchers Garage in Aboyne - odd how little things stick in the mind. All the kids in the district would congregate on the brae when conditions were good. The sledges would run on round the bend at the bottom of the hill and go on for up to another two hundred yards down the main road. The target was to pass the end of the factor's walled garden with its large roughly circular stone set on top and inscribed "PE -1747". Speeds were frightening; but those were the days when each had to outdo the other and the fastest got the furthest and won the blue riband.

The situation changed with the coming of the evacuees. As they had no sledges, we felt obliged to share with them, which spoiled much of the individual fun. Moreover, they were stopped from going down the brae because of the possible danger to them. Instead they were told to sledge in a nearby field, and we were also expected to comply with the new order. The result was that half the exhilaration was lost. It was not until they departed back to Glasgow that the thrill of the brae returned for a few years until we too had outgrown that experience and moved on. Imagine a lovely crisp moonlit night, with a light covering of snow on the brae. Half a dozen boys and girls, now in their teens, with other things on their minds, come down the brae on sledges, laughing with pleasure, while no doubt enjoying the odd stolen kiss. This is the kind of memory, capturing as it does, the quintessence of youthful rapture, which transcends those of later years and which makes recalling it and writing about it so worthwhile.

Pre-war, the Glen boasted a pleasant nine-hole golf course around St. Lesmos Chapel. The golf course was looked after by Mr Phillips. My mother played golf regularly and although I cannot think she ever became very good, it was undoubtedly of great therapeutic benefit to her. I often went out with her and had the use of her five iron but never foresaw that in retirement golf would become my major hobby. War brought an end to the golf course when poles were erected all over it to prevent enemy aeroplanes landing. Oddly enough, this worked the wrong way round for one unfortunate RAF pilot. Coming home from school in the first year of the war, we came upon a Fairey Battle two-seater that had crashed across the road at Braeloine bridge. RAF personnel were swarming all over it. Apparently, the pilot had begun to lose power as he came down the valley but, seeing the golf course, tried to land on it. Overshooting the end of the course, he crossed the Tanar and ripped off a wing on a huge beech tree on the top of the bank. Miraculously, both pilot and observer walked away completely unscathed. The golf course was never restored and the beech tree also never recovered. Today the old golf course is under cultivation, while this once beautiful estate has similarly deteriorated with time.

I had an odd experience while watching the RAF personnel dismantling the plane. A few of us were standing around, when one of the NCO's turned to me and said that I was from "across the water". I did not understand him but my pals immediately told him he was right and that I was really a Frenchman. The airman seemed an odd chap but with a penetrating gaze that left me feeling uncomfortable. He said that he had recognised that I was not one of them, a remark that left me totally bewildered. I was unaware that I looked any different from my fellows as my stature and colouring are all from my mother's side of the family; so what did this fellow see that singled me out so markedly? I almost felt he had some uncanny sixth sense as no one, even when teasing me, had ever made such a statement. This spooky remark made me give that airman a wide berth after that, just in case he might produce even more worrying insights!

War brought uncomfortable changes. Not only did the workers suffer, but also the landed gentry, whose comfort depended on cheap and abundant manpower, commodities that were now not readily available. Suddenly, young men disappeared to war, and no longer could paths be raked daily or Rolls Royces come and go at their owner's pleasure. The laird had added to his car collection just before the war: a big black Buick arrived first, followed by a superb cream Cadillac that was Lady Glentanar's pride and joy. These gas-guzzlers disappeared under dust covers and, throughout the war years, we would creep into the garage and marvel especially at the Cadillac. It was this vehicle that had so thrillingly transported us to cub camps in pre-war years. My father had three footmen and a hall boy in his house department. Suddenly, the pace of life was slowed to a crawl when they were all replaced by one parlour maid.

Father and Son.

Aged 17 – not much sign here of having inherited the continental appearance.

As the military were commandeering big houses for billets, the laird had to look smart in order to register the house as a school and find enough young ladies to justify this step. Luckily, as his daughter Jean was at the right age, he gathered a number of her friends, and daughters from moneyed families, and set up an educational establishment. The one girl who stands out in my memory was Zoë d'Erlanger. Tall and good looking, she was admired by my father as someone who was a delightful asset to the school, in addition to which she was kind and considerate to the staff. Jane McNeil, who later became a Norman Hartnell model was also another stunner. Married to the Earl of Dalkeith she is now the Duchess of Buccleuch and attracting much media attention after the theft of the da Vinci from Drumlanrig Castle. To us as youngsters she appeared very haughty and superior and not at all to our taste. Frances St John was by far the most approachable of the girls and I well remember taking her along to the horse-midden to dig for worms so that they could go fishing. Frances went on to be an occupational or physiotherapist. I was to meet her again when I was posted to Perth for my National Service and she was working in Bridge of Earn Hospital. Laughingly, she was to remind me of our last meeting with the two of us on top of a dung heap. We, however, saw very little of the school, although they did organise Girl Guides, which some of our local girls attended and seemed to enjoy and to be accepted. Gone, however, were the days of sumptuous entertaining, and the laird was reduced to having only one or two old friends to stay on occasions. Roger Moncrieff is a name that surfaces from those days, and was another person that my father rated very highly.

The Canadian troops had almost the same effect on the local population, as did the evacuees on us as children. They descended on Burnroot, situated opposite the present Aboyne Gliding Club. On this hillside, with their huge machinery and manpower, they built a camp of huts in no time at all. They then proceeded to fell trees at an unbelievable speed. Prior to this, Glen Tanar forestry seemed to consist mainly of Willie Ewen with his one horse and a couple of foresters. The felling of a tree and its removal from the wood by a horse was a big event watched with great interest by us all.

By comparison, the Canadians, with their massive caterpillar tractors and other sophisticated felling equipment, could have come from Mars as far as we were concerned. Swathes of trees disappeared in a day, which would have taken Willie Ewen a season to clear; while the Canadians themselves ran riot through the district with their uninhibited life-style. Suddenly, it seemed that half our young women were pregnant, a condition scarcely ever previously encountered in our area. The local dance, which took place once a fortnight in the recreation hall, was overflowing with these wild young men. They used to bring their own beer to the dances as there was no licence on the premises. From my bed at night, I used to watch them hiding the large cans in the bushes near our house and returning with their buddies, and perhaps the odd giggling girl, to slake their thirst.

What with the evacuees and now these North Americans, our lives were really turned upside down. One of our great treats was to walk half way up the Bungalow brae and then cut out over the fields along the edge of the wood over the hill into the Canadian camp on a Friday or Saturday night to watch the film show. All the latest films were available to them and in addition, we could taste Pepsi-Cola for the first time in our lives. We were given large slabs of Madeira cake, while occasionally chocolate appeared, which was almost non-existent in our rationed lives. They were a friendly gregarious lot, those Canadians, far from home and making the best of life before being transferred to the front line. Later, many were to die on the beaches of Normandy.

An unforeseen source of income followed in the wake of the tree-devouring Canadians, as they left behind all the brushwood after the big timber was removed. The green cones on the branches were in great demand for reforestation, I presume, and as boys we were paid the unbelievable price of £5 for a very large bagfull. Alfie and I spent many hours on the hillsides tediously picking, and I was to add £20 to my piggy-bank which, years later, went some way to funding my motorcycling. Remembering that at that time we were being paid two shillings (10p) a day to work on the farm or in the forestry nursery, £20 was the equivalent of two hundred days' work; so it is no wonder that we feverishly went pick-picking those little green gems.

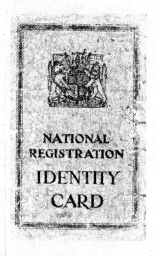

Identity Card carried
around everywhere –
no great hardship.

Although actual war never really touched the Glen the effects of it were all around us. The "blackout" with those heavy russet curtains draped over our windows blocking out the merest chink of light was accompanied by the visual propaganda of ARP (Air Raid Precaution) wardens shouting, "Put out that light". The ration books, clothing and petrol coupons, identity cards - SWAF 44:3, and that gas mask in its fancy red aluminium case, came to be accepted as our way of life. Khaki uniforms were everywhere with the Home Guard and soldiers on manoeuvres filling our lives along with the pretty Land Army girls on the farm The wireless took on a new meaning with us huddled round it every night plotting the course of the war as it seemed to draw ever closer in those first few years. The sinking of HMS "Hood" was a national disaster and with Lord Haw Haw claiming our aircraft carriers night after night we were uncertain who to believe, so often did his claims turn out to be close to the truth. The tide turned ever so slowly with our adoration of Monty in the desert balanced by our admiration for Field Marshal Erwin Rommel and his apparent chivalry. Stalingrad proved the turning point when we felt that at last the mighty Wehrmacht could be vanquished.

Another war memory is of waking on many occasions after midnight to hear the characteristic beating sound of the engines of a hit-and-run Heinkel bomber. It would come in from Norway to the Moray Firth and then come south until it reached the Dee at Aboyne, turning east to deliver its bomb-load on Aberdeen's dockyard. I never did experience an actual bombing, as the German raids had stopped by the time I went to school in Aberdeen in 1944.

War left Glen Tanar transformed from a millionaire's playground to a run-down shadow of its former self. My father weathered the war with a steady turnover of unsatisfactory staff, most of whom were unfit for war service and, for that matter, also unfit for much else. One footman was an epileptic, and one day when we were on our way home from school, we came across him lying in a ditch with his bicycle on top of him. My father had previously described these attacks to me, but I was scarcely prepared for the shock and the feeling of uselessness as we left him to recover on his own. Were we heartless, or was it apprehension that made us pass by on the other side? As we lived so far from the village, Father was given a small petrol ration and so was able to continue to use the car. I can remember the black headlamp-masks that were fitted to it so that the light beam would not shine skywards. Life on the farm was enlivened for us by Ian Livingstone, the dairyman, who had been taught to make cheddar cheese. We spent many happy hours in the special room helping him by turning cheeses and undoubtedly sampling not a few.

Having moved to school in Aberdeen in 1944, my days at the Glen were now reduced to the weekends. Travelling home on Friday to the Tower of Ess by Strachan's bus, I would be met by my father; and on Sunday night I would return by the same route for another week in the city. The ending of the war brings back no great memories for me. In fact it came as something of an anti-climax to what had gone before. The raucous evacuees were long gone and the stables stood eerily silent. Burnroot stood empty now with only rows of forlorn looking huts dotted up the hillside to remind us of a vibrant Canadian presence. The estate settled back into its pre-war torpor. But below the surface everything had changed forever.

The postscript to this chapter relates to *The Black Ship* pool on the Tanar, which pops up from time to time in these writings. Excerpts from the extensive *Glen Tanar Estate Papers*, in the possession of Aberdeen Central Library, give some background to the name of the pool and also to the danger of forest fires that frequently broke out over the centuries.

This is a direct quotation from the diary text as supplied to Lord Glentanar by a Mr Anderson, retired banker in Aboyne: "Robert Whyte and Ann Thomson, my grandparents, went to Glen Tanar about the year 1809. He went first as manager to the Earl of Aboyne in the cutting down of the woods and afterwards for many years he carried on a lucrative wood-merchant's business on his own account in the glen.

When my grandparents first went there, a village of fifty huts was built on each side of the road, on the southwest of the Tanar, about a mile and a half beyond the present Glen Tanar House. These huts were built to provide accommodation for the workpeople. During their twenty-five years' residence about a hundred and fifty children were born in this hamlet to the woodcutters and other workpeople. When my grandmother went as a bride to the glen, she planted a lime tree in the corner of their garden, and it is interesting to relate that after a hundred and seventeen years the tree still flourishes.

It is a magnificent specimen of great height and girth and is surrounded by a wire protection, presumably to keep the deer from eating its bark. The forest my grandfather was cutting was considered to be one of the finest in Scotland and Lord Aboyne was justly proud of it. He continually brought his guests to the glen to view the splendid trees and fine scenery, also to partake of bread and honey and sample the famous smuggled whisky. Many a Duke, Marquis, Earl and Lord with their ladies had my grandparents the honour of entertaining in their simple house in those days.

The quality of the tree was considered to be of the finest, and the wood was in great demand, many coming long distances to procure it. My mother told me that yearly, representatives of seed merchants came from England and collected the seed of the fir trees, it being in great demand. Sheets were placed on the ground round some of the finest specimens and the seed collected in this way. In June 1820 a great conflagration took place and at one time it looked as if the whole forest would be consumed.

Great was the consternation of the workpeople as the fire crept nearer and nearer. It was thought the whole of the huts including the sawmill would perish. So near did the fire come to the hamlet that all the workpeople were warned out of their houses – the women and children, with their goods and chattels being deposited on carts ready to be moved at a moment's notice. It was said that such a hold did the fire get on the woods and mosses that it was never completely extinguished until the winter snow came. Exactly a century later came the great fire of June 14th to 26th, 1920. The burnt area measured over two thousand acres and the number of trees so damaged as to have to be disposed of was over seventy-seven thousand."

My own father recalled this fire on many occasions as a major event. At one time, it seemed that the whole of Glen Tanar forest would be lost. Then, at the critical moment, troops and outside help were brought in, and the balance was tipped. This diary would appear to have been written about 1926. So this lime tree is now well over one hundred and ninety years old and still stands to this day, huge and powerful for all to behold. The Linden tree, as it was popularly known, was planted to keep ill spirits away in much the same way that country folk also planted the rowan tree outside their cottar houses.

These may still occasionally be seen among old ruins up our glens. This also explains why the tree standing on that large green area among the surrounding heather, abutting *The Black Ship* pool, always looked so incongruously out of place to me. Glen Tanar pine was used to build boats in the Aberdeen shipyards and there is a record of the schooner *Glentanar* built from this pine, sailing with a Mr Diack to New Zealand where he settled in 1858. Mr Diack then went on to establish the Glentanar Sheep Station on Mount Cook which is now renamed Glentanar Park, providing many outdoor activities over a wide area.

Another important tree, which Lord Glentanar is reputed to have treasured, is the Admiral's tree, some hundred yards beyond the Halfway Hut on the road to Eitnach. This old gnarled pine now stands surrounded by self-seeded saplings. In the past it was the solitary outpost for some ancient forgotten admiral spying out all the surrounding hills when out stalking. As with much else in the Glen, it is but another shadowy tale from the past, the details of which have died away with the passing generations.

The name *The Black Ship*, has had for me an almost menacing aura all my life, but especially so in those childhood days. My mother always told me that Good King Wenceslas lived in the dark shed by the pool, and for years I was uncertain as to whether this was supposed to be good or bad. Even to this day this spot has left me with a haunting sense of mystery when I reach it, especially now that I know that hundreds of adults and children lived out their lives in this very setting.

The Linden Tree - Huge Girth.
Planted by a Woodcutter's Wife almost
Two Hundred Years ago.

In all its Glory - the Linden Tree
in early Spring.

The Linden Tree in Summer
Foliage.

The Admiral's Tree at Half-
Way Hut.

The Tanar above the
washed-out Black Ship.

The remnants of the bridge and
behind the author, the dark building
where Good King Wenceslas lived
in the days of his youth.

Chapter 11
The Post War Era

The European war ended and peace came to Glen Tanar in 1945. A year later there entered my orbit a character who will always loom larger than life for me.

Arthur James Wilkinson was another only child, born of English parents from London. He was intent on making a living in estate management and was taken on by Glen Tanar Estate as a trainee. Housed in the old gardener's bothy next to the Archibalds in the Stable Yard, this extrovert soon made his presence felt to all those around him.

A few months younger than me, he had a long-standing history of asthma and had been left with the trademark barrel chest. For as long as I can recall, Jim was always taking a swig from some foul-smelling creosote type of cough mixture, which stood over his wash basin. In times of great hilarity he would convulse with a coughing spasm, upon which mouthfuls of this odious black concoction seemed to have absolutely no effect. Topped off with a ginger moustache and a rather prominent hooked nose, he always appeared to be experiencing a rather noxious smell from those around him.

Having none of the shy, withdrawn Scottish personality, he barged around the estate as if intent on sorting out every problem there and then. Yes, he was always self-important, but in time I came to feel a great empathy with this confident, cheeky Londoner. Well educated at Merchant Taylors School, he was extremely sharp in mind and action; but sport, such as football, played no part in his life because of a certain lack of co-ordination, which he never tried to hide. Despite the fact that I was a few months older than Jim, I was always happy enough to play second fiddle to this self-confident lad who never seemed stuck for an answer or an action, right or wrong.

With the departure of the evacuees, the Scout Troop had fallen on hard times and the factor, Mr R D Young took on the role of Scoutmaster, helped for a time by Albert Garland (1904 -1966). Albert had come to Glen Tanar before the war to assist my father and to take on the job of valet to Lord Glentanar. On the outbreak of war he was called up, leaving his wife and son Charlie to await the end of hostilities. Having returned to take up his old job and relieve my father of the dual roles of butler/valet, he used to come along to help with the Scouts and to teach us boxing. Suddenly, this all came to an end when, in a sparring match, I must have been rather too vigorous and broke a couple of Albert's ribs, which finished the boxing for good. Albert experienced chronic pain for months afterwards. He would continue to remind me whenever we met that I was responsible, but it was said with a hearty, if painful, laugh and we remained good friends.

1946 - The Glen Tanar Scout Troop on the Way to Auchengillan.

Back Row   The Author, Jim Wilkinson,
            Bob, Mr R D Young (Scoutmaster)
            and Douglas Young
Front Row   Charlie Garland, Donny Livingstone,
            Doug Forbes, Bill Archibald,
            Duncan Ross & Alfie Dawson.

Later on, Douglas Young and I would go along to help the Scout Troop when we came home from Grammar at the weekends. However, when Jim came on the scene, everything changed. Jim had been a very active scout in London and was in his element taking on the role of motivator. Suddenly, the scout activity increased. The initiative was taken to start a Rover Crew comprising those of us who were by now too old to be scouts. Doug, Jim and I recruited my old friend from Aboyne days, Alistair Taylor, persuading him to cycle from Dess to be with us to make up a foursome. We formed a core of older boys to help out with the scouts and take them off to camp during the summer holidays. Some hilarious times were had in Auldearn, Auchengillan and Penicuik, as well as at weekends nearer home. At times we linked up with the Aboyne troop under its delightful old Scoutmaster Brigadier Jackson who, with his rope-end to keep discipline, brought back memories of his British Raj days in India.

Our most memorable summer camp and expedition however occurred without Jim's presence. In 1950 Alistair and I took the Glen Tanar troop to Mar Lodge above Braemar to camp at the Corriemulzie Falls with my motor-cycle as the main means of transport. After a few days in camp we all took off to trek through the Lairig Ghru to Aviemore and then back over the top of Ben MacDhui, which is the second highest mountain in Britain. One by one I transported the members of the troop up to Derry Lodge. Then, leaving the bike in Jock Scott's care at his house at the entrance to the Lairig, we took off on the twenty-mile hike to Aviemore.

Having camped at the bridge at Aviemore for a couple of days, we then made our way up to the foot of Cairn Gorm. Climbing easily to that peak, we set off across the plateau to reach the summit of Ben MacDhui by mid-afternoon. We looked unsuccessfully for Cairngorm stones on the way. Descending into the Dee valley in glorious weather, I ferried the merry band back to our tents at Corriemulzie. It had been an epic journey, which would probably be considered too dangerous in today's climate of opinion. Certainly, if we had become lost in mist, the responsibility for getting the party safely off the hill would have been entirely mine. Fortunately, on this occasion luck was on our side.

1947 - Glen Tanar and Aboyne Scout Troops at Edinburgh Castle.
Delightful picture of Brigadier Jackson with such a great bunch of youngsters.

I look back with a feeling of great companionship to my young members of the troop, and especially to Alastair Strang the younger brother of my old school pal Jock Strang. Alastair was a delightful, intelligent companion full of good sense and it was no surprise that he went on to Varsity where he was to take an Honours degree in Engineering and to finish up as a senior member of the hierarchy of the well-known textile firm of Courtaulds. Retiring in his fifties, he returned to university to take an MA in Archaeology and then to go on further to do a PhD in this subject. Some people never do stop, but only at the cost of a triple heart bypass in Alastair's case. It is not surprising that he should have taken up archaeology as almost a second career. I remember a Scout camp weekend up at Corrievrach on the site of the old drover's inn at the foot of Mount Keen, when Alastair spent hours excavating for old bottles and relics from those far-off days.

Less fortunate was Donny Livingstone, the son of the dairyman who had introduced me to cheese-making. Donny was dourness itself; but beneath that exterior he was a good lad who failed to get into the Customs and Excise because he was not well enough read. He was sent home to begin reading the daily broadsheets, while I tried to guide his thinking. I regret that I did not continue to keep in touch with him, as over the years I believe he became more and more withdrawn, until eventually he became a recluse, having achieved nothing with his life. Another young scout who comes to mind was Ian Hepburn, the younger brother of my other pal who made up the Glen Tanar School trio of Peter, James and John. Ian was another live wire who became a joiner.

Scout Camp - Auldearn - 1949.
Alastair Strang, Duncan Ross,
Ian Hepburn, Jock McGregor,
Donny Livingstone, Roger Greig
and Author.

Mar Lodge - 1950.
Summit of Ben Macdhui.
Alistair Taylor, Alastair Strang
and Author.

Later, together with his wife, he opened an antique shop in Ballater, where he accosted me years later with the memory of those eventful days. Duncan Ross, the son of the head forester, was also in the Troop and sometimes required my boot of encouragement at some of our camps. In the years ahead he was to cock a snook at me when, during his spell of National Service, he learned to fly. Taking a delight in flying his Vampire jet up the Tanar valley at treetop height, he would curl round our house and then fly off over his parent's home at Belrorie. In so doing he seemed to be giving me the ritual two fingers. I'm sure he never even considered me, but I remembered him well from those early days. His premature death received a half-page obituary appreciation in the Scotsman, paying tribute to his work as the senior instructor at the Glenmore Outdoor Centre in Speyside.

Jim Wilkinson's bothy came to be a second home for me at weekends when we played records, listened to the American Forces Network from Germany and tried our hand at photography. We soon became familiar with all the intricacies of developing and printing our own photos.

Lounging in front of his open fire for hours on end, while putting the world to rights, produced a sense of escaping reality. A favourite tune called *Near You* was played by the Americans every night. This invariably sent us into ecstasies of pure delight, as we greeted it with whoops of "Yes! Yes!" We were very innocent then and adolescence still had that euphoric effect of making everything seem so fresh and appealing. Jim, or the Wilk, as we always referred to him, did nothing by halves.

So when he came to buy his first motor cycle, it was no common road machine, but a cross-country trials bike. He joined the Aberdeen Scrambling Club and would be off on Sundays, tearing up hill and down dale. He also had a very ancient Austin 7, which he regularly pulled to bits, much to our amusement. Once I went to Varsity, I introduced him to the Student's Union and he would attend our dances although he had no right to be there. However he could have carried

Wedding Day for the Wilk in 1955.
The end of an era in both our lives.

off the deception quite easily had he been challenged. He probably met Margaret Bowie, a student teacher, at one of these dances or perhaps the dances in the Dinnet hall near Aboyne. She was to become his wife some years later He was a true friend, eccentric and not always appreciated by the dour Scot; but his influence in my life brightened it with his can-do attitude and unfazed way of dealing with all adversity. In July 1955 I was his best man as he took on the responsibilities of married life and moved to work with the Air Ministry, at first in Aberdeen, before being moved south. In due course married life produced two daughters and the demands of family life were such that our contact tailed off except for the occasional letter. His death from prostate cancer in his mid-fifties came as a sad blow to me after those wonderful teen-age years together.

Through the late forties, my father continued in his role as butler. But the hectic parties of pre-war days had ended and the laird would just have one or two friends to stay for short spells only. My father now had little help, with the days of three or four footmen long past and I know that he became very tired at times. Yet he showed no sign of contemplating retirement. In retrospect, my education up until 1954 probably made it imperative that he went on working, as living in a tied house would present difficulties when the time came for him to go. By 1951 he had entered his seventies; but he never displayed a feeling of old age. As my mother was not yet sixty, he probably felt that there was no point in leaving the Glen quite yet. While never questioning the reasons for my uncertain progress through the years, I believe that he was quietly satisfied to see his son getting the chance that had been denied to him in his youth.

He was, however, very hurt by the implied derisory comments of one of the laird's guests, probably when I was in my third year. Professor Sir Stanley Davidson had been professor of Medicine at Aberdeen before being appointed to the chair in Edinburgh and was a regular houseguest at Glen Tanar. The laird, although an intelligent man, tended to be rather over-concerned with his health and was probably a soft touch for Davidson. When told that Francis's son was in his third year of medicine, Davidson turned to my father, as he was serving him dinner, and remarked that I would probably make an adequate GP. My father sensed the derogatory tone with the result that his dislike of Davidson became even more extreme than it had been previously.

My father always maintained that the jumped-up hangers-on who came to Glen Tanar usually showed their true colours when dealing with servants; whereas the true blue-bloods were invariably courteous and considerate of staff. The irony of this encounter, however, is that, as I check out my medical facts for these memoirs, whose text book of medicine do I have at my elbow but 'The Principles and Practice of Medicine' by Professor L Stanley P Davidson and who did eventually become an adequate GP?

Bill Archibald and I continued to make full use of our diplomatic immunity by being ignored by the ghillies when fishing the Dee. We found an ally in a recent new under-keeper whom I had known from my experience of grouse-beating at Delnadamph Lodge on Donside for Major Waddington. Jimmy Oswald was the son of the head keeper in the Upper Cabrach and really fancied himself as a tough man in those early days. At Delnadamph to begin with, he had tried to walk us off the hill and although initially successful, gradually as our fitness increased, we liked to think that the tables were turned and Jimmy was the one coming under pressure in the end.

He became a great companion however, once we had discounted all his bravado. He joined up with me in fishing the Dee when this should really have been out of bounds to us both. Years later, probably about 1957, when I was posted to the Gordon Highlanders Barracks in the last months of my National Service and living at home, a ghillie warned me off my happy hunting grounds of the Bank, the Kirks and the Waterside pools between Dinnet and Aboyne. Speaking a little later to Jimmy, now head keeper at the Glen, I found how times had changed as he shook his head at my wish to continue fishing in my old haunts, as I had done in days gone by. Suddenly I realised that I was now an exile from the Glen of my youth and that I had to come to terms with it. Time and people seldom stand still; but he was simply fulfilling his new responsibility and there were never any hard feelings between us. Now, Jimmy is recognised as an authority in so many different fields, especially capercaillie preservation and it is always a pleasure to sit and listen to him, as long as you have plenty of hours to spare.

Glasgow 1948.
The Glen Tanar Rover Crew,
Kelvin Grove.

Author, Doug Young, Alistair Taylor with Jim Wilkinson kneeling in front.

Hill walking continued to be a welcome interlude from the bustle of the city and the rigours of study. Climbing the Knockie hill, overlooking the mansion house, was a favourite amble. So Alfie Dawson and I would continue to wander wherever took our fancy. Mount Keen saw frequent visits and Alistair Taylor and I did some hikes in the name of Rover Scouting, with the resultant maps and details completed to justify it as being within the curriculum. These I still treasure.

In the early 1950's serious climbing was to broaden my appreciation of the mountains even further. This seems an appropriate time to introduce the subject, although the circumstances surrounding it are dealt with in a later chapter. Dr Tom Patey, then a medical student a year behind me, joined our merry band of grouse-beaters in our second year at Strathdon and he was to open a new window of experience for me. Tom, even then, was seen as being in the forefront of the new tradition of Scottish climbers who were leaving their mark on ascents across the continents. He was the most scruffy character ever to come out of a manse and he certainly never bothered about the niceties of behaviour. You took Tom at face value and he would never be a different person. He was tough and determined with a craving to do ever more new ascents. Climbing was a true religion to him and anyone coming into contact with him could not but be impressed with his single-mindedness and be swept along with it.

It was not long before he was recruiting us to accompany him at weekends to his favourite rock ascents on Lochnagar. Having had some experience trying to reach peregrine's nests on Mount Keen, I needed little encouragement to join him. So it was that I went on about five occasions, to savour the thrill of climbing with Patey on Lochnagar.

Reaching Loch Muick on our motor cycles, we would walk smartly up to the lochan below the cliffs of Lochnagar. The party usually consisted of three or four of us and the pace of the climb into the foot of the cliffs was my first surprise. There was absolutely no time spared getting to the start of the climb. It took me all my time to keep up with Tom even before we began the actual rock climb. Once at the foot, while others prepared the ropes and paraphernalia of climbers, Tom would already be a hundred feet above us trying the feasibility of a new ascent. "Would it go?" was the constant theme of finding yet another entry for the first ascent's library.

My memory of all the climbs is now hazy, but Parallel Gully B and Eagle Ridge still come readily to mind. Coming to one overhang, which I was apprehensively viewing from below, Tom shouted down, "Marie Newbigging led this ascent last week, so what's holding YOU up?" Remembering Marie from my Grammar School days, when she was a young 3rd year High School girl, I went up that overhang like a squirrel. Tom certainly knew how to shame one into action.

**Tom Patey as remembered by so many of
his friends and colleagues.**

My greatest experience, however, was on the crux of Eagle Ridge. The day
was very cold, with sleet enveloping us from time to time and my thin army
camouflage trousers were little protection either from cold or damp. I was
third in the order of climbing, with one of Tom's buddies at number two.
Roped next to Tom, he was extremely slow and at every minor hazard he
took an inordinate amount of time to surmount it. Standing below, I was
gradually freezing up and, by now, could scarcely feel my fingers. Coming
to a long traverse, he froze to the cliff wall and I remember willing him to
either get on or fall off. This type of distorted thinking was similar to what
happens to a person suffering early exposure. Some years before, in severe
conditions on Ben MacDhui, I recognised the same attitude of mind. He did
fall off, but held by Tom on the rope, he regathered himself and eventually
made it to safety.

The crux on Eagle Ridge has a drop of a few hundred feet out to the left and
you have to lift yourself up on to a sloping sheet of rock that rises to the right
at an angle of about sixty degrees. The knack is to lever yourself on to this
angled rock and then to stand up and walk up it, shutting your mind to the
sheer drop immediately behind you. Tom tried it first but could not find a
decent footing; whereupon he turned to me indicating that I should make the
attempt. As a virtual novice I levered my way up, but, to have the confidence
to stand up and walk without the protection of a rope above, was just beyond
me. Tom tried again, this time successfully. Now with the protection of his
rope, I stood up and walked up the rock face with little or no difficulty.

The thrill of reaching the top after such an experience was superb, and I can well understand how climbing can become an addiction.

After this, Tom tried hard to persuade me to keep climbing with him, as my head-down-and get-on-with-it style was exactly what he wanted in a number two. However, my life-style was unlikely to allow me to be very dedicated and, having experienced the thrill, I was satisfied to say I had climbed with the mighty Patey. Others with whom I climbed at this time were medics such as Mike Taylor from Peterhead, another fine climber, and my pal from grouse beating Delnadamph Lodge days, Johnny Wood who, like me, merely wanted to have an interesting experience. Tom's other great friend and fellow climber, Bill Brooker, has kindly supplied the atmospheric photographs which so typify that Patey of old.

Sadly, Tom was killed in May 1970, when working as a GP in Ullapool on the West Coast of Scotland. He fell while absailing alone from a sea stack. He is still recognised worldwide as one of the foremost climbers of our generation and I was greatly privileged to have climbed with him.

Mount Keen with the Corrach, where Bill fell, just visible
where the path goes over the ridge on the right.

A spin-off from these climbs was my desire to try a winter ascent when conditions are of course, totally different. In January 1952 with an ample fall of snow clothing Glen Tanar, Alfie, Bill and I would attempt a seemingly easy snow climb in the Corrach of Mount Keen. Walking into the climb, through

172

deep, soft snow was very tiring; but eventually we reached the hundred and thirty foot face, which presented only one real difficulty, namely, the penetrating of the cornice at the top. Climbing independently, we made good progress, with ice axes our only protection from falling. Approaching the cornice, Alfie and I were further over from Bill, when, all of a sudden, there was a loud rushing sound and the whole snow-face that Bill was on disappeared down into the valley in a whirl of snow-dust. Descending quickly, we found Bill sitting on the top of the avalanche holding up his haversack with the thermos in it. The thermos itself had been neatly crushed into a flat sheet of metal. Bill had been very lucky and we returned home a lot wiser, having learned that even seemingly easy ascents are hazardous for the inexperienced in the wrong conditions. I never attempted to make that proper winter ascent. Maybe the Gods were warning me off on that day on Mount Keen. When discussing this attempt quite recently with Ian Smith, the head gamekeeper at the Glen, he confirmed that the exact point of our ascent was the only place that a cornice could form on the whole estate.

Things began to change once more in Glen Tanar after that. Bill went off to the Navy and Alfie, a time-served electrician, worked away from home a lot. My trips back to the Glen became fewer as I started to get down to some serious studying. By now I was also having to consider doing house-doctor locums in preparation for the day when study would be behind me and forging a career and earning a living would become the way ahead.

Marie (Tink) Newbigging.
Patey's Secret Weapon.

Mount Keen - January 1952.
Lucky Bill (left) - none the worse after that 100 feet fall.

Glen Tanar Exile

Jim Wilkinson and I no longer had the opportunity to enjoy our evenings of music and laughter in front of Jim's bothy fire. Meeting at dances, each with his girlfriend, had displaced these encounters. The passing of this era of my life greatly saddened me. I felt this most acutely as I lay in bed often looking out over to the Knockie hill in the moonlight and wishing that time would stand still. To leave this wonderful oasis of my childhood was something I had dreaded facing for many years. Now, however, I sensed that just around the corner I would soon have to face up to a completely new way of life and be exiled forever from this beloved Glen.

The postscript to this chapter was a satisfying day spent back at Glen Tanar with Alfie Dawson on 31st July 2001. When speaking to Alfie the week before, he suggested a trip back up memory lane. So we quietly motored past the now wooded brae of the Burnroot Canadians to Glen Tanar School, where we were allowed access to those old classrooms, now so sadly dilapidated.

Glen Tanar - 2003.
Joiner's Cottage,
the Stable Yard.

Alfie Dawson back at his old front door. Where have all those seventy odd years gone, my boy?

Up the Fir Mounth we went into the estate to be greeted by the now head gamekeeper, Ian Smith, who arranged for his wife Cathy to show us around the ballroom once more. This was followed by a quiet walk round the lake stopping off in the boathouse and then on to *The Black Ship*. The bridge was gone and the old deep pool was now totally washed out, which seemed to mirror the changing face of life in this new century.

Back through the sawmill we went, to view Alfie's father's beehives and yes, there they were, now under new ownership. Into the joiner's shop to look at the skylight we had so often crawled through; and finally along the Stable Yard, past our two houses nestling cosily together and awakening so many memories. Across the Braeloyne bridge, marvelling at how the Fairey Battle pilot had survived that crash; then over the old golf course to St Lesmo's Chapel to view the gravestones of the Cunliffe Brooks and the Glentanars. There also, we came across the grave of Albert Garland. His incapacitating stutter had made me so sorry for him in the past. He was such a pleasant working friend and colleague of my father for so many years.

We continued round to the Fairy Lake, now full of the sphagnum moss which Alfie values so much for his bonsai hobby. And so homeward bound, having trudged around over familiar, favourite haunts with as relaxed and close a relationship as we used to enjoy all those sixty-odd years ago.

Chapter 12
Aberdeen Grammar School

The last days at Aboyne were a fitting climax to a very happy time there. Exams behind us, I had succeeded in passing my Latin by a small margin and also my French, with a mark surprising to both Miss Beinge, our teacher, and to myself. Thus all was set fair to proceed on to Banchory Academy. The last week of prize-giving having passed, together with the satisfaction of having achieved some worthwhile results, we were now all resting on our oars with our teachers' full agreement. A memorable class trek up the Fungle valley and out to the top of Carmaferg cemented a real camaraderie amongst the class after so many years together.

Summer holidays saw Alan Simpson and myself trek over the shoulder of Mount Keen and down into Glen Mark, carrying all our provisions and equipment in ex-army rucksacks. We carried far too much tinned food, which weighed the proverbial ton, yet which was half the amount we had originally intended taking. As we were uncertain as to how we would cope, on the previous evening we had a trial run up to the top of the hill behind the head-keeper's house, to what was called the Flagpole. Exhausted on our return, we threw out half the tins, but still carried far too much the next day. Camping in Glen Mark in drizzling rain for two days tried our patience sorely and made us return a day early. Although we were feeling tired and rather dispirited, we were pleased we had toughed it out. Little did I realise that this trip was probably the cause of an illness that was to herald a major turning point in my life.

The thought of Banchory Academy did not fill us with much enthusiasm as it had the reputation of expecting a very high level of performance from its pupils. In addition, as Banchory was twelve miles from Aboyne, I had to cycle four and a half miles to Aboyne before boarding a Bluebird bus to Banchory every day and back in the evening. We were packed into the bus like sardines, all standing sandwiched together in the aisle with the door squeezed shut behind us. It was a horrendous journey and within a couple of days I got home in the evening totally exhausted. I also realised that we were in an enlarged class of some very bright youngsters, especially the girls, some of whom had bussed all the way from Braemar, twenty miles further than us. So, why were we complaining?

On the Thursday of that first week I got home, feeling now more than just tired and convinced I was running a temperature. During the night I started having a stabbing pain at the base of my left chest each time I took a breath. And so in the morning, Doctor Willie was asked to call.

The Glen Mark Bothy.
*Two weeks later that smile had disappeared and
all was about to change for me.*

Dr William Brodie Brown was a tall imposing man, immaculately dressed and always smelling pleasantly of mild disinfectant. He had that wonderful kind of personality, which, by his very presence, reassured the patient that all would be well from now on. Quickly diagnosed as having pleurisy, I was informed that it would mean at least a month off school. I was probably treated with sulphonamides and had a blood test done to show the progress of the illness. This, the sedimentation rate, was measured weekly to determine when things were back to normal. I can well remember seeing the rapid settling of the blood cells leaving the pink fluid on top, which indicated I was far from right.

The weeks passed slowly and Marigold called in regularly with more and more homework. At first, I was far too off-colour to pay much attention; but gradually it dawned on me that I was going to have a mountain to climb with the volume of unheeded paper-work at my bedside. My pain had eased, but the sedimentation rate stayed ominously elevated with the result that Dr Robert Duthie, a physician from Aberdeen Royal Infirmary, was called in for a second opinion. Those were the days when tuberculosis was still prevalent; but no one ever referred to that in my hearing. He must have reassured Dr Willie that his treatment was correct. Nevertheless, it was nearly eight weeks before I was able to get an X-ray in Aberdeen to confirm that all was well.

Lord Glentanar took a great interest in my welfare, paying me regular visits and bringing me books to read. He was a great admirer of George Borrow and he infected me with his enthusiasm, so that I devoured most of them from his library. *Wild Wales*, *Lavengro* and *Romany Rye*, are titles I still recall with much pleasure.

Meantime at Banchory, my pal Alan Simpson had undergone a real upheaval in his life. His father, having returned on leave from the RAF, was somewhat dissatisfied with the idea of his son being educated at Banchory Academy. He therefore promptly went to see the then Rector of Aberdeen Grammar School, Sir James Robertson, to ask if his son could be admitted to that prestigious academy. The next I knew was that his mother had left Aboyne, rented a flat in Louisville Avenue and Alan had already moved to the Grammar. Mrs Simpson had always been very kind to me and she now proposed to my parents, that if I could also gain entry she would be delighted if I went to stay with them.

Prior to leaving Aboyne, our headmaster, Mr Mair, had told Alan and me that there were two places for us at Grammar should we wish to take them up. To me the very idea seemed too fantastic to be taken seriously - a local loon going to a fee-paying school where Lord Byron was educated sounded as unattainable as a trip to the Moon. Now, everything had changed and after attending for interview with Sir James, I was told to report for classes when I had properly recovered. My apprehension was balanced by the knowledge that the pile of homework could go into the bin and that never again would I have to face that dreadful journey to Banchory. True, my pleasant interlude with my secret love coming to see me every week had made life very tolerable; but, still being the same shy idiot, I had never made my feelings known. So life just moved on.

About ten weeks after the beginning of term I walked up the drive to the Grammar School, past the imposing statue of Lord Byron and in through the side door. There met by the head prefect, I was taken to the Rector's room where Sir James formally welcomed me and instructed me as to my timetable. The shock of entry to a fee-paying boys' school could not have been greater had I been going to Eton. A medical certificate ensured that I was excused gym and games. Otherwise I found myself in all the A classes, except for maths, where Mr Pimple Gray decided to keep me in his own C class to help me catch up with the syllabus after the lost weeks. The loss of schooling, the change of environment and the new experience of living away from home made life difficult both educationally and emotionally. My classmates' intense interest in the opposite sex was yet another new experience that I found disturbing in my own adolescence.

When at Aboyne, I had been the one who was academically ahead of Alan; but now the boot was very much on the other foot and I was dependent on him for the helping hand. Alan was very much a loner; but, in his case, the change of school was not associated with the additional complication of a change to a substitute parent. Moreover, he had not missed the schoolwork as I had during my crucial months of illness. My classmates were essentially from the middle and professional classes of the city, but at no time was I made to feel inferior. My health was bedevilled by bouts of sinusitis, which gave me bad headaches and also severe boils at times. Diet was much less healthy than that of the country districts, with carbohydrates filling young stomachs. Furthermore, I was not taking the exercise to which I was accustomed.

Glen Mark Expedition.
The Burn of Doune Waterfalls.

A further unsettling factor in my life was the fact that I went home to the Glen on a Friday after school, returning to Louisville Avenue by our well-kent Strachan's bus each Sunday night. The mind plays odd tricks, as I did not really want to leave my pals on Friday; yet the wrench of leaving home on the Sunday evening triggered an almost suicidal depressive state which I found profoundly traumatic. Looking back now, this is the point when my parents lost touch with what was happening to me. As a result they were unaware of the cause of my distress. From then on I was essentially on my own, making my own mistakes and often just drifting along. Professional and middle class parents have trod this path before, with the result that they can appropriately guide and advise their offspring. But in my case, even with Mrs Simpson's care and interest, I was breaking new ground in unknown territory. As I continued to plead inability to do games, this robbed me of two years of rugby. I never did go to gym during my three years at Grammar - all a grave mistake.

I felt most at home with English, under the delightful teaching of Charles Forbes. This is where I was able to compete with the best. While his reports used to enthuse about my class performance, I never felt that I did myself justice in exams - a recurring theme for future years. Pimple Gray kept me in his C class without giving me any individual attention, while I sat effortlessly at the head of his class with minimal effort. Driven to despair, as I could see my chance of a higher maths qualification slipping away, I insisted on a move to a class covering the full syllabus. I was thus relieved, albeit at the eleventh hour, when I was moved up to a B class. The attitude of many masters at the school was that each pupil had to look out for himself, whereas at Aboyne I had been spoon-fed by dedicated teachers, all bent on fine-tuning my abilities. Here, at the Grammar School, there was no real work ethic that I could discern. But with many of the best brains in the city attending Grammar, the school's success in the educational stakes was assured, no matter what happened to those who needed a measure of individual nurturing.

I truly loved the school and its wonderful traditions, going back to the thirteenth century. However, I regret never having fulfilled my potential either scholastically or in sport. Rugby was the game for which the school was famous. We had public holidays when Dr J.R.S. (Donny) Innes captained Scotland and when Dally Allardyce played scrum half for the Scots, as well as for Dr Doug W C Smith. Grammar FP's were unofficial champions of Scotland in 1947. There was tremendous kudos attached to playing for the school and the FP's team.

In my last year I decided that being a wimp had lasted long enough and I went along to enrol for rugby. Coming late to the game, I was pushed into the forwards, never having been grounded in rugby nor having received basic coaching such as the boys coming up from lower school had been given. Thus, I was at a distinct disadvantage. In my very first game, being totally unaware of the finer rules of the game, I suffered the humiliation of getting a withering verbal reprimand from our PT teacher who was refereeing. This was for throwing, instead of kicking, the ball into touch. Then, sprinting out of a ruck all on my own and going for the line, I was tackled beautifully by the full back whose collar bone snapped audibly in the process. That first game of rugby certainly sticks in my memory. I eventually played for the 2nd XV and for my house, Keith; but I felt that I had a lot more to give. However, having been

Winter 1946 -
week-ends at Home
from Grammar.

*Glen Tanar lake totally
frozen over with unusual
view of the boat-house.*

sheltered and personally shepherded in my country school, I had not assimilated the fact that initiative and self-confidence are qualities essential for survival in such a large institution and that hanging back gets one nowhere.

Desperate now to play cricket in the summer term, I found again that teams were already established and that there was no way in for someone totally untried and in his sixth year. So I turned to athletics. It transpired that I was a promising sprinter, competing reasonably well. But again, all this was achieved at the last gasp without any real preparation or practice, much to the PT master Jimmy Hunter's apparent annoyance. Once again, however, I never felt that anyone was really interested in assessing my potential.

In fact the school sports at the end of my sixth year provided me with the only real achievement of my time at Grammar. Coming in second in the hundred yards as well as anchoring the house relay team to victory compensated a little, but I was slightly deflated by Mr Hunter's comments afterwards – "And that was done without you training." A large big-headed young man from the year behind caused me to come in third in the 200 yards race. His name was Ian Cuthbertson and, having watched me come close to winning the 100 yards, he said to me that he knew that he could easily beat me and that he would now enter the 200 yards race. Sure enough, much to my disgust, big Cuthbertson duly came in second, which no doubt inflated his ego further. Ian was to go on to become a household name with his character parts in so many fine productions on film and TV: but I bet that I could easily beat him now over 200 yards.

With the war now ended, Pop Simpson was demobbed and Ma Simpson was expected to return to Muswell Hill in London to pick up the strands of the General Practice that they had left behind. This all occurred during my sixth and last year, 1946. Alan was now lodging with an aunt, so I obtained accommodation with a widow out at Woodside. As this was quite far from the school, I took to cycling again; but on the whole this was a totally unproductive year. I had already passed my Highers and added University Prelims to give me a better chance of University entrance. My health had been taken into consideration for my Highers, otherwise I might have toiled to make the grade. But the University entrance exam results came as a consequence of my doing some hard work at last.

1947 - Aberdeen Grammar School, Upper Sixth Year.

Back Row, extreme left - Alan Simpson
Second Row, extreme left - Jimmy Mitchell
and second from the right - Morland Craig.

Front Row, fourth from left - George Leslie
Second from the right - George A.M.Stewart
and third from the right - the Author.

In my Upper Sixth year I was among some of the elite awaiting University entrance and I badly needed guidance and monitoring at this point. As such career advice was almost non-existent, I simply idled and coasted through the year without anything to show for it. In retrospect, I was ashamed of myself and critical of the school's lack of appreciation and guidance of the individual scholar. Perhaps, however, it was not a wholly wasted year, as I lifted myself out of the rut of non-sporting participation thus paving the way for so much pleasure and camaraderie in my years ahead.

Glen Tanar Exile

In that last year I cannot now recall how I travelled to the school each day, although I am aware of having used my bicycle. Negotiating the cobbled streets out at Woodside Fountain and keeping out of the tramlines does ring a distant bell; but the route to school and even the cycle sheds are blotted from memory. It is so frustrating to have no recollection of those days except to know that I sometimes caught the tram out George Street. My amnesia must have been only partial, because I can well remember a stunning but remote redhead who travelled on the same route in the evenings after work. Years later, I was to come across her socially, married I think to a city planner, a puffed-up sort of fellow. Odd that the memory of a year is reduced to just this one attractive, but very isolated image.

Food rationing was at its worst at this time and I never felt fully satisfied after a meal, even though I seemed to devour more than my fair share and was left still looking for more. Carbohydrates again filled the void and I suffered from huge disfiguring boils on my back and legs, the scars being still obvious to this day. Life felt very confined in these lodgings and although I was treated extremely well I was pleased when the year came to an end and I moved on. However, during my stay at Woodside I may not have learned much academically at school, but living so closely in other people's small worlds helped broaden my experience of life.

The High School for Girls in Albyn Place, was the equivalent of our boys' school. The lads were keen to develop their contacts there, and I was surprised how quickly I got caught up in this mind-set. Madame Murray's in the Cowdray Hall was the scene of the local Saturday dance at which pupils from the various schools foregathered. Experiences there were eagerly discussed with my precocious friend, George 'Goofy' Stewart, behind the books in the library or in the corridors on a Monday morning. Madame Murray also ran dance lessons for the schoolchildren from Gordon's College, St Margaret's School for Girls, Albyn School for Girls and the Central School, as well as for the Grammar and the Girl's High School.

Alan and I enlisted for lessons during our fourth year and the intricacies of quarter turns, half turns, reverse turns, foxtrots, quicksteps and tangos tempered our enjoyment, but paid off handsomely for the future. Madame Murray however had the disconcerting habit of drawing attention to my frequent lack of finesse by addressing me in French, much to the hilarity of the class and my acute embarrassment. We tried unsuccessfully to form close relationships with girls, but my continuing shyness meant that I stood at tram stops for years with the same attractive girls and never opened my mouth. To this day I still know some of these elderly ladies and we laugh at what might have been if I had just loosened my tongue and made the first move. Bett Raitt, our close friend from Durris and ex-nursing colleague of my wife Kaye, remembers Douglas Young and me travelling to and from Aberdeen at the weekends when she was at Banchory. However she then has the audacity to add that it was only Doug she had ever had eyes for in those days. However, having spent Christmas Day with us for too many years to recall, her Manhattan cocktails have long since overcome that ancient insult from sixty years ago. My years in Louisville Avenue were really happy ones and I can still see the tram clanking down Great Western Road past the end of Ashley Road. I can so clearly recreate the carefree feeling of sitting out on its open-rear upper deck, with the sun shining down and the haunting strains of the *Trolley Song* in the background. What nostalgic memories are stored away from those teenage years of heightened awareness to be re-awakened, just very occasionally, when all is peace and quiet around me.

My friendships were many, but George Erskine Leslie, at six feet four inches tall and understandably known as Tiny, was probably my closest friend, apart from Alan, who was more like a brother. George had been born in India, where his father, having been trained at Kew Gardens in London, laid out the gardens in Darjeeling as part of his government job. Retired as a civil servant, his father received a good pension and was very comfortably off. George was a keen Scouter and this is where all his energies went when he wasn't lying in his bed. Tall with a slight stoop and often dishevelled, he was a good hockey player but was never one for the ladies. He and I enjoyed a very real friendship that has lasted even though we have been separated ever since.

1946 - The Aberdeen Grammar School Environment.
The Author and George E. Leslie studying hard.

185

Glen Tanar Exile

Wednesday afternoon was set aside for sport, but in my first two years this was my cinema time. The pictures were hugely popular. There were cinemas all over the city, from the palatial Odeon and Majestic down to the Playhouse and the Belmont, where, I believe, admission in the old days cost a couple of jam jars. The craze was for musicals, which appealed to the director's ambitions in Alan; or for the war-based films which were more to my liking. As various class members were excused games, we would join up together at times to visit the cinemas. As, on this occasion, my companion had no money, I lent him the sixpence (2.5p) for the cinema ticket. I never was repaid and the enormity of this transgression lives with me still. When one remembers that sixpence formed 25% of my weekly pocket money, the offence is probably understandable. Yet, the fact that sixty years later I can still recall it with so much emotion, seems almost absurd.

A similar event related to my rugby-playing sixth year when my mother bought me a new blue school rugby jersey to replace the second-hand one with which I had started. I was chuffed to be wearing it for the first time. But while I was in the shower it mysteriously disappeared leaving a much-faded replica in its place. I was truly shattered, not only over the loss, but by the realisation that, even in this type of company, a mate could turn out to be such a thief. It was altogether very disheartening. In later weeks, I came to be pretty certain who was wearing my shirt and his face is forever stamped on my memory.

The fact that I failed to take up cricket in my last year did, however, produce one small bonus. Mr Tyson the groundsman at our Rubislaw playing field, kindly looked out for me some old equipment from the pavilion, bats, pads and stumps to take home for our scout troop at the Glen. Over the next few years until I eventually left the Glen, we had many delightful days using this bonanza. The fact that I had never played cricket for an established team was yet another of those early regrets with which I now reproach myself. Opportunity often only knocks once; but it is only after the chance has passed that one realises what one has actually missed.

One of my greatest embarrassments relates to the cricket gear we were bequeathed from the Grammar groundsman. Jimmy Mitchell was also a close friend of mine at that time. We used to delight in singing close-harmony songs together in class, although I never had much of a voice. Having described my happy days playing cricket at the Glen, I invited Jimmy to come out to stay with us for a weekend at half term. That Friday evening, half a dozen of us were down on the golf course engrossed in a finely balanced game of cricket when I was aware of a stranger approaching. "Jimmy Mitchell what are YOU doing here?" I exclaimed, when all of a sudden I remembered my invitation.

Not only had I totally forgotten about it but, what was ten times worse, I had failed to mention it to my fussy mother. No one ever came to stay other than family, and I was very agitated as to how she would react. Once the initial shock had passed, we all settled down for a good weekend, Jimmy having cycled all the way from Aberdeen to be with us. But I doubt whether my reputation was ever completely restored in the Mitchell household.

The need to think about a career never seemed to occur to me and it was as if my father's ambition that I should benefit from an education to gain entry to university was an end in itself. My parents had not considered what I would actually study. To say I had absolutely no idea what I wanted to do is probably untrue; but the range of options had never been spelt out to me. The influence of Dr Willie's mystique, together with my close association with the Simpsons, gradually led me to consider the possibility of a career in medicine. This seemed especially true in Alan's case, as his father took it for granted that his son would be a doctor, although I could foresee that this imaginative, intelligent young man might be stifled in such a profession.

Another almost subliminal effect on me was the story that my mother, when attending a fair as a young woman, had had her fortune told by a scrawny old gypsy. She was told she would leave home for the big city and then travel widely in the world. She would marry a foreigner and have one child who would become either a pharmacist or a doctor. My mother, as a country girl living in a small market town such as Morpeth, where the girls all married locally and never moved more than twenty miles away, found this prophesy totally unbelievable. Gradually, however, as life unfolded as the gypsy had foretold, my future as a pharmacist or a doctor seemed to have been preordained.

Upper Six contained twenty-four of us, seven of whom would go on to study medicine. Thus, the strong influence of conformity was beginning to swallow me up. When the time came, I tendered an application for Medicine along with a place in Forestry as a second choice, just in case. What stupidity, as forestry as a way of life would have destroyed me. I had no real interest in that at all. This illustrates how we stumbled along with little or no guidance to help us in making our choice of course.

Apart from medicine, the most obvious professions to be considered were those of law, teaching, agriculture and forestry. As for the world outside Aberdeen, its opportunities were largely unknown. How things have changed for our young people nowadays - although medicine and law still seem to me the most popular pinnacles to aim for. This applies especially to the girl students. As I had only the basic qualifications, merely applying for a university place was no guarantee of success. However, following the interview with Colonel Butchart, the University secretary, and backed by a strong recommendation from my godfather Glentanar, I was accepted. Butchart seemed more interested in my Grammar background and my rugby-playing potential for the University, than in my academic abilities.

Grammar School Sports Day - 1947.
Keith House with some Future Doctors including
Sandy Cheyne on my left.
Ian Anderson and a very young Alister Nisbet behind.

Academic prowess is nowadays the sole criterion for acceptance into the medical faculty. This is in some ways sad, as medicine is essentially a learning and retaining skill, with little innovation and imagination involved. This level of expertise is well within the capabilities of a good average brain. Thus, our top students must be released to enhance the wealth and vitality of the nation. Instead, the kudos of being a doctor with its associated social status has led to many highly intelligent people finding themselves, after a few years, in an, at times, unchallenging profession in which they achieve the necessary standards while using only a fraction of their ability. One is left to ponder whether young, highly intelligent doctors will suffer from a general disenchantment and an aching for retirement when they realise that in General Montgomery's words "they will never reach the ceiling of their abilities".

I look back on my days at Grammar with great fondness, realising that, despite my blundering and misusing the opportunities offered, I was lucky to have reached my goal of university entrance. There is little doubt that I was ill-prepared for the 'take it or leave it' education offered at Grammar after the benefits of the intense teacher-commitment of Aboyne, along with my mother's driving influence. Throughout my life I have noticed that even a small amount of encouragement can make me perform one hundred per cent better. It is little wonder, therefore, that both Grammar and University found me struggling to cope without someone's big boot behind me.

The summer holiday of 1947 marked the end of my Grammar days, but with the future still very uncertain. As we would not be notified about our university acceptances until August, I had the prospect of some anxious weeks ahead. If successful, I would then be ready to start the autumn term in October. Alan, with advanced mathematics and mechanics on top of his basic requirements, could relax; but I was certainly not in that happy position. However, the Simpsons invited Jimmy Mitchell – another aspiring doctor - and myself down to London for a holiday and to see the sights.

London in 1947 was still recovering from the blitz. Londoners' thoughts and conversations were still dominated by its effects. Pop Simpson had just taken delivery of a new Austin Atlantic with which he was totally intrigued. New cars were for priority groups only. So, as a GP, Pop qualified to replace his battered old Flying Standard, which had stood jacked up in his garage throughout the whole war. The Atlantic was really a sports saloon with lovely modern lines and we all got a tremendous kick out of our trips in it. However, labouring up hills with Ma, Pop and us three boys aboard was a bit much for the car at times and I can still hear Pop laughingly shouting, "Scuff boys, scuff!".

I did not fancy a GP's life in a London suburb very much, as Pop seemed to be on call all the time, except for a half day on a Wednesday and a few hours off on Sunday. This was the start of the NHS and patients were using and abusing it to excess. Pop, a straight talking Northeaster, wasn't going to be persuaded to provide prescriptions for cotton wool to stuff patients' pillows. Some of his colleagues, however, with an eye to increasing their lists, gave lines for anything. Ma worried that, with this attitude, Pop would scare off the people whom they so desperately needed to help build up a practice that had faded away during the war in his absence.

The quality of Ma's life was even worse, in that help in the house was non-existent. Now she had everything to do, household duties, waiting room, surgery, answering phones and the door bell: added to which she had only a couple of hours on a Wednesday to dash out to the shops. I thought she had a horrendous life compared with the comfortable lifestyle she had enjoyed during her years in Aboyne and later in Aberdeen. It saddened me to see her suffer in this way, all the more so, since she had been almost a second mother to me. I do not think she ever delivered a cross word to me in all years I had known her.

Seeing the sights, doing some shows, especially *Annie Get Your Gun* and joining in with Pop's great love of tennis as well as swimming - all of this soon filled up our three weeks. So when I arrived home to open the dreaded envelope from the university, the utter relief of acceptance was unbelievable. I do not believe I had ever had to endure such strain before this and I am sure there are indelible traces of this in my subsequent life.

Often, over the years, I have dreamt of failing my Highers and being back at Grammar as a mature student, trying to get the necessary qualifications. It always intrigues me to think what else must be indexed away in the recesses of my brain that may one day reappear to shock me.

At this stage, however, reality was the open road, beckoning me to go forward and achieve my goal. Little did I realise that this particular road was going to lead not only to a mass of bends, but also to some very steep hills and very deep valleys.

Chapter 13
Books And The Scottish Colourists

Miss Pirie's little cupboard behind her desk at Glen Tanar School has much to do with my subsequent love for and treasuring of books. Not that her small prizes were my first experience of the riches contained in them, but I believe the achievement of winning them illuminated an awareness already present in the cradle. This awareness was engendered in the beginning by a small hardback that resided below my pillow, a book from which my mother read after singing me a lullaby. *The Little Ones, Peter Pan and Wendy*, retold for the Nursery by Mary Byron and illustrated by Kathleen Atkins, was first published in 1930. It measured only five inches by four inches and was my constant companion throughout those early nights. My mother firmly believed in the Truby King method of bringing up children and, just as Dr Spock advocated to future mothers, so did Truby make sure that lights were out by 7 p.m.

Mickey Mouse comics and boys' annuals came later but even at that stage they were never the real thing. *The Little Princess* given to me on my fifth birthday was the first bound volume I ever owned and became the bedrock of all that was to follow.

The next important occurrence came the following year when my grandparents in Morpeth sent me for Christmas *Sir Douglas Haig's Great Push*. This chronicled and frighteningly illustrated the events of the last years of the Great War on the Western Front in 1917. The horrendous depiction of the desolation and suffering kept me returning to this book for years afterwards. I was besotted with the pictures though I never read a word. Whether or not this was a sensible gift for a young child is highly debatable. On reading the book again, I see that my aunt Molly had bought it in 1917 and that she had probably passed it on as if it were a present from the grandparents. As parents and grandparents, we are very careful in our choice of what we give to our young on birthdays and at Christmas, but in a poorer age this was a luxury that few could afford.

Somewhat later, my less than honest approach to borrowing books is highlighted in another chapter; while even giving books to friends as presents proved difficult for me. I well recall purchasing a book from the Aboyne Station bookshop to give to my friend Alfie as a Christmas present. When I returned home, the dust cover and general appearance of the book were so alluring that I put it prominently on my bookshelf and sat down to consider what I should give Alfie instead. From very early days, certainly before I went to school, the *Mickey Mouse* comic loomed large in my life and the Tuesday delivery was the red-letter day in the week. I still recall many of the futuristic imaginings of the editors, which seem now to have been very prophetic. Then they were regarded simply as Jules Verne-type nonsense by the adults of that age. Having grown out of Mickey, *The Adventure* boy's magazine took its place as my favourite. Its delivery day was the one day in the week when I was never home late from school.

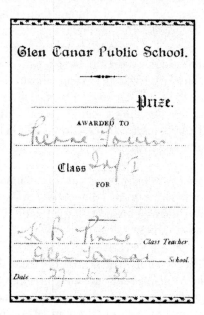

That First School Prize.
The well remembered signature
of the dreaded Miss Pirie.

Sporadically over the years, I also read the *Rover*, the *Hotspur* and the *Wizard*, but always came back ultimately to *The Adventure*. Special freebies issued with these publications were tremendously exciting, and those, along with the offers out of the corn-flake packets, brightened up many a week. At a time when radio was still fairly rudimentary and TV was non-existent, those comics formed the solid foundations for a love of reading. What with my mother's interest in singing to me as a small child, and having all the time in the world to read the usual bedtime story, it was not surprising that this captivating experience nurtured in me a great love of story-telling and the written word. In addition, there was a steady inflow of reading material from my aunt, so that I was being continuously stimulated to read more and more.

192

Another landmark book is dated 27th June 1935. *Rat Tat Tat, My Friend the Postman* may sound a rather uninspiring title, but it represented my very first school prize. I recently discovered it at the bottom of an old box in my loft. Inscribed on the presentation label were the words "Dr Ritchie's Prize for Infants One" and it was signed by my teacher K B Pirie. The reason for the award was not entered and who, I wonder, was Dr Ritchie anyway? No matter, this was to be the forerunner of many such awards over the years. But never, I am sure, did they give me such a thrill of achievement as this rat-tat-tatting postman.

While at Aboyne School, I went for lunch every day for six years to Mrs Halsey at *The Cottage* on Ballater Road. She was a marvellous cook and I was introduced to flavours, especially her puddings, which I had never savoured before. The only course which I had difficulty with during all those years, was her potato soup which was very thick and could contain whole potatoes. This triggered something in my palate reminiscent of the thick hare and potato soup at Glen Tanar School which had eventually stopped me taking school lunches there. I dreaded the day in the week when I was in danger of gagging as I ate the soup; but I was far too shy and frightened of upsetting my hostess by telling her of my dislike.

Mrs Halsey's late husband had either worked for, or been acquainted with a distinguished naturalist of the time, Seton P. Gordon. Mr Halsey had been given one of the author's books as a token of gratitude. I cannot remember there being great number of books at *The Cottage*, but that by Seton Gordon enthralled me. Over the years, I often took it down just to handle it and skim through its pages. It was quite a slim hardback printed on thick shiny paper, and entitled *Birds of the Loch and Mountain*. Published in 1907, it was the author's earliest work.

Over the years my aunt bought me one or two new books by Seton Gordon such as *In Search of Northern Birds* and *The Golden Eagle*. The 1907 book, however, always felt more substantial and of better quality. In the years ahead I always kept a lookout for a second hand copy. As time went on, I gradually acquired more of his books, especially those published during the 1920's, such as *The Charm of the Hills* and *The Cairngorm Hills of Scotland*.

However, there was never a sign of that well-remembered original book until years later. In 1954, while in Edinburgh, I was passing time in Thins, when, lo-and-behold I came upon a pristine copy for ten shillings. I flick through its pages now and feel the same thrill that I experienced all those sixty odd years ago in Mrs Halsey's home in Aboyne.

As a boy, I had little opportunity to feast my eyes on many new books as, especially during the war years, we rarely moved far from home. The only opportunity we had to browse through new books was at the bookstall at the railway station in Aboyne Square. Not that there was a lot to view; but, here I would buy some Christmas and birthday presents and, very occasionally, be allowed to choose something for myself. I remember being intrigued by a blue cloth-backed volume about building warplanes to scale with all the detailed drawings throughout the book. My parents told me that I would have to pay for it out of my savings. I must have made three or four visits to study the book again until, aware of the sales-lady's growing impatience, I bought it almost out of embarrassment.

Upper Deeside with Lochnagar in the Background.
Seton Gordon's Books Aroused a Life-Long Interest.

In my second wave of ownership my mother bought a set of twelve novels which had been published by the *Daily Express*. Various authors were featured, such as Jane Austen, Charlotte Bronte, Sir Walter Scott, Edward Alan Poe and Wilkie Collins. Over the years I succeeded in reading them all, and was very proud to have them in my possession. A set of Arthur Mee's encyclopaedias followed. By now the top of the wardrobe in my bedroom was becoming very crowded. My collection of the *Just William* books by Richmal Crompton gave me enormous pleasure; but *Spyflyers* by W E Johns was for years my favourite volume. Then, a few years later, during a thaw, disaster struck when a lead pipe burst in our roof space and water flooded on top of my wardrobe. *Spyflyers* looks very bedraggled and water-stained today, as do some of the volumes of the *Encyclopaedia*. The Richmal Cromptons have never surfaced again, and I believe that they probably landed up in some waste paper depot when my parents flitted from the Glen in 1955. My distress over losing the books is compounded by the fact that, nowadays, a full set of first edition *Just William* books would be worth a small fortune since a new generation of enthusiastic readers has rediscovered them.

The recreation hall housed the lending library, and every few months the books were regularly replaced from the large travelling van from Aberdeen. Over the war years, particularly, I remember National Savings being seen as a patriotic gesture; so I saved my five shillings every month by visiting the hall where Mr Ogston received these contributions. While I was there, I got into the habit of taking out a couple of books, particularly cowboy books, which was at that time my favourite reading. I must have read about every Zane Gray that was ever published and regularly put in my request for further books of this nature. Fortunately, this fad eventually passed.

For many years *The Daily Express* was my mother's chosen newspaper, and excerpts from it were regularly passed on to me. The adventures of Rupert Bear appeared every day, and it was to these that I gravitated as soon as the paper arrived. I was completely caught up in his escapades and I would never miss an episode, just as people today become addicted to soaps, such as *Coronation Street* or *The Archers*. Many were the Rupert Bear annuals that I collected over the years, but none was appreciated as much as the daily scanning of Rupert Bear in the *Daily Express*.

Throughout my life I have been an avid book collector, and my shelves groan with writings drawn from a wide selection of authors. One book that I purchased taught me an important lesson. This was *The Natural History of Deeside* by William Macgillivray, published in 1855. The fly leaf states *"This Work, printed by command of The Queen, is presented to Mr William Cocks by H.R.H. Prince Albert."* Bought at Thins of Edinburgh in the early 1950's, the volume cost me the princely sum of twenty shillings. However, also for sale, was a similar copy in leather and in mint condition priced at thirty shillings. This, I felt, was too expensive for me at that time. The collector's expertise to "always buy the very best you cannot afford", was a lesson I had yet to learn and it would take me years of experience in collecting fine paintings to realise that one good object is always worth far more than two mediocre ones. Not that I cherish my books purely for their value, but my Macgillivray might now be worth £50, while the mint one would fetch £350 at least.

As a boy I never analysed what it was about the production of a book that evoked the sensation of appreciation. It was not until I went to the Grammar School that I met someone who would open my eyes to what I was struggling to understand. Morland Craig, was the eldest son of John Craig, Professor of Paediatrics at the Sick Children's Hospital. Morland was brilliant at classics, but a poor mathematician.

So it was that I found myself with him, at the back of Pimple Gray's maths C class in fourth year at Grammar. Supposedly, I was being coached to make up for my lost months through illness and I was desperate to be moved up to an A or a B class. Morland, by contrast, was happy to be left alone. He was a dreamy, rather unworldly boy, but he left me with a deep appreciation of books. I can see him still handling an interesting volume in the library, caressing the leather cover with the flat of his hand.

He would then turn the book to run his fingers lovingly down the spine, while admiring and enthusing over the gold lettering of the title. The sensual pleasure he derived from this transmitted itself to me, giving me much future satisfaction when handling a book of real quality. Morland was never to fulfil his undoubted talents, being afflicted by some form of juvenile rheumatoid arthritis, or Still's disease, which was to leave him an invalid from his late teens. Nevertheless his influence has always remained with me.

Books also excited me in a totally different context. As we progressed through school, each year we were greeted with a new set of textbooks. Moving into my senior classes at Aboyne, I was overawed by a vast array of new books straight out of the packing cases, and I always found this experience one of the most exciting moments in the school year.

On arriving home, my mother would immediately spend hours covering the books most professionally in brown paper, so that they remained in mint condition when I came to pass them on. Looking back once more, I can see that an appreciation of the small things of the past has been overwhelmed by the abundance of benefits that are now available. Consequently, we have lost that wonderful feeling of ownership which comes with possession of a few valued objects.

Viewing my ornithological collection now makes me wonder what on earth I should do with all these lovely books, as my children show no interest in this field. Through the war years and into the 1950's, my aunt bought me every significant ornithological publication. Some wonderful books come to mind, especially those from the artist-naturalists. When my aunt gave me *Memoirs of an Artist Naturalist* by George E Lodge, published in 1946, it became the yardstick by which I measured all other publications. *Morning Flight* and *Wild Chorus* by Peter Scott, published during the war; and then later *Sketches and*

Notes from a Bird Painter's Journal by Philip Rickman in 1949; and *Bird Portraits* by J.C.Harrison, (1949) there are publications for which I would happily have taken up stealing again.

Graham Anderson - My Art Connoisseur.
*Encyclopaedic Knowledge of all things
related to Artists and their lives.*

As my eye for art improved, I found that here was another field that filled me with pleasure and one which would eventually lead me by devious routes to a love for the Scottish Colourists, Ferguson, Peploe, Cadell and especially for George Leslie Hunter. Thanks to linking up with Graham Anderson, another old schoolmate from Grammar School days, in the late 1970's, my appreciation was to be vastly improved through his expertise. However the initial interest was first kindled as a result of my association with the well-known local novelist, poet and lecturer, Nan Shepherd. I came to know her during my years of medical practice in Cults, a west-end suburb of Aberdeen, when I first attended her house-keeper/companion, Mary Lawson and later Miss Shepherd herself.

During this time, I was never fully aware of her writings or of the fact that she was already regarded as being one of the outstanding Scottish novelists of the 20th century. She left a lasting impression on me, together with the kernel of an interest that was to develop over the years. Hanging in her back room was a small, unremarkable oil painting of a beach scene in the west of Scotland. Casually talking one day about the painting of her porch by Barbara Balmer, also a patient of mine, she extolled this small beach scene as her real treasure. The oil of Iona by S J Peploe did not strike me at the time as being particularly memorable. But over the months, Dr Shepherd often remarked about how proud she was to own it. As my experience of art gradually expanded, I grew to understand her enthusiasm for the Peploe. Now Nan Shepherd's literature has also found a place on my bookshelves alongside Charles Murray. But my lasting memory of her comes from her association with that little oil painting.

Houseboats, Loch Lomond – Gouache on Board.
G. Leslie Hunter.

Lord Glentanar was a great admirer of the work of Sir William Russell Flint (1880-1969), well known today for his semi-nudes in French or Spanish settings. He was also a fine landscape painter and the laird commissioned him to do a series of watercolours of Glen Tanar. Painting many of the salmon pools on the Dee as well as scenes around the estate, such as St Lesmo's Chapel, a fine collection was formed. The laird had the series laid out for Xmas cards and I still have an array of Flint's work from those days of the annual Xmas card to the family.

The vast choice of books available nowadays can overwhelm one, as they come in all shapes and forms. Appreciation of fine quality productions seems to be a matter of secondary importance. Apart from the specialist publishers, the format and binding is done for a mass market where books are treated as relatively disposable items. The production of gorgeous leather binding, hand-cut paper and use of gold leaf is now a minority interest in these modern times. Although I have purchased a number of these recent books through the years, the pleasure I derive from them does not approach that obtained from handling a book like *Etchings and Dry Point* by James McBey published in 1925. The modern quality books strike me as being like reproduction furniture, which somehow fails to capture the romanticism of the past. Going back even further, a publication I treasure is *Scottish Character and Scenery* by Walter Geikie RSA (1885). With its hand cut paper, leather and gold it exudes history. I regret, however, that I have not the original edition published in 1841.

Yes, I suppose this all shows that it is my inherent desire to collect which drives all these interests. I can go into some of my friends' libraries and view their walls stacked with books which they have bought in the first instance to read; while I have often acquired mine purely for the love of handling them and the sense of ownership.

Writing this chapter has led me to pore over books long forgotten. But on viewing them again, the memories all come flooding back. Life without my books, I am sure, would have been very barren and I am thankful that I had an aunt whose love and interest fostered this great passion in me.

Chapter 14
University Life

October 1947 saw me assemble in Marischal College quadrangle with another hundred or so freshmen to experience the sensation of being students with the aim of ultimately qualifying MB.ChB. I look back in disbelief at my own casual attitude to it all, as if I was off on some sort of holiday adventure. The class of that year comprised both youngsters and ex-servicemen, with a number of girls and some students from the West Indies and India. The first year's study consisted of physics, chemistry and biology, which should have presented those of us coming from an upper sixth year at school with no difficulty at all. Most of the work, apart from biology, had already been covered. I certainly felt that I freewheeled through that first year, never really getting down to hard work. Apart from the odd hiccup, all went according to plan, and so we passed on to our specialist subjects.

Anatomy, with its associated subjects of Histology and Embryology, as well as Physiology and some Biochemistry, formed the workload. In addition, our introduction to the 'Drain' and dead bodies made us wonder how we would cope. Straight away, I realised that I was in a totally different world and that if I did not keep abreast of the work, there would be trouble ahead. The practice of four us together dissecting a cadaver brought one into contact with one's fellow students in a way never before experienced. Working as a two-man team quickly identified the strengths and weaknesses of each individual. The resultant level of co-operation and good-will contributed greatly to one's satisfaction.

Jimmy Davidson, a bright little chap from Peterhead, was always a jump ahead of the rest of us, both in preparation and enthusiasm around the table. Keeping up on a weekly basis with Cunningham's handbooks of dissection was always a chore to me and I was rarely abreast of the work. I went through the motions of studying my subjects without any real commitment and probably with very little interest. The ability of those around me varied from the bright clear-minded, through the doggedly determined, to the drifters and finally to the strugglers. I was certainly a drifter, enjoying the social interaction of such a diverse group while, at the same time, getting to know everyone. Work was of secondary importance to this enjoyment.

Coming, as I had, from such a distinguished city school, I went through none of the difficulties that so many country boys experienced of feeling socially out of their depth. However, the downside was that I was almost too urbane for my

201

own good and simply enjoyed the sensation of belonging to the inner circle. The grind of the occasional spotter exams in the Anatomy Department kept me at least relatively in touch; whereas, in Physiology, the class exams after each term were the only markers. The Second Professional Examination loomed like a huge unscalable wall in front of many of us, as it was common knowledge that to surmount it would enable us to obtain our final degrees, however long it took. To stumble here would mean a further year at best or total banishment at worst. Also, to know that in 1827 Charles Darwin had opted out of medicine at Edinburgh University at the self-same stage would have been of little consolation to any of us.

My nemesis had arrived; from that first day at Grammar through the wasted sixth year, retribution was at last about to overtake me. Having failed my Physiology exam, I was faced with the fact that in a few weeks' time I would have to resit everything. I was only too aware that next time I might fail some of the Anatomy subjects. I even started trying to resurrect my religion in the vain hope that someone out there would look down favourably on this poor sinner. No chance! I blew my oral in Physiology with such an elementary answer that old Dominie Walker must have sat up in his grave to ask me again what ten times nothing was and I would still give the same idiotic reply.

I was devastated by my failure. This was the first real setback in my life, and it was little consolation to find that I had done so well in all my Anatomy subjects as to be excused sitting them again. A repeat year was bad enough, but a further term had been added to the course because Biochemistry had been increased within the curriculum. Thus instead of being three terms behind my colleagues, I was now to be four terms. Devastation was all around me as others had failed everything, but I could only focus on my own troubles. Seven of us from my school year had started Medicine, but only four were through, including my 'blood brother' Alan. Many others would never return to University, while some, like school chum and George Formby impersonator, George A M Stewart, would change direction into an MA course. He became a teacher eventually, but never ceased to regret giving up Medicine.

The boat was leaving, the heavy hawsers were cast ashore and the medical year of 1947-53 set off upstream. There was I, a tragic lost soul on the quayside, unable even to wave them goodbye. For the first time in my life, I had to face up to failure and the consequences that it imposed on me and those around me.

My parents were totally supportive and at no time was there any question of them withdrawing their support. They regarded my failure as a hiccup and, my mother probably thought that one failure was, for me, excusable. My ex-service friend George McDonald from Fochabers had, like me, passed his Anatomy well, but failed Physiology. As we were both committed to attending classes in only half the subjects, we had to decide how to spend the rest of our time. George, a master at finding his way through the corridors of power, had his sister, Isobel, a senior ward sister in the Infirmary, to advise him. He arranged for himself to be installed in the Casualty Department under the direction of the chief, Dr David Proctor. For my part I reckoned that some pharmacy experience might help me in future.

Student's Charities Week - 1949.
The Torcher Procession – acting the Clown.

*John Pattillo and Sheila Duncan also
enjoying the Bare Facts.*

For over a year I would slap up ointments, fill bottles for the wards, count out thousands of tablets and, in truth, become an unpaid dogsbody in the Royal Infirmary Pharmacy Department. I probably learnt practically nothing that would help me in the future, but perhaps it did me little harm to get involved in the back-stairs running of a hospital. My contacts in the Pharmacy Department certainly made me an accepted member of the working class. Alec Reid was my unqualified and very pleasant supervisor down in the basement, while the chief pharmacist, Mr Kinniburgh, and his second-in-command, Mr Jack Fraser, reigned upstairs. Where was the University advisory service at times like these?

Either it just did not exist or I was too inexperienced to find it. Having first stumbled into medicine from school with little advice, I proceeded to spend a rather fruitless year in a backwater. I am certain that, had I been given guidance at this point, I would have benefited from opportunities to further my career by making use of my free time in a more worthwhile manner.

The necessity to resit the exams involved me in having to attend fewer than half the classes. This prevented me from getting to know my new mates really well. Quite a few were old school-fellows who had been either in the lower sixth or younger than me, or were just back from the services. I thus found that I had teamed up with no less than ten Grammar FP's. There was no difficulty in keeping abreast with the work the second time round, as being exempted from Anatomy made things so much easier.

Both George and I seemed to cruise through the course, being excused the mandatory oral exam for those resitting; so we must have done pretty well. One of the less savoury characters among our new classmates was heard to refer to us as 'throwbacks', a term which was true, but no less hurtful. The stigma of such failure is something that never leaves one, but often makes one strive even harder in future to prove that this setback is merely a temporary blip.

Temporary blip or not, I still had neither learnt the technique of swotting meaningfully, nor had I found any real joy in my subjects. Leaving the Marischal College campus and moving to the Foresterhill Medical School should have given me a sense of entering the actual world of medicine. However, I found that my colour blindness handicapped me to some degree when it came to studying Bacteriology. Materia Medica bored me, while Pathology initially awakened only a modicum of interest. My swotting technique was still faulty enough to make me think I knew and understood these subjects; whereas the searching test of a written exam would reveal only too well the flaws in my grasp of these fields.

Despite the odd upset however the aura of experiencing hands-on medicine began to seem attractive. After hurdling the third professional exam there came a dawning and a new understanding of my learning needs and a sudden realisation that I was in fact almost enjoying the course for the first time. A shaft of sunlight had come spearing through the surrounding gloom after all those wasted months and years. Now the clouds miraculously rolled away revealing everything around me in a different light. My spirits rose, my confidence gradually returned and suddenly the far off horizon became visible for the very first time.

Achieving acceptable standards in Medicine, Surgery, Obstetrics and Gynaecology, gradually made me realise that I was no longer fated to be a 'throwback.' Instead, I could now be someone who could more adequately contribute to discussions and in clinics. What brought about this welcome change? I believe the move from my digs at No.75 into the student residence brought me into an atmosphere where students shared their knowledge and difficulties. Here I could derive the greatest benefit from being surrounded by people who were really anxious to learn. Previously I had every intention of swotting, and, despite long hours spent with my books, I just did not seem to retain what I was reading and I tended to skim over apathetically what I did not understand. Now, in my new accommodation, I was writing résumés, underlining passages and, above all, being able to recall the facts at the end of my reading. This was the technique that had eluded me for so many years. George McDonald's presence in the room next to me also played a great part in my continuing improvement. His determination was infectious and he was always there to revive any lagging enthusiasm.

Alan Simpson continued to take a paternal interest in my progress and for him to turn round and note my achievement in exams as being better than his, was praise indeed. It did seem at this stage that I was achieving more on paper than he had achieved, even though he was a year ahead. But there is no doubt that he was unenthusiastically studying a subject which did little to inspire him at the time. I have always maintained that his great talents were wasted in medicine, despite the fact that in 2002, at over seventy years of age, he is still working as a consultant anaesthetist in Waterloo, Ontario.

Obstetrics awakened my keenest interest and I found a new confidence in discovering that, when I was really interested in a subject, I could hold my own with the best. Looking back, I now realise that I can function either very well or very badly according to my level of commitment. I seem to have no easy middle course, as so many of my peers demonstrated. They proceed, never really excelling, but also never failing. Some of my colleagues were blessed with that raw native wit which sees them through all crises by using their heads and making the most of what little knowledge they have; an ability that is not part of my make-up.

During our study of psychiatry, our Intelligent Quotients (IQ's) were assessed. I achieved a reasonable score of 128. I would have been happier with ten points more but considering that, even the bright sparks did not score a great deal more, it did not seem to me to matter all that much. It is obviously up to each of us to use our special talents to the best advantage, while being fully aware of our weaknesses.

University life should encompass much more than the course itself and, here again, it is very difficult for the freshman to get the balance right between study and the extra-curricular activities. Again, there seems to be no happy medium. Some give themselves over to snooker, sport, drinking or other student activities; while the John Knox fraternity hold their hands up in horror and advocate nothing but hard graft. I was certainly fully aware of my responsibilities and neither the billiard saloons nor the pubs ever saw me. Rugby took up Wednesday afternoons, with a rugby fixture on the Saturday followed by the student dance in the Student's Union, the Mitchell or Elphinstone Halls. Fear of not applying myself to my studies stopped me from taking part in the student shows. Furthermore, any thoughts of flying with the Air Squadron were dashed by my colour blindness.

Alan was a workaholic. I can still see his fixed, slightly slanted, stare whenever I seemed to be lifting my nose from the grindstone. The ethos of the Leslie household was also about hard work; too much pleasure being rather ungodly - certainly in Mother Leslie's eyes. Also there was a feeling abroad that medics had really to keep at the books or fail, while some other degree courses allowed much more freedom, which was probably true.

I always felt that the practical purpose of so much detailed learning in the dissection room was aimed more at developing the student's ability to concentrate, rather than learning anatomy for its own sake. Certainly, by the time I came to do my surgical house job, my anatomy knowledge had blown away in the wind. I was nevertheless confirmed in the certainty that the medical course required great determination and stamina.

Rugby gave me great pleasure and the camaraderie of the team was an inspiration. Having taken up the game late at school, I had been drafted in as a forward, whereas by choice, with my speed, I should have been on the wing. Also, being tall but of slender build, I was not really cut out to go far playing among the tough burly figures in the scrum. For most years I became the regular leader of the 2nds pack and was also a first reserve and played quite often for the 1st XV. One of my most memorable seasons, was probably 1950. Under the captaincy of my fellow classmate Marshall Munn (at scrum half), the 2nds were unbeaten throughout the whole season and scored the greatest number of points ever recorded up to that time.

The memories from those days are many, but two others will suffice. The pinnacle of my rugby career from my point of view came about in season 1951. It so happened that my classmate and captain of firsts, Sandy Cheyne, together with our Scottish international second row forward Ernie Michie, were away playing in a district's trial match in Perth. As a result I was promoted to take Ernie's place in the scrum, packing down with my large energetic classmate Gordon Smyllie in second row against Grammar FP's. This was one of our most prestigious fixtures, because FP's, although not quite the force in Scottish rugby that they had been in the late 1940's, were still the team to beat outside of our inter-university matches. The match was to be played on the FP's ground at Rubislaw, and we were not really rated to give them much of a game, especially with our weakened side.

Back Row
C S Philip, D S Robbie, E J S Michie, H G Smyllie, R A Greenshields,
F L P Fouin, A J M Gunn

Mr Webster
Colonel Butchart

Front Row
J D Smith, A B R Sharp, K McLean (Vice Captain), J M Munn (Captain),
J G C Munro (Hon. Sec.), A I Cheyne, D R Pratt

On Ground
H B Paterson, G W C Hunter.

*Of the sixteen players in this photograph -
seven came from our Medical Year.*

Among the FP's were many well-remembered players; but for me the two Hunter brothers, Jimmy and Eddie were of particular significance. Jimmy Hunter had been my PT teacher at Grammar when I had crawled out of the woodwork in my sixth year to belatedly take up rugby. As I have related previously, he had taken my very first game for the also-rans, when I had fielded the ball and, under pressure, had thrown it into touch instead of kicking it. I can still remember his amused, incredulous disbelief as he whistled me up and explained that I should perhaps learn the rules of the game before trying to play it. Now, four years later, this idiot was to have the temerity to come back and play on the very same pitch as he had shown his ignorance of the game and, what's more, dare to play against the crème de la crème.

Whether or not this memory spurred me on, I really don't know. But that day I really played a blinder. Getting out fast in the loose play and wreaking havoc among their centres, I felt for once inspired, especially when giving Jimmy Hunter a rough time. That day we ran the FP's ragged and, to crown it all, we achieved a pushover try under their posts. Both Gordon and I fell on the ball to score almost at the same moment; but of course, Gordon being Gordon, he convincingly claimed it. I did not mind as the whole game had been a bonus for me, and running out worthy winners, we basked in the glory for a week. Years later, when playing for Perthshire Accies while in the Army, I came back into contact with Eddie Hunter, now playing impressively for Accies. It seemed a small world but by this time my best days were past and I was but an unfit shadow of the player who played that satisfying match at Rubislaw.

I was lucky enough to play against Gordonians on a number of occasions. With my height and jumping ability I was useful in the lineouts and the ball was frequently thrown for me. It happened that during one match I was playing opposite the moustached Adam Tullett - also a classmate of mine - when I was upended at the very first lineout, even before I had touched the ball. There was no doubt I had been given a firm message by a master and thereafter knew exactly the treatment I was in for. The Gordonian pack was undoubtedly the toughest, hardest, set of players that I can remember playing against. Not really dirty players, but intimidating from first to last. Over a pint after the match, we enjoyed some good-natured banter. I can still hear Adam's deep guffaw through a bristling moustache, as he commented "You mamby-pamby little boys come to Seafield to be taught how to be men!"

Our medical year spawned an impressive bunch of rugby players and about ten of us were spread between firsts and seconds and this led to a great bond of companionship. I played regularly in the scrum in the 2nd XV together with my ever-present classmates Herb Longmore and Ian (Boom) Reid. Herb, whose occasional caustic comment about my youthful tendency to over-exaggerate, lived on with me in the years ahead, reminding me to stick with the facts and stamp on that ever present desire to over elaborate. We must have played for about four seasons together in sun, rain and snow with few, if any, injuries of note. No matter what time we got back to Aberdeen, we always had enough energy to dance the night away. In the early days, the redoubtable Dr Francis Clark, 'Fishy' to us all behind his back, was an ever-present member of firsts. As we had consumed our fair share of alcohol after away matches, getting into the Mitchell Hall dances could be difficult. Told by the bouncers at the door that the dance hall was full, we always waited for Francis to appear as he would never accept being turned away. The doormen knew Francis well from years

1949 – Lassie and the Tiny Leverets.
University Rover Crew outing to Mount Battock, Feughside

of experience and, while they converged to manhandle him if necessary, we would quietly creep in behind and shoot up the stairs. When Francis had graduated, my fellow classmate and Scottish University's Heavyweight Boxing Champion, Gordon Smyllie, took over the role of battering ram for a time. Thereafter, I had to use more subtle methods like getting to know the doormen well; but it was never so much fun as in the days of our two bold heroes.

I had hoped that, as time went on, I could establish myself as a regular in the first team. But always someone new came along, with the result that in my final year Webbie, the old groundsman, said to me, "Concentrate on your studies laddie. You're not going to make your living from rugby". That shrewd advice made me think that, just maybe, he was right. So I joined my three pals, Jim Taylor, Doug Stuart and George McDonald, with whom I had shared the adversities of previous exams; and, together, we made use of our Wednesday afternoons to learn from one another.

Also in the early years at Varsity a Scout Rover Crew was established by a number of us with my friend George Leslie much to the fore. For two years the Crew thrived and some good excursions resulted but eventually it petered out as people graduated and the medical students moved on into their clinical years.

An event worth recalling was our hitchhiking trip to Ireland in my second year. Jimmy Davidson, from our dissecting table, together with Johnny Pattillo and I, rigged ourselves out in kilts and thumbed our way to Glasgow. Having sailed to Belfast, we went south, camping on the beach at Galway before proceeding along the coast and back to Dublin. The year was 1948 and food was still scarce at home. So here we made absolute pigs of ourselves in O'Connell Street, consuming huge steaks followed by peaches and cream, something we had almost forgotten existed.

Listowel near Limerick.
*Jimmy Davidson and I relax
after a dip.*

Bantry Bay.
*Farmer Dan & wife rescue
us from a storm.*

I vividly recall various incidents from that holiday, such as when the BBC radio played God Save the King when we were in a tough Dublin pub late at night. We three stood to attention, only later realising we had taken our life in our hands, as everyone stopped to stare and growl. On another occasion I was sitting in the front seat of a car being driven westwards through the Republic when a magpie flitted across the road ahead. My ornithological interest was immediately aroused as magpies were uncommon in North East Scotland at that time. The driver's brusque response, however, stopped me in my tracks, when he pretended that he had never seen the bird and added that it was known to bring disaster. He scarcely spoke again for the rest of the journey and I recognised that this superstition was no joking matter.

The fat, ever-present priests did not impress us very much. In fairness, they treated us wonderfully as individuals. However, our contacts with them enabled us to identify some of the roots of Irish hatred of the British nation. The country at that time, especially to the west, seemed to be in a time warp. Beggars haunted the streets and their persistent attempts to extort money was upsetting. On returning to Ireland even a few years later, we found that conditions were improving. Nowadays the country is a centre of prosperity.

One other person in that year was to play a major part in my subsequent life. Geoffrey Gill, son of Dr James Gill of Inverurie, was a keen scout and we had the beginnings of a friendship from our very first year together. Geoff at that time was one of the most single-minded people I had ever come across. Walking up Union Street after classes, I would wish to cross over to look into some shop or other, whereupon Geoff would just wave goodbye and proceed on his way. There was no question of his coming with me; he was just single-mindedly doing his own thing. While I was faltering in second year, Geoff just kept going in his usual imperturbable fashion, eventually to enter General Practice with his father in Inverurie. I have been golfing with him nearly every week for the past thirty five years during which time he has certainly mellowed and, although the loner trait is still with him, it is suppressed enough now to keep us usually beating a mutual course together down the fairways.

Single-mindedness personified.

Geoffrey M. Gill.
The RAMC takes him to Japan.

Norfolk Broads cabin boy.

Also from that year ahead, consultant obstetrician and gynaecologist Dr Garden Swapp was to reappear in my more mature years. Along with his wife Anne, the four of us enjoyed exploring the world together. Those happy times were saddened with Garden's death in 1997, but together with Anne we still toast the memory of his meticulous planning and great companionship, while we continue to uncover the beauties and interests in far-flung foreign lands.

Summer holidays throughout my student days meant grouse-beating and the glory of lovely sunny days high in the heather-covered hills; or being wrapped in a damp morning mist, making it very difficult to keep in touch with one's neighbours along the line. Shooting grouse is a tradition in which I was steeped from the pre-war days when my father took the lunch up to the shepherd's hut at Eitnach to have it ready for the toffs, when they would come in from the grouse moor at lunchtime. I shall never forget the thrill when my mother and I were taken in the estate's Albion bus to the bottom of the road leading to the hut. We were dropped off there to lie hidden in the heather, waiting until my father appeared at the hut door. He would wave a towel to let us know that the meal was over and that the shooting party was off back to the hill. Having stretched our legs climbing the brae to the shepherd's hut, we found that Dad had set out our places and we sat down with him and Jock Begrie the chauffeur to feast on pâté de foie gras. This was followed by cold grouse and salad, washed down with copious amounts of stone ginger beer, after which we finished with a delightful sweet. Those were red-letter days when the sun always shone and no cloud appeared to make it other than an idyllic experience. Growing up, I came to be a participant in this royal sport as a beater, first as a youngster in Glen Tanar in the immediate post-war days and then, later, when a student.

The Grouse Seasons.

The Very First Season
–aged 5.

Now Aunty Molly
Joins Us.

Dad and Jock Beagrie.

Shepherd's Hut - 1935 to 1937.
The Lunch made them just Wonderful Days.

Major Waddington, well known author of various fishing and shooting books, used to rent Blairfindy Lodge on Speyside as well as Delnadamph Lodge on Donside. He rented these lodges for the grouse-shooting from which he made a livelihood by having paying guests. In 1949 he had applied to the University to recruit half a dozen students to live at Delnadamph Lodge. They were to be supplied with a jeep in which to drive over to Speyside on the mornings when he was shooting on that side of the hill. Somehow, I found myself not only driver, but leader of the group which included Johnny Wood, the fellow climbing medic from the year behind who was mentioned earlier.

The omens were not good as Waddington was not a very pleasant person and some of my colleagues were not the sort of people to be easily led. Waddington promoted me to being his loader. This meant that when he was standing in the butt with the grouse being driven over the guns by a line of advancing beaters, he was using two guns, one being reloaded by me while he discharged the other. Although this sounds simple, in the heat of action tempers get frayed, especially if the birds are coming over fast and furious. Taking the discharged gun with one hand while proffering the loaded gun with the other needs precision timing and direction.

Delnadamph Lodge, Donside – 1949.

(Jim Hardie, John Farrant, Bill Mathieson,
George Paterson, Johnny Wood & Harry Forbes)

*Mrs Moir, our cook, with the unruly Gang
and that unlucky Jeep.*

Practice makes perfect, but Waddington wasn't the most patient of men and I dreaded crashing the two very expensive *Purdeys* in mid-exchange and then being blamed for damages.

No such disaster occurred. But it was a very stressful experience made worse by two incidents involving the jeep. Coming down the hill into Blairfindy Lodge one morning, loaded with a jeep-full of beaters, I took the sharp turn into the Lodge too fast, and had to spin the steering wheel back very speedily in order to miss the granite entrance gate. Scraping through, the side of the truck just caught the pillar and a young lad who was aboard the jeep had his lunch-bag and thermos flask crushed flat on impact. Waddington and his guests, sitting in the lounge, had a grandstand view of my manoeuvre. As a result, I got a sharp wigging. Nevertheless, I was so relieved that it had been no worse.

A lesson had been well learnt for the future, but that jeep was still to have the last word. The Major had firmly laid down that we were not to use the truck to go socialising in the evenings. Various temptations were present, however, to make it highly likely that we would eventually disregard this order. Among my band of merry men there were a number of rebels who had a bloody-minded attitude towards our arrogant employer. Moreover, my current romance with a certain Ballater lady made it hard to resist their clamour to have a night on the tiles. Against my better judgement, I agreed to drive them all down and everyone had an excellent evening. But, on the homeward journey my exuberance got the better of me. The result was that I burst a rear tyre when driving too fast over a humped-back bridge.

Here we were, ten miles from Delnadamph, in the wilds of Glen Gairn, at one o'clock in the morning and with no spare tyre. What were we to do? Walk and leave the truck, or drive along quietly on the rim and hope for the best. The latter choice seemed criminal, but I was overwhelmingly outvoted. And so we crept home, shredding the cover on the way and buckling the rim. Lying is not one of my strengths, but next day I tried to convince the Major that it had happened on our way home from Speyside. Unfortunately a lady acquaintance of his reported us as having passed her house at two in the morning, so the cat was out of the bag. Why he didn't sack us on the spot with no wages, I shall never know, but I stayed for a further three days having to return home to swot for exams. The rest of the lads were there for a further two weeks. Then, four days later, he sacked the lot for insubordination and made them walk over twelve miles across the Lecht from Speyside to Donside. So justice was done, while at the same time the real culprit had shamefacedly escaped.

Upper Donside saw us appear the following year under the leadership of Sandy Smith from the year ahead when we came to Edinglassie estate. Sandy was the banker's son from Bellabeg just down the Don valley. Accommodated in various outbuildings and above the garages, we numbered about ten of us from various faculties, medical students predominating. The Tennants who owned the estate lived in the big house and employed two keepers, Jimmy Smith being the head keeper.

I must have gone there for four years for nearly a month at a time from the start of the season on the 12th August. Every day was a bonus to me. I loved the company, the camaraderie, the local worthies and above all the wild beauty of the countryside. Mingled with this, by contrast, was the feeling of sadness and nostalgia, which the remains of deserted homesteads and crofts aroused in me. There they were, scattered here and there in the little valleys; a poignant reminder of a rural life that had once echoed to the voices of happy bare foot children while their parents toiled to make a living from sparse resources. Where were all the descendants of these hardy folk now and did they ever come back to meditate on a time long past?

I was very much at home on the hills and I came to be an end-of-the-line man, who brought in the beaters at the right time and to the right spot in relation to the butts, while also keeping others in their places along the hillside. It was a marvellous life, and in the years ahead I would myself come to stand in the butts and experience that thrill of having the impressive wave of grouse driven to me instead.

To turn to the more difficult subject of girls, I find I am loath to go through the ups and downs, heartaches and happiness, distractions from study and all the emotion that this whole whirlpool stirs up. Sexual education was taboo in those days, and consisted of my mother presenting me with *The Mastery of Sex* by some reverend gentleman at age fourteen. This non-explicit book muddied rather than cleared the waters, so that my real understanding was picked up piecemeal from the playground and put together like a jigsaw. An innocent abroad, I reached the Grammar school to be reminded of dark-haired Lynette Petrie, tom-boyish Marie (Tink) Newbigging and gentle Rosemary Strachan, all from the Girl's High School. There was fair-haired Aileen Reay, also at the High School, whose input into this book is recognised in the Acknowledgements. She stood with me at the Louisville Avenue tram stop for two years and neither of us uttered a word until a full twenty years later.

Margaret Rezin - Mar Lodge 1950.
Blamed the motor cycle for coming between us.

Glen Tanar Exile

Margaret Rezin, a North East Beauty Queen and later the Students Charities Queen, was my first true romance in 1948. Cycling long miles to make those frequent trysts at Cambus o'May seems a million years away now. She was a year older than me and an uncertificated teacher. To woo her seemed at first beyond my wildest dreams. However, after achieving the impossible, I then proceeded eventually to fall out of love over a period of three years, leaving behind a rather unhappy person who never deserved to be so treated. My own immaturity over affairs of the heart was undoubtedly one reason, while her not sharing my love for tramping the hills and the wide open spaces created a fundamental gap between us. Men are all little boys under the surface and perceptive women play along with their interests knowing that that is one sure way to their hearts.

In 1951, I was now foot loose and fancy free, when Kathleen Rose Angus just happened to be having her own boyfriend trouble. An invitation to a class picnic the next day, at the Queen's Loch at Aboyne was accepted. But instead of going by bus as arranged, Kaye persuaded me to take her by motorcycle. I was never very sure at the time if it was me or the motor cycle which was the greatest attraction. Her strength of purpose however had unwittingly found the key to my inner soft centre. Despite vigorous denials and shows of independence, I was still attuned, as an only child, to a firm female presence, so a strong woman was always going to be the one to sway me and influence my actions. Over the years this romance flowed smoothly for periods, only to reach at times the occasional rapids of turmoil. The fact that we were both studying, she for her RGN and I for an MB ChB, did not always help our romance. That we eventually married in 1958 is still some way off, but many years later, I was made to pause and consider the whole question of picking a suitable mate.

My colleague from Maternity Hospital days, Dr Val Farr, recently reminded me that the girls had all selected their males earlier and that for us to think that we men did the chasing, was pure delusion on our part. On reflection, it does strike me that this observation is much in keeping with the thoughts of Professor Dawkins in *The Selfish Gene*. Here he suggests that women consciously or subconsciously make the decisions, so ensuring the best outcome for their prospective young.

I certainly responded to a strong woman's attitude and, although Kaye would bridle at the thought, I was destined to marry someone who possessed not a few of my mother's characteristics. The uncertainty in such a marriage is whether this power is used in a selfish fashion or for the wider benefits, such as a mother might do. The proof of the pudding would be in the eating, but so far that test has endured for over forty years.

216

No matter how well you think things are going, the Finals have an ominous ring to them. I doubt whether even the brightest students approach them with total confidence. As it was, I felt that the papers were set in such a way as to give me a great opportunity to pass without too much difficulty. It was a great relief to me that my areas of weakness were fortunately not revealed. Given such an opportunity, I made the most of it, being aware of the need to make a good showing on this occasion as, next time around, it could all be very different. The students' attitude to these hurdles is based on the idea that if you can't know everything, at least aim to know just enough to clear Beecher's Brook - with a little to spare.

Over the years, I subsequently learnt, my fellow students used to wonder how I ever got through an oral examination. Not, I may say, because of my probable lack of knowledge, but because of my dreadful taste in clothes. The dress code for us during an academic year, attending clinics, was expected to be collar and ties with passable jackets. For our oral exams however we were expected to present in our Sunday best. My Sunday best was impeccable except that my colour coding, without a mother at my shoulder, could see me in a green shirt, red tie and blue suit. Hideous, but only in later years did my colleagues guffaw over it to me at our reunion dinners, never having said a word to me at the crucial time.

My lasting memory of those final hours occurred during my surgical practical exam as I was walking along the corridor to the male end of Ward 9 Surgical in the Infirmary. The tall ghoulish figure of Mr George Mavor came towards me holding up his index finger and, as he passed, this reminded me what it was used for. Of course, it transpired that my patient had a rectal carcinoma and I was home and dry. I often wondered why George tipped me the wink, when I remember how he had humiliated me in a clinic some months before over the various diagnoses of the thyroid gland. Could it have been an act of contrition?

Throughout that whole clinic he hounded me unmercifully in front of all my peers and the patient until I was unsure whether I was standing on my head or my heels. At the end, walking down the ward, he said, "Now you will never forget about thyroid disease". He may have been a brilliant surgeon, but he had just made certain that humiliation had ensured that the learning process never stood a chance. The result was that in future I would develop an almost total memory-block whenever the thyroid was mentioned.

Most of our tutors were well-intentioned, but the psychology of teaching was not even basically understood by many. In my later years as a University lecturer, I often remembered George and some other talented doctors who, through sheer ignorance of the art, often destroyed the very thing they were trying to impart.

Graduation Day - 1954.
The Author, George McDonald,
Jim Taylor and Doug Stuart.
The Four Musketeers.

At about 5pm on a June day in 1954, the results of our final exams were posted on the notice board in Marischal College quadrangle. Not only was it a long way from Foresterhill, but it was not the easiest place to read the results in the presence of others crowding around. The apprehension gave way to unbounded joy as we Four Musketeers, as Jim, Doug, George and I termed ourselves, found our names posted on the list. The euphoria of envisaging the title *Dr* before our names was unbounded for the next twenty-four hours. However, once the graduation ceremony was over, we quickly adapted to the prospect of a new life ahead.

In retrospect, I regret that I did not play a fuller part in University life, but a medical course probably makes it difficult to find the time. I think that the student advisors left a lot to be desired and failed us. I can only hope the

218

modern generation gets a fairer deal. The quality of teaching was not uniform, ranging from excellent to the indifferent; but in defence of the latter, many lecturers were handicapped by the lack of proper resources.

Prof. R. D. Lockhart.
*His great loves -
Anatomy, Roses &
Rhododendrons.*

Prof. Sir David
Campbell.
*Exuded the power of
the Establishment.*

Prof. Sir Dugald Baird.
*Spurned his offer of
making me into an
obstetrician.*

Among my teachers, Professor Lockhart remains in my memory as an excellent head of the Anatomy Department. In the passing, his impressive secretary, Miss Hathaway, ever helpful, is also well remembered. Johnny McKenzie, in the same department, was a fine teacher who was sadly incapacitated as the result of an accident, which occurred some years later. Professor Sir David Campbell, Dean of the Faculty, was always a presence in the Medical School representing the power of the Establishment. Glowering over lowered glasses, Sir Dugald Baird, with his stooping stance, was a memorable figure who filled us with awe, but who was to be disappointed in me in the future after I spurned his offer of making me into an obstetrician.

Much later, meeting him at Fettes College while I was watching my son, and he his grandson, demonstrating their canoeing skills, he remarked in his typical caustic manner that he often read my letters in the British Medical Journal. "Fouin do you not yet realise that politics is the lowest form of medical endeavour and that obstetrics would have kept you out of such mischief." That wise old owl may well have been right although his own international reputation had been built on many public health issues that had a strong political flavour.

There were many more lecturers whom I later came to know as colleagues. Some of these possessed admirable qualities while there were a few whom I did not rate quite so highly. Even at this early age, I was critical of the motives and attitudes of many of those around me. Was I justified in holding this opinion or was I merely a cynic?

The study of physical Medicine never really fired my enthusiasm to explore the practical minutiae of the subject as it had inspired so many of my colleagues. For too long I studied without much commitment and regarded the years of training simply as a series of hurdles to be overcome. Looking back, I now realise that diagnosing obscure diseases and showing off my knowledge of intricate syndromes never excited me, whereas understanding how human beings functioned in society was enthralling. This is best illustrated by the analogy to the car. What was going on under the bonnet was only of passing interest, whereas how the car handled and its peculiarities had me firing on all cylinders. With a greater understanding, not only of the world outside, but of my role in it, I therefore believe I could have harnessed my enthusiasms in many different fields. Unfortunately, however we all pass this way but once and looking back is too late.

I was now equipped to make the most of a life that had been made possible by my committed parents; and not only by them but by all those dedicated and caring teachers who had nurtured me over the years from those far-off days at Glen Tanar School.

Aberdeen University - 1954.
Medical Class Graduation.

Chapter 15
Digs And Two Wheels

That this subject should justify a chapter to itself may appear strange. However, I feel that to skim over the experience of those first years living away from home in lodgings requires more than just a cursory note. There is some overlap of facts, as my life in lodgings relates both to the chapter on the Grammar School and on to the University, but not enough I hope to detract from the overall picture.

17 Louisville Avenue was the home of little Miss Jessamine who was afflicted by rheumatoid arthritis. She lived there with her niece Hilda Liddell. The workings of a small city mafia are such that everyone seems to know or have contact with everyone else, especially in the business world. Mrs Simpson's brothers, the Strachans, were in the leather trade with a small shop opposite Marischal College in Broad Street.

The Liddells had also been in business and Hilda and her brother Charles had been brought up in '17' with Charles graduating as a doctor in 1937. As Hilda and Mrs Simpson's sister-in-law Phyllis were close friends, the top flat was made available to Mrs Simpson when Alan's father insisted that Alan should go to the Grammar School. Little did I think that any of this would have a bearing on my later life. Yet in the years ahead, Dr Charles Liddell was to become my senior partner in General Practice. But this was still fifteen years away over the horizon.

By the time I had recuperated from my pleurisy, the Simpsons had been in residence for over three months and I was given my own bedroom at the top of the house, with Alan in the adjoining bedroom. His mother slept downstairs on the first floor, on a bed-settee in the lounge and her kitchen was in a box-room, which would have been used as another bedroom in days gone by.

Life from the start was totally relaxed, and, as I had stayed on occasions with the Simpsons for parties in Aboyne, I found no difficulty in settling in. Ma, as Alan and I both called her, was a delightful woman of firm, and at times blinkered, Conservative beliefs and a total disregard for public opinion regarding her way of life. At times she lost her temper with Alan, but never directly with me, as far as I can remember. In fact, Alan maintained that I could do no wrong in his mother's eyes. I felt it had more to do with my apparent support for Alan in the years gone by. Ma was ever my unfailing friend throughout her entire life.

Ma smoked heavily which irritated Alan considerably and his constant complaint was that there was always ash in the mince. She was a great fan of Victor Sylvester and his Ballroom Orchestra. Their music was frequently played on the gramophone, later to be followed by pieces which Alan favoured such as *Claire de Lune*. Alan's father had enlisted in the RAF as a volunteer, probably without considering the full implication for his wife and son. They were just expected to cope on their own. Ma was always very sympathetic to the plight of overseas service men, and the fact that they were far away from home. As a result, her Aboyne house became a home-from-home for many of the Canadian soldiers.

Alan Simpson with his
BSA 500cc Twin.

Alan was always an intriguing personality; solitary and introspective at times, always of a serious disposition and very concerned about the inequalities of life. He was enthusiastic in whatever he took up, whether it was the appreciation of music, love of the musical movies, or showing sympathy for the underdogs of this world. He tended to be a perfectionist and an obsessive with an overwhelming sense of duty and responsibility. This was to emerge clearly in his future dedication to his patients, but I always felt that with his talent and imagination he should have followed a career in which these particular attributes would have been more appreciated. In eventually choosing a career in anaesthetics, he probably found satisfaction in devoting the bulk of these good qualities in the area between the mechanical and the caring aspects of his chosen field. He always maintained that he got little from his student days or from those around him. Despite the fact that we were so different in our personalities, we rubbed along very well together in what was almost a brotherly companionship, where we accepted each other's foibles and just got on with our lives.

As previously recorded my health was plagued by frequent bouts of severe headaches, which came on regularly about midday and which were finally diagnosed as chronic sinusitus. Having always considered myself perfectly healthy, I was unnerved by these lapses in my well being and had no real motivation to get involved in the sporting activities of the school. Weekends at home broke the continuity of my life in Aberdeen, which was an unsatisfactory state of affairs.

With Alan already well established in his schoolwork, I had to come to terms with the fact that I needed his help to keep abreast of my work. I found it quite difficult to settle down to swotting and homework in this new environment with its many distractions. Alan's ability to study late militated against my desire to retire by eleven o'clock. Wasting an evening talking or messing about pillow fighting on the stairs ate into my study time, whereas Alan could catch up by a concentrated effort later on. Looking back, these excuses all seem irrelevant. Adolescent stirrings, taken together with a change in environment while living in a middle-class home, prevented me from achieving my own hoped-for standards. This was not helped by my poor health at this time. Despite these drawbacks, I was always perfectly happy in the Louisville Avenue home while also coming to love the school and all that it stood for.

In keeping with the Simpsons' past Aboyne parties, we leaned on Ma in our fifth year to throw a similar one in Aberdeen. With rationing very tight, my lasting memory is of the 'banana' sandwiches made with parsnips and flavoured with banana essence. The very thought of that concoction still makes my stomach turn over. Did we have girls at the party? I can't remember that, but I certainly remember those sandwiches. Two Dunfermline PT College lady students were lodging next door in '15'. Alan and I spent ages watching them coming and going despite their being a few years older than us. Across the street lived red-haired Alison Geddes, also known as 'Rusty'. She was a High School girl who was a year younger than I was. She used to study in the front room upstairs, the window of which became the focus of our interest. Alison, a delightful person, was later to graduate with me in Medicine in 1954 and she regularly attends our class reunions; but alas her hair is no longer carrot red.

What amazed me about city life was the sense of privacy that so many people displayed. Despite having lived in the street for countless years, neighbours would hardly ever pass the time of day with one another. This reserve seemed utterly unreal to a countryman like myself. Old established streets across the city still retain much of this isolation even today.

Albert's BSA *Bantam* experience was to lead to this machine in the not too distant future.

In his final year at school Alan convinced his parents that a motor cycle would get him around more easily and he became the proud owner of a 250cc BSA machine with a lovely silver and blue tank. This made me very envious. I always found it surprising that his parents agreed to the purchase as, even then, motorcycling was a dangerous business. Danger apart, it seemed to me that this hobby was one that was really worthwhile; so it induced me to take on holiday jobs to finance the purchase of a similar machine.

Albert Garland, victim of my boxing prowess at the Glen, had bought a BSA *Bantam* motorcycle with a small 125cc engine. Recognising my enthusiasm for the hobby he invited me to take the *Bantam* out for a spin as far as Ballater. A lovely warm summer's day saw me transported into another world with the thrill of a new experience completely overwhelming me. Any lingering misgivings I may have had about bankrupting myself in future in pursuit of this hobby was now well and truly dispelled.

The end of the war saw Ma return to London in 1946. As a result, I was forced to look for alternative accommodation during my sixth year at school. It was suggested that I should lodge with a mother and daughter who at that time lived in Great Western Road, just a couple of hundred yards from Louisville Avenue. However, by the time the summer holidays had passed they had bought a semi-detached house in Woodside and I found myself in digs at the opposite end of the town in much less salubrious surroundings.

An immediate pre-war two bedroom semi-detached house was a far cry from the granite built large terraced house in Louisville Avenue. By contrast, Woodside had the run-down feel of a largely working-class area. I had obviously become accustomed to a middle-class environment with the result that I felt very conscious of my new surroundings, and never really adjusted to them. Living in a small house as the only lodger involved me very closely with everything that went on in the family and I became the sounding-board and receiver of all manner of information. After a time, I was treated as one of the family, but it had none of the satisfaction of life with the Simpsons. We all live fairly narrow lives and this came home very forcibly to me in this setting. Lacking any deep empathy or common interests with the family, it was probably a relief all round when the year ended.

About to embark on my University course, I felt it imperative that I should find more suitable accommodation. But where, then, was I to stay? The Morrisons in Beaconsfield Place were friends of my father, Mr Morrison having also been in service. So my parents approached them. They ran a small boarding-house for genteel retired people. They offered me the use of a small downstairs room, which I could have until something else came up. From the start, it was obvious that this could only be a temporary arrangement as living with a lot of elderly people did not strike me as being much fun.

Meantime, Alan had somehow got settled in with my old friend Tiny (George) Leslie, in their large house at 75 Fountainhall Road and I leant heavily on George to wheedle his mother into shoe-horning me into the house as well. Mrs Leslie was a large good-hearted lady who had difficulty in saying no to all the waifs and strays around, so I was duly accepted into the world of the Leslies. This proved to be one of the most satisfying and enjoyable periods of my life and the memories of this time far outweigh all the self-inflicted trauma of my student years.

'75' was to my eyes a very large house, with access to the servants' quarters up a separate stairway. So the two bedrooms with a wash-hand basin on the landing became home for Alan and myself for the next four years. Others in the house included George's eldest brother John and his wife Enid. John, back from the war, was following in his father's footsteps by studying for a BSc in Forestry. Also in the house at times was George's sister Anne studying Home Economics and Alistair McDonald from Aberlour reading Classics before going on to Oxford University.

The Leslies had owned a mansion house, 'The Dowans', in Aberlour, before it was taken over by the military. When this occurred the family decided to move into Aberdeen to facilitate their family's education. Alistair McDonald had been at school in Aberlour with the Leslie children and, like Alan and myself, was one of Mother Leslie's waifs. Tiny was to study for an Honours Physics degree over four years, so there was no lack of company at '75'. Over the years the faces changed, as people graduated and moved away to be replaced by other odd strays, as Mrs Leslie never seemed able to turn them away.

Having lived with a household of servants in Darjeeling, both Mr and Mrs Leslie were anything but house-proud. Yet somehow, the domestic chores were dealt with in the fullness of time. A rubber of bridge was the highlight of their lives and there was many an evening when no meal arrived on the table until the rubber was complete. Mr Leslie was a very quiet, almost absent-minded old man, who said very little, but I always had a high regard for him. On some occasions when George and I would spend an evening tearing the world to bits, Mother Leslie would invariably get up about one in the morning, lean over the bannister and call down to us "Daddy says you boys have to go to bed." Daddy, of course, never ever voiced such an instruction, but we always had a good laugh as we could frequently hear him snoring away in the background.

Mr John Leslie
Trained at Kew and laid out
the Gardens in Darjeeling
in the 1920's.

*Many excursions into Tibet
and the Himalayas to
collect specimens for
Darjeeling and Kew.*

George was another person who could talk till midnight and then go off and do a couple of hours swotting; whereas my eyes had long since closed. Alan had developed a determined routine in which he shut himself away after tea to study until perhaps half-past ten, and I took an aversion to this single-mindedness, which I outwardly detested but subconsciously admired. He would then take the family collie 'Lassie' for a longish walk and would come back to do another stint at his books. Alan was a dyed-in-the-wool blue-blooded Tory while George and I were socialist idealists. Many were the evenings that Alan would flounce out in high dudgeon after the two heavyweights ground him down with us flaunting our caring philosophy as against his apparent dogmatic realism.

My lackadaisical sixth year spent in the digs in Woodside left me totally unprepared for the rigorous study regime required for the medical course on which I was now embarking. This, coupled with the fact that I now approached my new subjects with a lack of enthusiasm, gave me cause for concern. The highlight of our evening was when George came down to make supper at about ten o'clock. He would cook up a mouth-watering haggis in milk or cream and spread it on toast. He and I would then talk or go out for a walk and, although this produced much intellectual stimulation, it certainly made sure that studying was further delayed.

The Leslies' weekly routine was invariably the same. On two days a week Father Leslie would take himself off downtown to the library or to browse round the bookshops. This was followed by a visit to Milnes' auction rooms in North Silver Street to enjoy the excitement of buying all sorts of odds and ends, especially books.

Although he never did show a preference for any one of us in his house, he did present me on two occasions with books that he had bought. I still have in my collection two volumes of Goldsmiths *Animated Nature* and I found it a touching gesture from an inscrutable man who did not readily show his feelings. When he smiled, however, he radiated a tremendous sense of calmness and goodwill, which I found immensely warming. A quiet, solitary man, he would sit by the fire in his big leather armchair, reading or perhaps staring into the glowing embers. Over the years, he never appeared perturbed by the continuous presence of a band of lively students.

Around the room were framed photographs of the Himalayas and the gardens in Darjeeling, which hinted at a man who had done it all and was now at peace with himself. Mother Leslie, some years younger than her husband, had been wooed and wed on one of Mr Leslie's trips home, which was how things were done in the days of Empire. They were an unlikely couple, but the marriage seemed to work. Mrs Leslie was a big woman with a simple faith in God and dedicated to being kind and thoughtful to all around her. She always appeared very overweight and her shopping expeditions during the week used to exhaust her. Yet she battled on like a mother hen trying vainly to control her brood.

She had her favourites; Alistair was seen as the brilliant young man, while she looked on Alan almost as a young son in need of her understanding and sympathy. Perhaps it was his solitary independence that tugged at her heartstrings. Whatever the reason, there is little doubt that he was her blue-eyed boy. She treated me as she treated her son George as if we were big enough to stand up for ourselves and didn't need any particular coddling, which suited us both ideally. The Leslies looked forward to their weekly trip to Dunecht in the big black Humber Snipe to buy eggs and butter from a local farm. Despite their comfortable life style, they were simple folk who had both come from humble beginnings, and I thought them the salt of the earth.

Living in a large household among many people was a great experience for an only-child such as me. Alan and I had stayed together amicably in his Louisville Avenue home where the question of share and share alike never seemed to arise. In the setting of '75' things were totally different, the Leslie boys having had to come to terms with each other over the years. In our now extended family, there was a necessity to look out for oneself; especially when, for example, the eldest son, John, would be the first to choose his sweet cake before even commencing the evening meal. This selfish attitude pervaded the atmosphere and stimulated in both Alan and myself a fervent belief in fair play. Sharing the last cake, Alan and I would study with mathematical precision the mid-way point before agreeing a line of incision.

My experience of living at Woodside with a rather fiery young woman proved useful when it came to dealing with George's sister Anne. Those of us blessed with equable temperaments can only try to understand and be patient with such female volatility. Luckily at No '75' I was buffered, as there was relative safety in numbers. Anne had a particular bee in her bonnet about the boys thieving out of the food store, a suspicion that was probably well founded. George had a voracious appetite, especially late at night, and we were not slow to share in his plundering. There was always a bawling match at breakfast next day when Anne discovered that food was missing. We kept our heads down, sniggering in the background, while George, with his easy manner, blamed it all on the mice. I now realise that at times Anne was shamefully treated by us. Nevertheless, I was very fond of her, as her bark was always so much worse than her bite. Altogether, I have happy memories of a family to whom I can never repay the kindness offered to me over those difficult years.

In my second year at Varsity I had saved just over a £100 from summer work in the forestry nursery and on the home farm. I was also a total miser with money received from relatives, which I hoarded in the best tradition of Scrooge. Now the temptation to blow it all on one item had arisen, and to be able to ride my own motorcycle seemed the ultimate ambition for a student. Alan had progressed from his 250cc BSA to a 500cc BSA Twin, that was way out of my reach; but I felt that I could afford to buy a 350cc AJS with a little help from a friend.

That friend turned out to be my father who coughed up the extra £25 that I needed to get me on the road. Looking back, I am amazed and humbled, not only at my father's generosity when faced with my living expenses, but also by his confidence that I was not about to kill myself. Neither parent ever raised the subject of danger and seemed implicitly to trust me which, as a parent myself, I find almost unbelievable. It should be remembered, however, that traffic in those days was very much lighter than it is today.

Alexanders in Union Street stocked the AJS and Matchless range and I bought my '350' for about £128 from the then manager Sandy Kellas, who had been a cycle racer in the old days. The world of motorcycling brought me into contact with a totally different set of people, from the salesmen through to the workshop, where, apart from the mechanics, all the biking fanatics would gather at times.

There was an agreeable informality in that you just drifted in and talked motorcycling to all and sundry: or you picked the mechanics' brains, while none of us stopped to consider that the men had their work to do. It was all very reminiscent of Peter Murdoch's saddler's workshop in the Square at Aboyne, where old Peter would be sitting at his work bench at the window, while two or three local worthies sat around his fire in the corner and just blethered. A companionable feeling of informality prevailed, as the world dashed past outside, while all was still and tranquil within the little shop.

The thrill of my first bike trip is still with me. I can recreate the feeling of riding over the Bridge of Dee and up the hill past Kincorth, with Alan riding close beside me. The magic of that first day has lived with me ever since. My recurrent desire to get back to motorcycling in my later years was halted when I realised that my children, Peter and Nicky, were keen to get themselves involved also. My father's understanding totally deserted me and I was just another anxious parent imagining all the dangers, but none of the delights. When the children left home I never got round to fulfilling the dream. There are nights when the satisfaction of riding on a motorbike can return in my dreams, only to disappear on waking with the reality that there is no fancy AJS 500cc Twin in the garage.

Kid with a New Toy -
AJS 350cc.
GAV 77 - 1950 Model

Bigger & Better -
AJS 500cc 1952.
HAV 540 with Jam Pot
rear suspension.

Two motorcycles parked on the pavement outside '75' became a normal sight for some years. After eighteen months, I replaced the '350' with a 500cc model. It had a jam-pot rear suspension and a very fancy double seat with a chromium rail around the back. A windscreen was the ultimate accessory and I was now the complete motorcyclist. Not quite, perhaps, as Alan's father was determined that Alan should wear a crash helmet, something which was never seen other than on a racetrack. He bought two racing helmets and added a slip-on visor, which enhanced their appearance. I had an AJS transfer put on the front and from then on wearing a helmet became almost second nature.

Looking back, we were in the forefront of this movement, as it was not until many years later that wearing a helmet caught on and was eventually made compulsory. At night the cycles were parked either up the side of the house or alongside the Snipe in the garage. Cars were almost non-existent among my fellow class-mates, except for my ebullient friend Michael Emslie, with his little MG sports car, but a fair proportion owned motor cycles of varying age and condition. Among my motorcycling contemporaries this was a bond, which drew us together, and at class reunions we still reminisce about those far-off days.

My parents' faith in my good sense was mainly well founded, since during six years on the road I was involved in only one accident, and this was probably avoidable. I planned to visit my Auntie Belle in Edinburgh by riding over the Cairn o' Mount and then on to Edinburgh. It so happened that on the previous day Les Graham, the racing ace, riding an AJS in the Isle of Man TT had been very badly injured. Then, on the day of my departure, my old schoolmate, John Strang, and his pillion passenger, Colin McGregor, riding a big BSA, struck a fence on the Swan's Neck at Glen Tanar.

As a result they each sustained a fractured leg. I was, therefore, particularly careful while riding over the Cairn o' Mount; but while negotiating a corner at too slow a speed, I caught the sand on the edge and skidded off the road into the heather and down a small bank. A slightly sprained wrist seemed to be all the damage until, when I hauled the bike back onto the road, I found that the telescopic front forks were badly twisted. I made my way home very carefully while holding the handlebar so that the steering position was at a different angle from the front wheel. This was difficult, but once achieved, I repeated the manoeuvre the next day on my way to Aberdeen and deposited the bike into the hands of the trusted mechanics.

Unhappily, motorcycling appeared to be the cause of my first romantic break up. Margaret Rezin, the lovely daughter of the owner of the newsagent in Ballater, had been my first true love. Once my new powered transport had liberated me from courting by bicycle, Margaret always maintained that, from that time on, she became second-best. Although I never believed this, it was a fact that our romance faded, while my obsession with motor- cycling increased further as the years progressed.

For the first time a holiday around Ireland with my new girl friend, Kaye, along with Alan and his girl friend, combined both passions. The following year, Kaye and I made another long trip, this time to London and the South coast. These were never to be forgotten halcyon days. My first contact with Kaye's aunt Ashie and her husband Don in London occurred on this trip. The young man, who at first appeared to be a foreigner, came to be totally welcomed into their family. Out of this meeting grew a truly wonderful friendship with Uncle Don and some memorable sailing holidays together on the Norfolk Broads.

The Intrepid Sailor.
*Uncle Don on the
Norfolk Broads.*

How did a loon from a working class home manage to aspire to living a better-off life so early in his career? My own thrift enabled me to buy the bike, while my aunt Molly, with her generous few shillings a week, made sure I could afford a gallon of petrol weekly. In addition, money earned working in the holidays covered the cost of the licence and insurance. My parents never funded me after giving me the initial £25, although I continued to receive my usual pocket money of a few shillings.

On occasions, my father would ask if I needed any more, but I was quite proud to say that I was managing my finances very well. I was also very aware that my stumbling progress was probably something they had not anticipated. Despite the fact that I needed an extra year to see me through Varsity, I never remember a word of criticism from either of them, nor did they reproach me for being a financial burden.

In writing this, it really comes home to me how lucky I was to have parents who believed enough in me to continue their support when things looked bleak. I may have been an only child and important to them, but they never made me feel that they worshipped me. Their help was freely given, as it would have been if I had had other brothers and sisters. Their ability to support a larger family would have been reduced had there been more children, but my parents' commitment to education and betterment of their offspring would have seen them making sacrifices in order to give their children a proper chance in life. Altogether, I was extremely fortunate in having two such patient and considerate parents.

My 'honeymoon' at '75' came to an end in 1952, when I had to go into the student residence to do my maternity training. I was then accepted as a long-stay student until my graduation. Alan had moved out of '75' the year before, and with George having graduated, the household was reduced now to the parents and myself, together with Lassie the dog. As Anne had already married and moved away, Mother Leslie was increasingly finding the house a burden and my presence was not making it any easier.

The good days were past now, the house was silent, and I realised sadly that the time had come for me to go. I often returned to walk Lassie and keep in touch, but it was obvious that '75' was now too big for the old folks' needs. They moved south to Chester some years later to be near their son John, and we stayed with them in the early sixties, while on our way to a holiday in London. In failing health, they eventually moved back to East Kilbride to end their days with their daughter Anne.

The motorcycle lasted, as a best friend, up until I completed my house jobs in Aberdeen Royal Infirmary; but, when called up to do my army National Service, I bid my old friend an emotional goodbye in July 1955. Having been posted back to Scotland, on my first leave I revisited my old mechanic friends in Alexanders to be directed to a pile of twisted metal in the corner of the workshop. The double-seat with the chromium rail jumped out at me as I realised that my pride and joy was now just scrap. The lad who had bought it, had crashed on the very Kincorth brae up which I had ridden with Alan on that first day so many years before. He had escaped with his life, but serious injuries would probably end his motor cycling career, and he left me with a lasting memory.

I had always longed to own an AJS 500cc Twin, and I saw in the window a second- hand, low-mileage machine, such as I had dreamed of. I was sorely tempted to buy it, since a foreign posting was now unlikely; but I hesitated to commit myself, and the chance passed. Never again would I enjoy the thrill of the preceding years on two wheels. During my life I have owned a selection of cars, from sports models to quality machines; but nothing has approached the exhilaration of feeling the wind swirling past the windscreen and the delight stimulated by the poetry of motion. Six months later, a small Austin A30 took me on to four wheels and, sorrowfully, the years of my early youth had silently slipped away forever.

Chapter 16
The Apprentice

Graduation may have been a tremendous hurdle to overcome but, having been successful, I now felt that I had emerged from being hemmed in for years by the towering cliffs of the Grand Canyon. The scenery had been wonderful and the experience unforgettable, but it had not prepared me for the vast open prairie of adulthood. Life before had been circumscribed with limited room to manoeuvre, while now the world was wide open for me. I was thankful that the experience of my mature ex-service colleagues had at least prepared me for what to expect.

Months before, my friend, George McDonald had sounded me out as to my intentions once the exams were past. At that time I could see no further than the notice board in Marischal College quadrangle displaying our results. By this time, however, he had prepared his own way by completing locum house jobs in both surgery and medicine and had been quietly told that the surgical job in Ward 10 at Aberdeen Royal Infirmary was his for the asking.

By encouraging me to take up the next locum post in Ward 10, he opened the door for me to stake my claim for one of the prestigious jobs in the hospital. I felt at the time that I was unprepared for such an onerous responsibility. In the event, I survived the first week without too many mistakes. I must have acquitted myself reasonably well because my application to spend my first six months as a doctor in Ward 10 was accepted. So George and I set forth to work closely together to learn our trade.

As with many fences in life, the obstacles seem increasingly insurmountable the closer one approaches them. Yet once airborne, one seems to clear the hazard without difficulty, and subsequently to wonder why one had been so apprehensive. Life as a house doctor was hard. Long hours, and the pressure of being on call for all and sundry, was unremitting; but one could easily cope with the actual work. Although neither of us wanted to be surgeons, we had a wonderful six months during which we derived tremendous satisfaction in caring for patients.

The nursing staff were true professionals and I developed a huge respect for their discipline and commitment as well as an appreciation of their general smartness and attractiveness. Since that time, however, some of these attributes often appear to have declined. Our chief was Mr Andrew Fowler, with his second-in-command, the redoubtable Mr Sidney Davidson. Andrew was a charmer who had a large private practice and carried out many operations in the local private nursing homes. We used to assist him, and were happy to obtain the experience without receiving any remuneration. He was a careful, meticulous operator who, by revealing my ignorance of anatomy, confirmed me in my decision not to become a surgeon. He and I had an odd relationship. While he appeared to be a competent and caring doctor, especially in the eyes of prospective private clients, he would catch my eye while watching him and I could sense that he knew I was laughing inwardly at his patter. On these occasions he reminded me of a schoolboy caught licking the jam spoon, hoping no one was looking. With his Bentley, large house in Rubislaw Terrace and handsome income, he had really made it in the world of Aberdeen medicine. He was kindly, without ever giving one the feeling that one's career really mattered to him, whereas the formidable Sidney was quite the opposite.

Mr Andrew Fowler. *A most kindly chief, who uncovered my lack of interest in anatomy.*

Mr S G Davidson. *Terrifying, but the first doctor to take an interest in my career.*

Mr George Mavor. *A raised index finger in the Finals, and I was home and dry.*

Mr Sidney Davidson always made me feel anxious right from the days when he lectured to us or took us for clinics as students. To find myself working directly with him reinforced all those previous conceptions. His manner was brusque and to the point, yet he also had the unnerving ability to go off at a complete tangent to the original subject, so that you were never quite sure what was coming next. Marching into the ward with his arm around your shoulder he would say, "Yes, yes, my boy, let me see what you have got here?" Without warning, he would stop and draw your attention to some trivial detail outside. Then he would immediately demand to know what tests you had done and what conclusions you had reached regarding the patient behind you. He would go nod-nodding around the ward, listening to your report and then asking what he should do without making any helpful comment. Walking briskly out of the ward, again with his arm around your shoulder, he would say, "Thank you, Thank you" and be gone.

In the operating theatre I had to pay close attention to his conversation which would range widely, often accompanied by his singing his favourite hymns. The sudden question of whether I had had a long night on duty would be immediately followed by the instruction to pull harder on the retractors, as I was obviously flagging. He was a real character. As the weeks passed I gradually relaxed with him, in the knowledge that he was interested in me. So long as I kept on my toes, all would be well.

I was once admonished for not phoning him in the middle of the night to tell him I had admitted one of his private patients. This was my sole black mark, and it was a relief to reach the end of those six months without further upsetting him. Yet he was most generous to us for assisting him in the nursing home and seemed genuinely appreciative of our services to him. At the conclusion of my six months, he thanked me for my time with him and told me that, if he could ever be of service to my future in medicine, I should not hesitate to contact him. This was the very first time any doctor had shown the slightest interest in my career, and I was tremendously lifted by this unexpected encouragement from a man I had viewed with much trepidation.

The surgeon who made a great impression upon us at this time was quiet, withdrawn, Peter Kinnear. He was a small man whose speed of technique, combined with his skill in keyhole surgery, was to be admired. The older surgeons seemed to distrust keyhole surgery because it seemed to run counter to their teaching. They, of course, always made adequately large incisions in case further contingencies should arise.

Operating experience was limited in such a large unit with the registrar grades requiring the bulk of the cases to expand their expertise. Injecting leg veins and haemorrhoids was a fairly mundane procedure, so that we, as residents, were allowed a share of their operations. My first venture at injecting haemorrhoids demonstrated the inherent dangers awaiting the unskilled and unwary. Under the anxious gaze of the registrar I injected the anal haemorrhoid with phenol - a carbolic acid to thrombose the dilated blood vessel.

After lunch a rather anxious patient returned to mildly complain that passing urine was causing him severe pain. My needle had obviously penetrated through the pile into his prostate, but my registrar airily waved his worries aside telling him to drink plenty of fluids and not to worry. I felt very humble but grateful to my colleague as the outcome of my learning could have had serious consequences. He insisted however that we must not be deterred by our failures and that we should go on to refine our skills for the benefit of the many.

I also carried out a few appendectomies and a hernia under supervision, as well as the regular bougieing of First World War veterans. Difficulty passing urine, the result of their venereal escapades in France, had narrowed their urethras. The only method, then available, to keep them patent, was to pass curved steel rods up the penis, gradually increasing their size until the canal was enlarged enough to last for the next six months, when the procedure had to be repeated. This seemed a barbaric method, but the old boys all took it in good spirit. As I came to each narrowed area of urethra one old worthy would regale me with the tales of exactly where and when each had occurred among the prostitutes of Amiens and Paris. He seemed to regret nothing and reckoned it was all a lot more satisfying than a Bosch bullet.

I enjoyed the appendectomies and could well understand the thrill of surgery once you had mastered the techniques and gained confidence. Left to get on with it on one or two occasions, I had as my hand-maiden, a young lady proffering me the next instrument before I realised what I required and who kept telling me where to put each subsequent stitch when closing. On marrying her a few years later I found that her skill in anticipation holds good in so many other spheres. So nothing has changed from those very early days.

After six months I felt I had experienced this field of surgery long enough and was quite ready to move on. About two months prior to finishing this first house job, I had eaten some rather dried-out sandwiches that I had found in the sister's room. At 3 am I had thought little of it. But a few hours later I became violently sick and continued to vomit over the next thirty-six hours.

I was admitted to the staff ward where Dr Robert Duthie, who had visited me in those far-off days of my pleurisy, suggested setting up an intravenous drip within the hour if I had not stopped vomiting by then. Marvellously, the retching stopped and, as I was discharged next day, Dr Duthie asked me if I would like to do my medical house job with him in Ward 3 at ARI. Naturally delighted, I felt that even the gastro-enteric bugs in the sandwiches had worked for my benefit.

Knowledgeable patients dread admission to the wards in July and January, as the new residents have just started, and the chances of becoming black and blue from failed drips and blood tests are very high. Moving from surgery to a medical ward, however, is less traumatic for the young houseman, as he has usually already cut his milk teeth. Again, this was a very enjoyable ward in which Sister Sangster, mother-hen-like, protected her ageing chief from too much work or hassle. Dr Duthie at this time must have been in his sixties and was suffering from valvular heart disease. For a cardiologist, it was a terrible irony to be afflicted by a problem for which he had treated so many others in the past. I recall him telling me that he had been wakened one night by a loud sound and a sense of vibration. It took him some moments to realise the noise and vibration came from his own chest, and these were his very first symptoms. He was a kindly man, but becoming forgetful, so that when I returned to the ward a year later, he had forgotten who I was. It was not very reassuring to think that I had made so little an impression on him, although I can well understand the reason as names and faces also elude me now.

Dr Robert J Duthie.
A charming man in the twilight of his career.

To be his houseman, after his involvement with my
pleurisy in childhood, showed how small a world it
can be here in the North-east.

The approach to problems can vary enormously from one doctor to another. For example, one night a young girl was admitted deeply unconscious from an overdose. We assessed her and under the direction of the senior registrar, we proceeded to monitor her in a relaxed manner. Dr Tommy Morgan, from his ward at Woodend Hospital, would sometimes descend on us on a receiving night to see how we were coping. On this occasion he blew his top at the SR's inactivity and had us scurrying about with drips and stimulants for the poor girl. There is no doubt in my mind that without his intervention she would have died by morning. It is interesting to speculate as to how many deaths result from doctors' attitudes as much as their competence. Furthermore, might not this account for variations in mortality figures from hospital to hospital?

Coniston Water - 1955.
Holiday in the Lake District.
Kaye basking in the sun.

My prolonged period in bed with pleurisy had left me with one very distressing problem. An anal fissure may sound trivial but, when bowel routine is altered, constipation can cause real agony. My surgical residency often turned night into day, so I was frequently in dire trouble. Where better, however, to have your surgical problem sorted out than on the spot? So Andrew Fowler proceeded to do the necessary with me and I was off work for only a few days. The healing procedure takes time and, when I attended for my National Service medical, I faced the possibility of a six-month deferment to be followed by reassessment. This delay did not suit me and, on appeal, I was fortunate enough to be put into a home posting category. The farewells from a ward full of appreciative patients, with presents and mementoes to take into my army life, left me with a feeling of true satisfaction. This had been a time of real progress along the road to my becoming a competent doctor.

A holiday in the Lake Disrict with Kaye and the trusty old Austin kept my army service at bay for a couple of weeks. Staying at Coniston, we did a number of ascents including Skiddaw, Helvellyn, Scafell, Scafell Pike as well as the old Man of Coniston. Steep gradients required various manoeuvres with the old lady at times. One such memorable occasion involved the enforced reversing of the Austin up one of the passes, due to the car's lack of power. Ben Nevis was to follow a year later but before that Her Majesty urgently required my services.

238

Reporting to Crookham Barracks, outside Aldershot, together with a large number of my own colleagues, recreated life back at student level once more, albeit with a lot of army bull and shouting on the parade ground. The army intake also included a large proportion of doctors from what we disparagingly called the red brick universities of England. The smirk was rapidly removed from our faces when it turned out that many of these graduates had already taken the first parts of their degrees in specialised medicine and surgery, whereas the Aberdeen graduates had scarcely got round to thinking that far ahead. It suddenly made us realise how parochial we were, and that Aberdeen was not the hub of the universe at all, but was really a peripheral outpost. Eventually, having been posted to the Black Watch Queen's Depot in Perth, it seemed to be my destiny not to travel to far-off lands. This was in marked contrast to the experience of my parents, who had ranged all over the world. As there was no accommodation available in the mess, lodgings were found

Crookham Barracks, Aldershot 1955

Herb Longmore and the Author enjoying the Good Life.

for me in the St Leonard's Bank Hotel. A rather grand name for two houses that had been joined together, but which did have a lovely outlook over the South Insch.

The owners, Kay and Preston Smith, were kindness itself, and I spent eighteen months with them very happily. Staying with them was Preston's mother, who was the widow of a successful retailer in Dundee before the war. Her money, I imagine, would have been behind this venture. Preston, another only child, had been completely spoilt throughout his childhood, and the effect of this was still evident in his forties. Old Mrs Smith's dogs, dandy dinmonts, seemed to swarm all over the place; and what one saw behind the scenes in the hotel kitchen did not always fill one with confidence. Preston was very shy, and his main daily

Idler on the Broads.

Kay and Preston in the cockpit.

239

activity was to creep up in the evening to a local bar, where he would sit quietly, downing the odd pint of beer.

Kay, who was much more outgoing, but very deaf, would nearly always go with him. Latterly, there were times when I also got caught up in this ritual. Preston's great hobby was sailing and he much enjoyed navigating his twenty-two footer on the Norfolk Broads. This was their regular destination twice a year. In the future I was to sail his boat, the *Idler*, a couple of times, before taking up the truly exhilarating hobby of inshore and flotilla sailing. On these occasions I was to share this pleasure together with my family.

1955 - Kaye and the Trusty
old Austin in Oban.

Directly under my command at the Medical Centre, located in a self-contained unit within the barracks, was my RAMC staff. However, the discipline of the Depot was the responsibility of the Black Watch, with the result that my soldiers could be hauled up for dress and conduct by the BW adjutant or the sergeant major. This, at times, caused difficulties. I found myself complaining to the CO about having to resolve the conflicting responsibilities of representing my men, who claimed victimisation, and the demands of the BW, who accused the RAMC of lowering the standards of a Highland regiment. The CO took such complaints in a very paternalistic manner, obviously viewing an amateur RAMC captain with some amusement; but on the whole I was left to my own devices. My duties related to the routine examination of new recruits, their immunisations, etc. and the daily traumas suffered by such young men. Going sick was not encouraged among men who were being taught that they belonged to the premier Scottish regiment, whereas the 87th Company RASC, attached to the 51st Division HQ, were not imbued with such high ideals.

The 87th Company, consisting of a mixture of regulars and national service men recruited mostly from the Glasgow area, reminded me strongly of those scruffy evacuees I had first seen in 1939. If, in those days, I had viewed the Glaswegian character from a child's angle, I was currently seeing them from an adult's perspective; and it was equally disturbing now. These young men took every opportunity in the book to evade duty, with excuses ranging from going to their grandmother's funeral to the most bizarre of illnesses. As soon as I had noted that their grandmother had died more than once, I began to get as fly as they were; but at no time could I outfox them. It was all a game, and my own RAMC personnel were certainly not blameless. Yet, who could reproach them for trying it on, as most had not volunteered to join the army in the first place?

At first I had a warrant officer as second-in-command. Being an old soldier, he could also put it across me. But when he was posted out, my sergeant dispenser took his place. A fellow National Serviceman, Paul Richards was a recently qualified chemist from Manchester where his father owned a chain of pharmacies. A delightful person to have, he relieved me of much of the routine and took on a lot of responsibility. The only real medical crisis in my whole service career occurred when Sergeant Richards took to his bed with abdominal and back pain. Although he made light of his symptoms, I still felt anxious, as his presentation reminded me of a case of retrocaecal appendicitis which we had missed in Ward 10 of ARI. I breathed a huge sigh of relief, when, on his admission to Bridge of Earn Hospital against his will, my diagnosis was confirmed at operation. Had I failed to recognise this condition correctly in the case of one of my own staff, it would have been a black mark against me. But, as things were, I could enjoy his family's great appreciation of my brilliance!

He was demobbed some six months before me, and Sergeant Rhodes, another young recently qualified pharmacist, replaced him. Having set up in business as a pharmacist in Blairgowrie some years later, he called to see me in the 1970's when we reminisced about some of the good times and a few of the bad.

The formality and elitism of Scottish regiments, especially the Black Watch, the premier Highland infantry regiment, has to be experienced to be understood. The officer corps, drawn from the cream of English public schools and a few Scottish ones also, was grafted on to the regiment, which resulted in a formidable combination. One poor officer at the Depot had been to the

Grammar School some years behind me and was treated as an inferior being, as he had not been to the 'right' establishment. The officers, regulars and conscripts alike, all exhibited a confidence characteristic of their class. It was therefore difficult to evaluate them superficially. Even with my insight as a doctor, it used to take me many weeks to distinguish the idiots from the men who were worthy of respect.

In the setting of the armed forces, however, this was obviously a strength, as only the confident can really lead in battle and these Black Watch officers had certainly plenty of that. Having seen them only in the setting of their Depot and not out with the regiment in Guyana, I have no clear idea how they bonded with their men. I believe, however, that a mutual trust would have developed despite the barrier of social class.

I recall one episode, highlighting the hidden barriers that occurred, when the BW played their annual game of rugby against their great rivals, the Gordon Highlanders. Having gone back to playing for Perthshire Accies, I was regarded as being part of the BW team and found myself alongside a mixture of raw recruits and regular officers in this fixture. We had been beaten by a single try in Aberdeen in the autumn and were desperate to reverse this result on our home ground. Puffing up behind my pack and not nearly so fit as these young recruits, I found myself almost out on the wing when the ball came back. It was picked up by the adjutant, Captain Orr-Ewing, and as I was the only one outside him, I shouted his Christian name, 'Eddie, Eddie', again and again, to let him know I was there. I saw him hesitate in mid- flight before he passed the ball for me to score under the posts and so win by this, the only score. Later that evening in the mess he remarked that he had been so taken aback by being addressed by his Christian name by a possible ranker, that he almost stopped to put the culprit on a charge. Instinctively in the heat of battle, with so much at stake, he obviously felt officers are still officers.

Playing rugby regularly for Perthshire Academicals second string, with mid week work-outs in the gym, attempting some semblance of fitness, formed the social side of my Perth posting. However a partially torn cartilage in my

Lt. Dave Brien tempting the
Reindeer on Cairngorm.

knee made the days after a game very uncomfortable, so it was becoming increasingly obvious, that at twenty eight, my days playing this boisterous game were numbered.

Attending, as the MO, at various military exercises, based at the Rothiemurchus Hut near Aviemore, saw me revelling once more in the mountainous surroundings I so loved. Having accepted a fellow officer's invitation for a week-end climb and hike through the Lairig Ghru and GlenTilt to Blair Atholl, we arrived in Aviemore one fine spring morning. After spending the night at the Rothiemurchus Hut, Dave Brien and I next day reached the Shelter Stone, thence on to Ben MacDhui and down to the Corrour Bothy for the night. Feeling very fit, I thought nothing of trekking the twenty two miles to Blair Atholl on the following day. I arrived at Blair Atholl railway station literally on my knees, with the stiffness and pain in my joints making the subsequent exit from Perth station a nightmare, by this time I realised just how badly I had overestimated my capability. My young colleague just shook

his head in disbelief at my frailty as he himself looked fit enough to do the return trip there and then. It had been a wonderful few days but the lesson for the future of "not biting off more than you can chew," had been painfully learnt.

While living in the hotel, I must have looked really scruffy to the NCO's of the regiment, with my tarnished unpolished belt and seamless trousers. Nevertheless, they saluted me smartly every morning as I entered the barracks. I was allotted one Black Watch orderly in the medical room to liaise directly with the BW orderly room in dealing with recruits. He would often take away my belt for polishing, as he could not abide its dull appearance, which made me feel that I was letting him down in the eyes of his mates. Private Clokey had been to the 'right' school and

Perth Army Sailing Club – 1956.
The Author, Col. Fearon (Commodore), Frank and Geoff with the Nationals.

his family had attachments to Oxford University; but despite this, he had failed to qualify for officer training. Stationed at the Depot, he was allocated to me as the medical orderly, and he turned out to be very proud of his position. He had absolutely no fear of rank and was as likely to be found chatting up a visiting brigadier, who had come to see me, as telling my colonel in HQ that I was too busy and would he phone back later. He got into all sorts of hot water, but this never deterred him. Paul Richards and I used to be thoroughly entertained watching his confident attitude towards authority, all the more so, as neither of us ever had the nerve to challenge those of a higher rank.

Whether or not it was case that the army mistrusted these apprentice doctors, a civilian GP was attached to the unit to help out. He was Dr Willie Davidson, someone I could always trust to give good advice. It was with great sadness that I learnt later of his death at an early age from a coronary thrombosis when pulling his dinghy out of the Tay. I knew exactly where this must have occurred as I had been dragooned at the outset into the sailing club by Major Frank O'Regan. Frank, my immediate superior at 51st HQ, was an Irishman, a regular soldier and also a doctor. He was a bundle of energy, and it was due to him that I became keenly interested in sailing. Sailing Nationals on the Tay came to be my foremost hobby at this time. Under the watchful eye of Captain Jock Morgan of the REME, we built a GP14, of which we were inordinately proud. These fourteen feet dinghies were all quite tricky to sail and it took some experience to manage to race them across the Tay, while taking into account wind, current and the state of the tide.

Nationals Racing on the Tay.
*Author getting the thrill of sitting
out, but coming Second.*

After a time, Wing Commander Bunce and his wife came to be billeted in the hotel. He and I became good friends. In command of the Scone Flying School, he was engaged in training foreign pilots, mostly from the Arab countries, in the basics of flying. Hearing of my past keenness to fly, he offered to have me taught under his command, which I enthusiastically agreed to. The then Prime Minister, Anthony Eden had different ideas, however, and the attack on the Suez Canal put a stop to all these arrangements. Wing Commander Bunce was quickly posted back down south and my flying career stopped before it had begun. Perhaps the Gods had again looked down and decided that, after all, my fate did not lie in this direction.

A car had become a necessity for me, and I had persuaded a fellow officer to sell me his black Morris Minor, until at the last moment he changed his mind. I then bought a blue Austin A30, which after a time started leaking water down the door. This was a true example of the shoddy British workmanship of the time. Looking around Grassick's garage, I came upon a second-hand white Triumph TR2 equipped with every extra under the sun, as well as hard top and tonneau cover. This sports car was in a more expensive class than I could afford. Nevertheless, I bought it, and I was to enjoy a period of carefree living such as I never again experienced until my retirement.

Dad in retirement still treasured his old
Austin despite the march of time.

The Triumph TR 2 nestles happily beside the old lady.

Posted to Barrie Buddon camp, outside Carnoustie, for my last three months of duty, I found myself looking after the formidable Gurkhas. However, as they never seemed to fall ill, my services were rarely required. Dr Peter McKay was

Desswood, Lumphanan.

Dad at 77 so proud of his house and garden. Aunty Molly admiring the results of all the hard work.

one of the local GPs in Carnoustie and was a very keen rally driver. On a couple of occasions I acted as navigator for him driving his VW Beetle. This fantastic little car really excited me and, when I returned to civvy street, I bought one in place of the impractical Triumph. It was now 1957, and there were only one or two of these machines being driven in the North East, so we enthusiastically flashed headlamps at each other to show our individuality. It is odd to remember this when the VW range is so popular today.

With my period of National Service almost at an end, there was a hiatus before starting my house job in the Aberdeen Maternity Hospital; so I agreed to stay on for another three months. Posted to the Gordon Highlanders barracks at Bridge of Don, I had by this time practically completed the full circuit of the premier regiments. I had done relief duties with the Camerons and with the Seaforths; while a spell at Pinefield in Elgin doing medicals for the troops who went to Suez, had given me a fair insight into the Northern military.

At Bridge of Don I came upon an unlooked-for kindness from the civilian-attached GP, Dr Betty Morgan who, with her husband, had a practice in King Street. She was looked upon as the bane of hospital residents' lives. Whenever she would phone to admit a surgical case, we would despairingly remark in anticipation, "Another of Betty's constipations or urinary infections." Knowing that I was from Deeside, she unselfishly told me to go off and live at home with my parents while she would always cover for me. This was a service which, on looking back, I accepted without much thought. But in retrospect, I now realise that it was an extremely generous gesture on her part. Later, I was to learn in what high regard she was held by her patients and that her workload was often such that she had to make snap diagnoses. This meant that she would often refer many more patients for admission than would have been referred by doctors with more time. It taught me the valuable lesson that judging hastily without knowing the full facts often leads to wrongful evaluations.

About the time I was posted to Perth, my father had at last decided to retire. With the help of a consultant colleague in Bridge of Earn hospital, I was able to arrange for my parents to buy Desswood, an attractive modern bungalow in Lumphanan in Aberdeenshire. Not a place I would have chosen to live in, but the house was the deciding factor, especially for my father, as it had a lovely big garden and greenhouse.

Leaving the army to return to hospital practice and then to spend a career in General Practice covering Cults and Peterculter, outside Aberdeen, would push the memories of Glen Tanar into the background. National Service had taught me little medicine, but it had prepared me for life. I had met people from all walks of life and under very differing conditions. I look back with no regrets at spending two years in the army and am a strong believer that some form of voluntary service would be beneficial for all our young people and would contribute to the improvement of their subsequent life-styles. In retrospect, I would have loved a foreign posting to Germany or, better still, to Japan, as I am sure that this would have broadened my horizons immeasurably.

Sharing in My Pride - 1957.
The Parents - Happy together in Retirement.
Probably their best years together.

Because, having spent my army service entirely in the Highland HQ area, I had ample opportunities to return home to the Glen. Sadly, now came the time for the removal van to bring to an end the forty-one years that my father had enjoyed in this lovely valley.

By now, well into his seventies, he remained as spry as ever and for years to come would continue to remove tons of stones from his new garden plot. The enjoyment he derived from his new house was wonderful to behold and he richly deserved such a fulfilling retirement. Lying there in my familiar bed on that final night, the moon was yet again shining brightly, illuminating the little room. The final act had been reached at last, the curtain was falling and the ending was as emotionally draining as I had always feared it would be all those years ago.

Chapter 17
From Christian To Humanist

On the 12th of February 1929, I was baptised into the Scottish Episcopal Church, at St Lesmo's Chapel, the little family church of the Glentanars, and I have the solid silver porringer and spoon on display, duly engraved with those dates. This offering came from my godfather, Lord Thomas Glentanar. Miss Molly Watson, my mother's oldest sister, was my godmother and she was to be my principal benefactor well into my early twenties, although religious sentiments never crossed her lips.

My mother had been brought up in the Church of England and so it was fitting I should belong to its Scottish version, the Episcopal Church. Many of the Scottish aristocracy also belonged to this anglicised church, as many of them appeared to view all things English as superior to anything that backward Scotland had to offer. The Glentanars belonged to this faith, and so the services in St. Lesmo's were taken by the Rev Tom Gray from the mother church, St Thomas's in Aboyne. These were held on alternate Sundays, if my memory serves me correctly. My father seemed to have no strong views about my religious upbringing, allowing my mother her head, as his experience of Roman Catholicism in France had left him disillusioned and totally apathetic.

Religion was central to my mother's upbringing. She came from the small town of Morpeth, in Northumberland, where life in the late 1800's was very simple. Attending church, often three times on a Sunday, was quite normal. Church-going was a social event for girls, such as she, and these girls would often attend events at churches of other denominations as well as their own. They loved being in each other's company and singing hymns together. Thus a camaraderie developed that reinforced her religious beliefs. It was not surprising, then, that these beliefs would endure throughout the rest of her life.

My father, living in a Catholic country, had been only too aware of the tyranny of the Church in such a setting. The story, which affected me from an early age, was his recollection of the night the priest came to call after the harvest. My father, who was still quite young, probably about eight, was wakened by the sound of raised voices. He crept out to the top of the stairs to hear his distressed father in the kitchen pleading for a postponement of his dues to the church as the harvest had failed and he had six young children to feed. His mother's weeping also fell on deaf ears and the priest left telling them to pay up or have more than the wrath of the Lord upon them. From that day onwards, he disowned his membership of the Roman Church and, despite many Catholics asserting that his faith would return on his death bed and he would ask for a priest, he died at ninety-seven in some distress, but true to his own beliefs, without any priest.

St. Lesmo's Chapel – Glen Tanar.
*The grave stones of Sir Cunliffe and Lady Brooks
are to the left of the church entrance.*

My own early memories of church are of counting the gilded stars with convex centres of silvered glass and the antlered ceiling of St Lesmo's Chapel. The sermons went over my head but the enumeration of these details seemed to hasten the final blessing. Ladies' hats in the 1930's were large, broad-brimmed and often quite gaudy. My mother appeared to have accumulated a collection of the most hideous of these specimens, and Sunday was the day on which they were displayed. I recall my acute embarrassment at the time, sitting next to her in a Scottish kirk while she wore one of these hats fashioned in the latest London style. As I grew older and bolder, I would refuse to sit with her and, instead, would join my pals and their more sensibly clothed parents. Things never improved and, with my sense of embarrassment never far from the surface, I would increasingly bridle at regular attendance. It would seem, therefore, that from an early age something was missing from my spiritual approach to religion.

Although the more puritanical extreme of forbidding all activity never really affected our activities, there was always the sense of desecrating the day of rest with too much jollity. In those pre-war times we, as children, derived little pleasure from the Sabbath. Certainly, the thought of playing a game of football in front of the recreation hall could never be entertained. A general air of disapproval hung over the scene that both added to and safeguarded the atmosphere of sanctity of the Lord's Day, especially among the older citizens. The coming of the evacuees to Glen Tanar probably hastened the loosening of these shackles. They were all Catholics but, nevertheless, by the time that midday arrived and they had completed their religious duties, they became free, boisterous spirits for the afternoon. Our local Protestant parents found this hard to comprehend and it became increasingly difficult for them to make us understand why we should not also become free agents after midday. Once the barrier was breached by many of us there was no going back, although some parents did keep their children firmly apart, religiously, long after the end of the war.

Those Embarrassing Hats.

Aunty Belle & Mother in the '20's - but just as bad in my church-going days.

I must have been a very naïve and trusting child in my early days. For example, Santa Claus persisted in my imagination as a reality long after my cohorts had discarded his persona: they laughed increasingly at my gullibility. I attribute this innocence to my status as an only child totally influenced by my mother. If she said there was a Santa Claus, I would believe her, just as I believed that she was forever twenty-one years old. Children seemed to have a fascination at that time with the age of their parents, but I obviously never questioned her honesty when I asked this of her. A year or two later I realised that I had been deceived and had been made to appear stupid in front of my worldly-wise friends.

Having been deceived and demeaned twice, I quickly developed a habit of doubting anything that seemed vaguely dubious and, significantly, religious belief fell into that category. Being urged to have faith sounded uncommonly like a call to believe in Santa Claus - and I was already becoming sceptical. This, in turn, led me to think that my mother was being rather gullible. However, to question religion at that time was still blasphemy, and I entered a period when I felt vaguely out of touch with it all. Yet I could not understand how so many influential people could be wrong. Surrounded by so many expressions of religious faith - such as the recital of the Lord's prayer at morning assembly, the singing of hymns and the learning of biblical screeds - no child could fail to feel that this was reality. Going to church and having to listen to meaningless sermons had left me totally bored and disenchanted. I became uncertain of my surroundings, much as I had felt when I realised that

251

Glen Tanar Exile

I was colour blind. But was there something here to which I was also blind to? What was I overlooking that others could easily assimilate? And, if I were blind, when would a lightning bolt strike me and reveal the existence of a great Promised Land? Luckily, despite my mother's devoutness, she never dragooned me into going to church. However, at times she did appeal to my better nature not to let her down. I obeyed her wish while she was alive, even after my children were born; and for many years afterwards I still felt the need to attend church from time to time. Looking back, I believe that I have honoured a discipline according to the best Victorian tradition; in other words, if it does not hurt and does not disturb one's comfortable way of life, it is not doing one good. Perhaps that, in itself, is an excellent training for life, but in my case it has nothing to do with religion.

What further worried me, however, was that while religious belief seemed so questionable, superstition remained and even flourished. Freud maintained that all superstition derived from our primitive ancestry and our need to believe in something. Then why should I doubt the apparent mythology of Christian belief and yet never fail to touch wood, avoid walking under ladders or never leave a house by a different door from the one I entered? Black cats held all sorts of implications while the Garden of Eden and the Resurrection sounded totally implausible.

Church-going continued to be onerous for most of my youth and the only time I ever felt inspired by what I heard was in my last year at Aboyne. The Canadian soldiers, felling trees for the war effort at Burnroot, had their own chaplain. At the end of summer term, a service was usually held in the church behind the school and on this occasion the chaplain had been invited to take the sermon. We all slouched into the church and were prepared to be totally bored. But, suddenly, this inspirational preacher seemed to reach out and awaken a real interest in all of us. Many came away amazed at how much we had enjoyed the experience and only regretted that this could not be repeated in the future.

In those days of my youth, if there was a more dreary religion than the Episcopal Church, it must have been that of the Scottish Presbyterians. The dourness and drabness sometimes associated with the Scottish character was amply reflected in those days, both in its ministers and in its form of service. In Aboyne, the Reverend Hamilton ministered to the villagers' needs and a more sinister figure I have seldom encountered. This impression may well have been unjust because my only contact with him was simply passing him in the street. But when he wore his black cloak, offset with a black slouch hat, he seemed to embody the evil of Satan rather than the good of God. The villagers were so in awe of him, if not in fear, that many would avoid him by crossing the road on his approach. It is well to remember that the power of the church in our district, even in the 1940's, was still capable of dominating a small community making people consider it wise to pay lip service to it.

With a godfather like Lord Glentanar, the ceremony of confirmation could not be avoided and, when I was sixteen, many of my Saturday mornings were spent being prepared by Dean Wattie in his study in St Thomas's Rectory, Aboyne. On Thanksgiving Sunday in May 1945, under the auspices of the laird, Bishop Hall confirmed me during a special service at St Lesmo's Chapel.

I have a lovely photograph of a very slender young man standing outside the chapel with Bishop Hall and Dean Wattie. I am not proud to have participated in a ceremony which, by that time, I had come to think of as little more than a meaningless ritual. Such was the pressure exerted by my mother and by my godfather, that I did my duty, despite the fact that I was no longer sure of anything, but had not the courage to state my case. With all around me appearing to adhere to their beliefs, I obediently went through the motions of the service.

By 1948, my experience of University life and living with the Leslies at 75 Fountainhall Road, led me to examine my doubts more closely in the hothouse of student debate. Mrs Leslie was a member of the Brethren, a sect that is one of the more fundamentalist forms of Christianity. Honed in the fishing villages around the North-east coastline, this narrow exclusive faith probably derived its beginnings from the harshness and dangers of fishermen's lives.

Mrs Leslie's youngest son, George, and I were both sceptics and gave his mother a rough time on occasions by asking her to spell out the basis of her beliefs. I came to feel very sorry for her, as the simplicity of her faith could not match our intellectual arguments. She could only state that she held strong beliefs and that that was all that she had to say about it. This was a valuable lesson to me because I realised that, to undermine other people's convictions without putting anything in their place could be a totally destructive act.

Despite all my doubts, both my children were baptised because I considered that they themselves should decide whether or not to continue to observe a religious life when they eventually became mature. In a society that still has a strong Christian tradition, I would not have wished them to reproach me in the future for not offering them the option to take the road to salvation. In the event, they both appear to have inherited my scepticism. Some might ask, "Were they, perhaps, not brought up in the right atmosphere?"

Thanksgiving Sunday - May 1945.
St. Lesmo's Chapel - The Confirmation.

Bishop Hall and Dean Wattie officiate.

An intriguing appointment was to occur during my career when I was selected to serve on a committee directed to oversee the health of Church of Scotland ministers. Having been put forward by a local minister, I was eager to view the inner workings of John Knox from 121 George Street, Edinburgh. With my previous experience of the puritanical religion, I was surprised and delighted to find the clergy on the committee broad-minded, sensible and with an excellent sense of humour. The secretary at that time was the past moderator, Sandy McDonald, and I developed a very high regard for the open way he tackled the problems surrounding ministers and their wellbeing. My anxiety arose, not from the religious fraternity, but from my medical colleagues who made up a high proportion of the committee.

Presumably selected from a devout background, it was they who radiated the narrowness associated with the church. Medicine requires of its practitioners a clear, unbiased attitude. I do not object to my colleagues holding their own beliefs so long as they do not obscure their duty of providing the optimum outcome for patients. Another problem that beset me on this committee was my alignment with the difficulties that young ministers and their wives had when adapting themselves to modern manse life. My experience as a GP is that wives no longer wish to be shackled to practice life and this was mirrored in the problems experienced by these young couples. A person with that attitude was probably regarded as a thorn in the flesh by the Church as it had been to the medical greybeards in my own early days.

In the past the village GP was expected to be a pillar of the Kirk and, although many of my generation continued to pay lip service to this tradition, the practice is slowly dying out as they retire. I was never very certain whether the GPs were just conforming to expected behaviour or whether they were true believers. Hypocrisy lies nearer the surface than most of us would like to admit. This opinion was offered by a senior medical consultant some years ago. The occasion was when GPs were considering a proposal to introduce merit awards. The consultant shook his head and ventured, "If the Devil was handing out the top merit awards in my hospital, there would be precious few Christians left among us". This seemed very cynical at the time, but as I have grown older and wiser I feel his opinion was probably not too far from the truth.

Throughout my career, despite my views, I have always been prepared to assist in patients' hopes of recovering by backing their religious beliefs. The power of the mind is still scarcely understood in this field and so it is imperative that as doctors we are sensitive to everything that will help in a patient's fight with adversity. The fact that patients have survived horrendous accidents and illnesses completely beyond medical expectations highlights our ignorance of the power of the mind in this matter. I feel certain that science will unravel this mystery in the years ahead, and that the full power of the brain will be employed to stimulate the process of recovery that will make much of present medical practice redundant. Science is also now beginning to explain the visions and visitations experienced by the devout through the ages by finding a specific area of the brain which is sensitive to these stimuli. Epileptics are particularly affected by these phenomena, which seems to indicate that the brain's *God centre* simply consists of hypersensitive neurones.

While I observe that some of my well-respected and clever colleagues are very religious people, I sometimes wonder whether I am missing something. Medicine is based on facts and proof, while religion appears to regard a questioning attitude as being close to blasphemy. I therefore look on blind belief as illogical, but I understand the nagging need of so many to find some explanation into such unanswerable questions as "Why are we here and what for?"

I have searched both ancient Greek and modern philosophies, as well as the books of Richard Dawkins (*The Selfish Gene*), Ludovic Kennedy (*All in the Mind*) and Jostein Gaarder (*Sophie's World*) to discover a reason for existence. Along with the views of these authors, I am led to the conclusion that no obvious reason does exist, except that we are here to procreate in order to continue the species. This is true for all other living things. To believe that humans have any other choice is to deny that the hormonal drive in most of us is directed at fulfilling this purpose. True, some dedicated individuals override this drive and remain celibate, but this has no bearing on the quest and, in any case, celibacy has no survival value! A somewhat larger group appear to have developed atypical drives, which society at present is being brain-washed into perceiving as normal, but which are actually one of nature's anomalies. As with celibacy, these again possess no survival value.

Our basic instinct in perpetuating the race is obscured by the fact that mankind energetically pursues education, careers, prosperity and enjoyment, almost to the exclusion of all else. Woody Allen, that famously eccentric American actor and film director, seems to worry about this all the time. He observes that those around him will turn to dust in a few decades, so why do they bother to work so hard and for what? The rest of us meanwhile are so distracted by what is happening in our lives and around us that we are spared from becoming as neurotic as he is.

If I feel I have gone some way to answering the conundrums of life - the 'how' and the 'what for?' - I am certainly no nearer than are the religions of the world in finding an answer to 'why?' That there is a mythical answer to explain such a well-structured and successful continuation of life through millions of years, beggars belief; but when all becomes obvious what will happen then to all man's fantasies? On the other hand, thank goodness for those amongst us who can also poke a little fun at all our sermonising and agonising; none better than Woody himself, who brings life down to its true perspective with that wonderful quote. "Not only is there no God, but try finding a plumber at weekends."

I have come to believe that all religions are more or less mythological concepts but that they are, for a vast majority of the population, an essential part of life in that they cement communities together. They encourage individuals to care for one another and can bring out the very best in man. The terrible atrocities that have occurred in the name of religion at all stages in the past, and in the present, are the other side of the coin; and they continue to divide close communities today. The missionary spirit has driven many fine people to sacrifice their lives, not only to bring a better way of life to other cultures, large and small, but also to spread the spirit of yet another brand of beliefs.

The betterment of the under-privileged is totally acceptable, but I have never agreed that disturbing the lives of a people by forcing them to adopt an alien religion could ever be fully justified. That these religions could displace old beliefs so readily, in both primitive and advanced societies, also surely demonstrates the superstitious frailties of the human mind.

From Christian To Humanist

With waning interest in religious practice in this country, what is there to replace it? I would despair if this would lead us to become mindless consumers and selfish hedonists. Also, in a world in which some militant religions are gaining strength is there a danger that a weakened Christianity could be replaced by far more dangerous destabilising forces in our society? As in the past, the masses will always follow the strongest, so should we humanists keep our views to ourselves and not undermine what is after all a fairly non-threatening set of beliefs which has kept our country relatively stable now for generations?

Witches and warlocks still form a part of our lives, despite what many of us may assert. This is vividly illustrated for me on my computer. Threatened with ill-luck and misfortune if I break a chain letter sent by E-mail, I hesitate for a moment and still need considerable willpower to dismiss the threat, just in case something nasty should occur to me or my family.

The emotional reaction to the words *agnostic* and particularly *atheist* has preoccupied me for many years. In the past, to be labelled with either of these words seemed to place me in a peculiar anti-social fringe-group that was perceived as trying to undermine the fabric of our culture. Even today the words sound alien, so I much prefer terms such as *humanist* and *pragmatist*. This conveys the impression that people who have applied reason to their stance have reached a rational and logical point of view.

Hitler's Pope, by John Cornwall and *The Spanish Civil War*, by Antony Beevor would have been read by my father with no great surprise as he believed the Roman Catholic Church had totally failed his generation. These two books raise the question of whether our present generation has learnt any lessons at all from the past, or are we all still basically barbarians with only a veneer of goodness to make us feel saved?

That my mother looked on religion as the bedrock of her existence and that my father was completely indifferent to it, reinforces an observation that women often appear to demonstrate a greater commitment to their faith than men. It is also interesting to note that many pious men seem to have a strong background of devout mothers or wives. How then did I escape from this spell?

The tale that describes the destruction of my father's subservience to Rome has always been present in my thoughts; but it was probably our personalities and not the story that influenced us mostly. While some of us appear effortlessly to make the jump from logic to belief, others just cannot rationalise it. Just as my colour blindness makes me totally unable to visualise what I am missing, so does my character and experience prevent such an act of faith. It is quite understandable however, that the less introspective and thoughtful amongst us today just drift along in the wilderness, unable to disown their religion, yet evading any actual involvement in church ritual.

If I stand and contemplate a beautiful clear night sky, with millions of tiny specks shining down on me, I just know that our little world is but an infinitesimal cog in some mighty great wheel. Man may dominate life here on earth, but in the universe he is of little consequence. It seems rather pathetic that our pride and sense of importance in being the masters in our world should make us believe that there is a higher being out there who is only interested in us. Yet, notwithstanding the evolution of the human brain, man persists in calling upon the mysterious to justify his existence without getting any closer to answering the question, "why?".

A minister once remarked that, despite all my apparent pragmatism, I used an excessive number of religious expletives and references to the Lord. It was said with a marked sense of sarcasm and was, of course, very pertinent. It is perfectly true that I utter such words; they were once used in sheer mockery but now seem ingrained in my psyche. In my more whimsical moments therefore, I do wonder if after all, there is an omnipotent force infiltrating my brain in order to make me recognise the error of my ways? If I was therefore to be proved totally wrong and could meet up again with friends and family in some 'higher' place, then there would be no one more delighted than me.

Chapter 18
Thieving, Cynicism And Health

Looking back to my childhood, I feel that as I grew up I imagined two little pixies seated, one on each shoulder. The bright little fellow on the right exuded openness and integrity, while the one on the left was devious, not to say dishonest. The influences around me should have made the right pixie thrive and grow while the rascal on the left should have gradually shrivelled and fallen off. Essentially, I believe that this did come about, but the little devil on the left proved to have great staying power. Perhaps, even to this day, although I can't see him, he is still probably clinging on there somewhere.

The name Foin, Fouyn or Fouin has various meanings, but the one generally accepted in France means 'hay-maker.' However, the second derivation is *'surnom d'une personne finaude'* which translates as 'surname of a sly and wily person'. Not very complimentary and it gives rise to gales of laughter and much nodding of heads among some of my friends. So perhaps the left pixie has every right to stay where he is.

The Life of Jesus Christ in Pictures appeared from the bottom of a box in the loft the other day to remind me that I was once a thief. Aged five, I had coveted this book belonging to Willie Archibald from that day in his house when I first set eyes on it. Battered, with well-thumbed dog-eared pictures, it appears now like something ready for the waste-paper basket rather than on a shelf of special volumes. But who knows why I was attracted to it? It was not as if I had no books of my own; in fact our house overflowed with reading material, especially boy's books, but it seems that I had to have it by fair means or foul. Borrowing Willie's book, apparently in good faith, I believe that I never had any intention of returning it, instead giving the lame excuse that it had just got lost. It now seems incongruous, in the light of my future doubts that I should steal, of all things, a story about Jesus Christ.

Another act of childhood sleight-of-hand took place a year or two later when my old adversary, temporarily-turned-friend, Peter Strang was baby-sitting for the Dawsons next door. Wills new set of cigarette cards *Railway Engines*, issued in 1936, found us all feverishly striving to complete the set. Hey presto! The day after Peter was baby-sitting, that last missing card appeared in my album. Not a murmur of puzzlement came from my friend Alfie on finding his much sought-after card No 47 *Streamlined Locomotive 'Commodore Vanderbilt' (New York to Chicago Railway)* gone. Willie's book, on the other hand, presented me with a sobering lesson.

My father had returned from Norway bringing me a lovely multipurpose penknife with stag horn sides. It was unique and I was devastated to find that it was missing shortly afterwards. A little later Willie was playing with a similar knife, which his father, in my presence, said he had given to him. My own knife was nowhere to be found and it was obvious that this was tit-for-tat revenge, the moral of which was not lost on me. In some strange way, however, this loss did seem to salve my conscience.

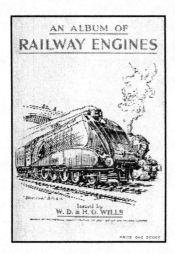
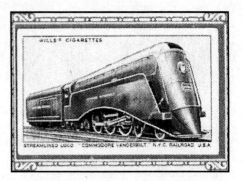

The Collecting Craze – I would stop
at nothing to complete that Set.

Stealing, however, could also come into another less contentious category of acquisition. Climbing on to the roof of the joiner's shop, prizing open the skylight window and then entering and filling our pockets with every size of nail available, was simply deemed to be 'taking'. That Alfie was always with me; together with the fact that this was his own father's domain seemed to legitimise the operation. However, removing wood from the sawmill was somewhat different. Nevertheless, we did not regard even this as stealing and we would have been horrified had we been accused of theft. And my conscience was clear on this issue.

In my first year at the village school, my pals found a little summerhouse in woodland just off the main road. To our amazement, it proved to be full of toy soldiers and guns. They obviously belonged to the children of some wealthy parents, and these toys really made a wonderful sight, all laid out in their serried ranks. I took my share of the booty, but not without some pangs of conscience. It astonished me that my mother believed me when I said that my pal, Bob Rose, had given the models to me. She surely must have realised that no village lad ever owned toys of this quality. My friends, of course, dismissed the act as "just taking"; but I sensed that this was in a totally different category from our pocketful of nails, and I was never again to repeat it.

An in-between category between out-and-out stealing and "just taking" was the raiding of the apple orchards and fruit gardens. The plots at the side of the recreation hall were the showpieces of so many keen gardeners and their produce was greatly prized. Mr George Allan, the estate's electrician was particularly adept at growing huge juicy blackcurrants. So one fine summer evening Willie and I decided to sample a few. Creeping along from two gardens away, under raspberry and gooseberry bushes, we eventually reached the blackcurrants and lay munching happily until, suddenly, an angry face appeared above the bushes. With a roar of rage and a spade in his hand, Mr Allan gave chase. Never have I bolted faster in my life, before or since, feeling that this spade was about to descend on me at any moment. Mr Allan never took any further action, as I'm sure he reckoned we wouldn't try that trick again. Perhaps like us, the adults felt boys will be boys and, after all, raiding orchards has been the subject of romantic tales throughout the centuries. So, our behaviour was taken in reasonably good part.

Were we potential felons who should be kept under surveillance by the police, young though we were? Should we then have been flogged? Or perhaps in some societies even hanged? In my mind, I continually see the righteous hangers and floggers in conflict with the mild liberals in society and wonder who has right on their side. I came from a reasonably secure background with kind and well-meaning parents and from an environment in which I suffered no great hardship. Yet, as a child I could have drifted away from honesty and clean living into a darker world.

If we were to descend a few layers into an even poorer society, we would observe the little pixie on the left shoulder as the survivor. Hanging and flogging would then appear more reactive than proactive, preventing us from fully understanding the reason that converts the naughty child into a hardened criminal. I knew right from wrong, but it requires direction and determination to avoid following these overpowering evil influences.

As a child, I was ever watchful for the signs that I might become the whipping boy for certain bullies and would make myself scarce before their beady eyes could settle on me. Thus, I became so successful in avoiding beatings and fights over the years that I cannot remember getting into any real trouble. Some youngsters appear to thrive on getting into fights and I have no doubt many consider this a normal growing up process. However, tales of cruelty in our armed services, both directed at their own recruits as well as the enemy, have never surprised me. My experience at the Glen school illustrated the level of harshness that such societies accepted as normal. Add one or two potential psychopaths into this setting and little wonder we breed individuals who are a menace to all.

The only time that I ever got the literal bloody nose was one evening when I was with the evacuees waiting for our Saturday night film to begin. I was involved in mild, aimless horseplay with one of my old school buddies when suddenly he lashed out with his fist and left me pouring with blood. The ferocity and suddenness of the attack was so unexpected that I simply retreated to stem the bleeding, completely mystified as to the reason for the assault. It left me sadly antagonistic towards this unpredictable chum, and probably ended any form of real friendship between us. Much the same reaction, however, comes from a friend's unguarded word, which can also leave one bitter and resentful. The old adage 'least said soonest mended' is a wise one. Whenever it occurs the odd cutting remark is rarely forgotten, whereas other more relevant details fade into obscurity.

The danger of getting into the wrong company is something I have been aware of from an early age. This has made me take an interest in those around me, irrespective of whether or not I liked them, but because I was fascinated to discover why they functioned as they did. My interest in observing human behaviour has gradually increased over the years, without my realising that I was trying to develop an ability that would stand me in very good stead both as a General Practitioner and in the wider sphere of personal interactions.

As a child, I was frequently instructed to be kind and considerate and take those around me at face value. With maturity, over the years, I have found such advice an unreliable procedure. In one's formative years, when one is so vulnerable, it pays to know your colleagues and be able to assess them accurately. In the world of medicine, shifting responsibility on to the shoulders of juniors to preserve your reputation was far from unknown. This had happened to me on one or two occasions and, as a result, I quickly learned to size people up, to avoid being a victim of their incompetence. That all this tends to breed a level of cynicism towards your fellow man is unfortunate, but I have always found that building trust from bottom up is by far the soundest principle.

Once, when walking out with a few student colleagues to attend a clinic at Woodend Hospital, I was giving a highly critical negative assessment of one of our lecturers. Suddenly, my couthy friend, Jim Taylor, turned on me, observing dryly that I was becoming a total cynic. His unexpected remark took me aback; even more so, because I realised that what he said was true. This was, however, the forerunner of many such remarks I would make when provoked by the sight of my peers ingratiating themselves with their superiors - or acting God.

Over the years I have found the finger of scorn frequently pointed at me because I am an only child, with all the weaknesses this apparently engenders. That there could be an element of truth in being an only one I do not doubt, but society always seems so ready to put one's problems down to colour, creed or anything else that sets people slightly apart from those around them.

There is little doubt, however, that my complete sense of relaxation on being alone is because I spent so much time in solitary, but happy isolation in childhood. I remember receiving great praise from my English master, Charles Forbes at the Grammar, when I turned in an essay entitled 'The Hero of My Dreams'. In it, I outlined how I filled my quiet waking hours by telling myself hundreds of stories in which I was my very own hero. Whether it was one of W E Johns' fighter pilots doing battle with the Red Baron in the First World War, or imagining myself making a Don Bradman-like century at Lords, I could fill hours of peace and quiet in this manner. Climbing Everest with Mallory or solving a Sherlock Holmes mystery by my sheer brilliance never failed to send me off into a sound sleep. Waking in the morning, I would usually find I needed yet another episode, before achieving my eventual triumph. This habit lasted well beyond my early years and in a reverie, even now, my imagination can produce scenarios, which I might have recorded in my youth. Is this fantasising typical of the egocentricity of a lonely child?

Alcohol appears to have varying effects on different individuals and my early memories of my father, turning from a mellow easy-going man into an argumentative rather unpleasant person, occasionally upset me in childhood. At Hogmanay the local gamekeepers, gardeners and other employees would first-foot my parents and the often ill-tempered noises of drunks filled me with apprehension as I tucked my head below the bedclothes. Scenes outside the Boat Inn in Aboyne at closing time were also imprinted on my mind, as I cycled past one night on my own and felt frightened at these ruffians arguing and jostling one another in total inebriation. Are we perhaps a little more civilised now, or am I mixing with a different sort of people, as I no longer associate drunkenness with physical violence? My student colleagues could become noisy and obstreperous, but fists were rarely raised and in adult life, I cannot remember seeing much aggression. I feel relieved that my father's trait has not been passed down to me; but why should one person react to this drug in a completely different manner from another?

"There is no such word as *can't*" and "If the job's worth doing it's worth doing well." My father would repeat these sayings to me throughout my childhood as I frequently stumbled in my attempts to live up to his standards. I wonder to what extent these maxims affect our future lives and should we continue to live by them in the present age? All those old sayings, which were repeated to me at Glen Tanar School, flood back into my memory and they have shaped my attitudes and behaviour throughout my working life. Now, in retirement, I find that a tendency of mine to procrastinate is increasing, and I have difficulty in motivating myself to embark on a new project. However, once thought through properly, I find that the old driving force is still there and I shall persist with the task until it is completed. These memoirs are a case in point since I had begun to think that my old grey cells were dying off so quickly that I had better use the remainder to finish the project before they vanish.

It is strange that individuals, from even the same family, can have such differing strengths and weaknesses, interests or culture. My mother, with only a basic education, had a wide knowledge of literature including the works of even many of the more minor poets. Yet, I, with the benefit of further education, derived less satisfaction than she did from poetry and, in particular, Shakespearian drama. Not even did her vivid description of memorable London theatre productions stimulate me; while a Donald Wolfit season at His Majesty's Theatre scarcely excited me at all. On the other hand, I respond with immediate pleasure to the wonderful insights and vivid expression of Charles Murray in poems such as *The Whistle*, and *There's Aye a Something*, and the lesser-known *Dockens Afore His Peers*. These works speak to me in a way that many English poets fail to do. This special affinity with the Doric poetry is not surprising, as during my early years I was attuned to the local dialect, so much so, that it gives me a thrill to recall it in print and to roll the words around my tongue when reading them aloud yet again. I have to accept the fact that I am still a country lad at heart, with tastes that have been formed in a rural setting.

Turning to health, I am so conscious of the stress and unhappiness that goes hand in hand in our lives when illness strikes those whom we love so dearly. Some families seem blessed to never experience such traumas, whereas others go from one tragedy to the next. My mother in her sixties developed abdominal pain, eventually requiring hospital admission. As a fourth year medical student, I had the dreadful sensation that the most likely cause was an advanced cancer of the bowel. Watching the wheels of examination and decision-making grind so slowly left me with a lasting appreciation of the anxiety experienced by patients and their relatives. In my mother's case, we were relieved to find that adhesions from a previous appendix operation were the cause of her trouble. But the experience served to bring home to me that, while a doctor must learn not to be emotionally involved, he should be able to empathise with a patient's anxiety.

Life without good health is a dreadful burden. My parents always seemed to be healthy. My father had almost died in the dreadful 'flu epidemic of 1918, which killed millions around the world; but apart from the odd sore back and touch of bronchitis, he seemed to keep very well. From time-to-time, his bad back used to poleaxe him completely. I can still recall the stench of those mustard plasters and the Sloan's Liniment that reached every corner of the house. The dreadful accident, which wrote off my father's pride and joy, the Austin 10, in 1968, resulted in both parents suffering multiple fractures from which, luckily, they made an amazing recovery. Unfortunately, at the age of 97, during a short respite stay in Aboyne Hospital, my father suffered a broken hip from which he never really recovered. Having returned to the Aboyne hospital from Aberdeen Royal Infirmary he died in some distress from bronchopneumonia on the 20th October 1978.

Over the years, my mother suffered from headaches and an unsettling tendency to feel faint and pass out which reminded me of the 'vapours' of the leisured classes in Victorian times. This drew little sympathy from me in those early days. Such giddiness was possibly due to a type of postural hypotension. We, as doctors, would have dismissed this condition as being relatively unimportant. At midnight on the 1st of June 1989, in Nazareth House, my mother just faded away with what I would have thought was just a 'vapour.' She died of nothing serious - just a very peaceful 'vapour' at ninety-seven years old.

'Consumption' was a dreaded word back in those early days and it was uttered with not only a sense of foreboding but almost as a derogatory term. Tuberculosis, to give it its correct name, was still rife throughout the country. Inconceivable though it is to us nowadays, to have contracted it seemed almost indecent in those days. Similarly, when diphtheria and scarlet fever flared up, I can remember the sense of anxiety at school if someone was infected. Certain names immediately bring forth a scene or some association into one's mind.

The words 'scarlet fever' take me instantly back into the cookery classroom in Aboyne. There I am sitting up at the back listening to the official announcement that half a dozen children had been admitted to the isolation hospital with scarlet fever. The sense of anxiety that pervaded the whole class is with me still, although no one close to me ever did contract the fever.

The early morning stropping of the razor followed by a vigorous slapping of the chest were my waking sounds, as my father got ready for a new day at seven in the morning.

My Cousin Marie Aillerie approaches her Century.
Living into their nineties seems commonplace for the Fouins.

Following his near death experience with the 1918 influenza, he always had a tendency to bronchitis. Some perceptive early physiotherapist must have advised him about self-treatment, as the habitual pounding of his chest to loosen accumulated phlegm was a routine that never varied. His other unfailing habit involved the daily dose of fizzy health salts, such as Andrews or Fisons, from a liver-shaped tin. My mother, on the other hand, took no fancy extras; but I was dosed with Allen and Hanbury's Cod Liver Oil and Malt through winter to spring every year, and I loved it. In the very early days, I remember wearing a medicinal locket around my neck to protect me from coughs and colds. When the big boy of the evacuees, Mick Tully, was provided with the luxury of Virol tonic by his Glasgow parents, I also wanted to change to this special tonic. How odd we are sometimes to be so influenced by what others do. For although I detested the taste of Virol, I persisted with it for a couple of years.

Nowadays, with our beautifully centrally heated double-glazed residences, we tend to forget how bitterly cold our houses were back in those days. My mother, first up, would get the range going and I would descend from my frosty icebox to clothes warming in front of the fire. It still took a determined effort to leave the cosy bed, but I bet that not many of my friends were spoilt with a warm sark in the morning. The one luxury item that our house boasted was a large chromium-plated hot-water towel rail in the bathroom. It was a delight on entering the bathroom to sense the strong masculine smell of my father's shaving soap and hair oil. Having brushed my teeth and hurriedly sponged my face, I scurried off to school to the accompaniment of Mother chiding me for being late as usual. The other lasting memory with its medicinal associations is related to the Victorian fixation on constipation. Health was dependent on a regular bowel habit and the need for a weekly dose of an aperient was something that obsessed my mother. I can still involuntarily retch at the thought of sitting by the range with the bottle of castor oil warming on the hearth. When eventually I did swallow this foul mixture, I was invariably sick. This finally convinced my mother that the less effective syrup of figs would have to do.

When I was about six and becoming somewhat difficult to discipline, my mother bought a very heavy schoolmaster's tawse to keep me under control. Amazingly, it hung on the back of a cupboard door for years and years without ever being used. I now understand that it was obviously a deterrent. I could never understand why my mother, who had little money to spare felt that she needed such a weapon to keep a reasonably civilised child under control. I never took the threat seriously and always regarded it as a bit of a joke.

Health is something most of us take so much for granted, almost like expecting our modern-day car to continue to run with no servicing. However, when illness does strike, we come to realise how frail our bodies can be. As a doctor, I am very aware of this, having repeatedly seen people snuffed out like a candle with precious little warning. During my childhood days, cigarette smoking was an attraction to many of my pals, but oddly enough, with both parents smoking, I never did take it up. Occasionally, when spending an evening on the riverbank, I did succumb to smoking as a deterrent to the midges forming a haze around my head, but the habit had no attraction for me. Nowadays, awareness of the risk to health posed by smoking and by other hazards seems for some to be no greater than it was, and I am also dismayed to observe young people apparently becoming more and more unfit.

Looking back on those years of old wives' tales, I find it amazing that many of us have grown up with so few hang-ups. While I was lucky enough to have been brought up by two sensible, worldly-wise people who could mostly distinguish fact from fiction, there remained an air of mystery and myth surrounding many health matters. It is not always appreciated, even by those of us who lived through those times, how much education and scientific discovery have since dispelled many of these misconceptions.

Thanks to my parents, I am still living a sensible and healthy life. Now, having exceeded my biblically allotted span of three score years and ten, I can but hope that there are, nevertheless, still some good years left for me to remember; a hope that is assisted by a stiff dram every night.

Chapter 19
From Random Thoughts
To Threshing-mills

There can be few among us, who, when looking back over the past, ponder whether taking that left fork in our lives instead of going right would have led on to greener pastures. As I review my life, images from the past slowly appear and I begin to feel astonished that, from an early age, so many long forgotten forks reveal themselves. The fact that these almost forgotten choices did not haunt me throughout my life should be a positive sign that I was content with the route. But on reflection, this is perhaps a very superficial view.

Being born into an atypical family with a foreign-sounding name certainly brought some stresses, but also occasional benefits. The name makes you remembered by others when, unfortunately, you have long forgotten who they are. Early schooling was the most difficult time I remember, when certain children could cut you to the quick by name-calling alone, while the threat of physical violence was never too far away. Then there were the sly remarks about one's love of frog's legs, one's excitable Latin temperament or even being a Romeo. My studied indifference to all this leg pulling took years and much patience to develop and perfect.

Later on, more sophisticated friends still found it difficult to understand why I should feel so little affinity with my French background and in particular with what was, to me, a surprisingly difficult language. A situation in which my father never spoke French in a home where my mother disparaged everything of a foreign nature was a state of affairs that few were able to comprehend. Moreover, my father was rarely at home at the time when I could have benefited from his knowledge and, I believe, such was his struggle when learning English, that he wished to protect me from similar pressures when learning French.

Whether it was the result of feeling like a young duck among chickens, there is little doubt that my apparent foreignness, at times, often tempted me to take up an independent stance. I detested the sheep-like deference of so many around me, causing me to overreact by distancing myself from such conformity. On the other hand it would have been pleasant, on the odd occasion, to be just another Jock Tamson with local roots, who was easily accepted, and did not have to suffer the quizzical look of local strangers working out who this odd fellow might be. Certainly, by the time I was seven,

I had seen more of the world than over ninety-nine percent of my fellows, all of which further accentuated the fact that I seemed rather different.

Aged seven, standing with my father on the edge of a small French airfield, and watching the aeroplanes come and go, I was surprised to see Father strike up a conversation with a helmeted young man. Before I knew it, Father was telling us that the pilot would be delighted to take us up for a view of the countryside. Although my mother refused to go up, she encouraged us to accept the offer. Characteristically, I turned down the invitation. It would be well into adult life before such another chance would present itself. My regret stayed with me for years, and I used to belligerently blame my father for not giving me a stronger lead. In 1937, the opportunity to fly was not readily available to the general public so, perhaps my Dad, too, had just the slightest misgivings.

Aged fourteen, I was lucky enough to be able to break with the tradition of many working class children, by not being expected to pick up a message bike to become a Co-op or butcher's delivery boy. After opting for secondary education, I sensed that some of those in the Aboyne environment felt that I was obviously getting too big for my boots. To go to the Aberdeen Grammar School was definitely a step too far for many. Five or six years previously, I seem to recall one scholar going on to Gordon's College. Otherwise, Banchory was expected to be the limit for any child from Aboyne. The fact that Alan Simpson and I set a precedent, led the way for three boys in the year behind us, Douglas Young and William Alexander, the chemist's son, coming to the Grammar with Ian Watt going to Gordon's. In the fullness of time Doug took a BSc and became an agricultural adviser, Bill graduated in law and later became a schoolmaster, while Ian returned to his roots as a vet in Aboyne and Torphins.

The tremendous benefits available to those children belonging to an educated middle class family compared with those from a less academic home tended to be overlooked or forgotten even by the educationalists in those early days. Brilliant brains usually rise to the top from any background, but the less gifted will struggle if the environment is not advantageous. Parents with little insight and understanding of their children's learning needs should have been offset by the efforts of those trained to help children from an educationally deprived background. The fact that this did not seem to happen for many young people, and in my case at both Grammar and at University, shows a lack of awareness of the boy or girl as an individual. As far as the authorities were concerned, one regime fitted all, despite the needs of so many for counselling and advice. Is it little wonder, therefore, that we in Medicine lost so many good potential doctors in those early years?

From Random Thoughts To Threshing-mills

In most of us there is the desire not to be undervalued and this manifests itself particularly in Japan and China as the fear of losing face. This desire has at times driven me to take some hair-brained risks while on occasions I have walked away from a challenge for fear of being ridiculed. Probably self-doubt gives rise to this apprehension. The unfortunate truth is that no one else is conscious of or concerned about one's misgivings. It is very reassuring to discover that this problem affects others who rate themselves highly. My bête noire of student days, that eminent surgeon George Mavor, was a friend of my senior partner Charles Liddell, and so I got to know him much better. When I enthused about my love of game-shooting, he also expressed an interest, and so I suggested that he should come out with me one day to shoot pigeons. His response was an immediate refusal, saying he would only appear in public when he had become reasonably proficient at the sport. Disappointed, but recognising the very quality that made me apprehensive about letting myself down, I did not press him any further.

I have not inherited my parents' desire to roam widely around the world, except on holiday. This urge is something we either have or have not. My inherent canniness over a lifetime has also prevented me from taking too many chances. However, in retrospect, I do not regret having remained at home instead of emigrating to sunnier climes, as once envisaged, by going to Canada in 1959. A number of my colleagues did however disappear to Hinton in Alberta, where my rugby-playing colleague Ian Reid was to rise to some prominence in the politics of the Province.

Politics has always been an interest of mine from the days when my father used to sing the praises of Joseph Stalin. In retrospect, my share owning, independent-thinking father was certainly an unlikely communist. However, those around him would unfailingly return a landed or titled Tory to Parliament at every election, in those old days. Talk about turkeys voting for Xmas, but such was the power of the upper classes as employers, that workers instinctively knew where to put their crosses. My father used to shake his head in despair at this herd-like mentality and his irritation quickly spread to me as I reached my teens.

Lady Grant, later Lady Tweedsmuir, sat as Conservative MP for South Aberdeen in the post-war years. Alan's mother was always a fiery "blue rinse" Tory and I was introduced to canvassing at elections and tendering general support, just to please her, when staying in Louisville Avenue. Once at University, however, my socialist leanings took over and I became an ardent nationaliser of all the major industries. Involved in heated student debate, I certainly became an idealist, believing that with social decency, hard work and

Father

*On retirement in 1956
aged 75.*

Mother

*At the same time
Mother reaches age 64.*

common sense we could cure all the post-war ills of Britain. After only a few years I was to realise that these attributes were sorely lacking, so heralding the first signs of my increasing cynicism. It is so sad that the experience of life changes so many of us from joyous romantics to such surly pragmatists - something I had deplored so readily in my buddy, Alan Simpson, in those early arguments in our lodgings together.

Even today, some of our country districts still tend to pay homage to the blue of the privileged Tories, as if inheriting their ancestors' genes of subservience to their betters. That this seems to irritate me now as much as it irritated my father all those seventy years ago, also tells me something about my own genes. Apart from her dislike of Mrs Thatcher, my mother did not become nearly so heated in political debate, although she did often point out to Dad in retirement, how incongruous his stance appeared, considering that he was a property and share-owning capitalist.

August 1954 found me standing, rather self-consciously, waiting to open my first bank account at the Queen's Cross Branch of the Clydesdale Bank. No sooner had I reached the teller with my request, than a broad Banchory voice summoned me sternly to "Come awa in here laddie and let me see what you are up to". John Chrystal, sitting in his manager's office with the door wide open to watch over his clientele, seems a hundred years away now from our present impersonal banking service. That his keen hearing and observation had alerted him so quickly to a new client, I have always considered remarkable.

Viewing my first salary cheque from my hospital post, he completely took over my financial thinking. "Two sets of people are feels with money - kirk ministers who haven't any, and doctors who always seem to think they have more than they have, so we won't have you making a feel of yourself." For years ahead, old John became my financial mentor and father figure. He bought me my first shares in a property company called *Capital and Counties*. I still have the small "with compliments" slip that accompanied the certificate, with written in his own hand "For better or for worse and dinna blame me" In his retirement I would often visit him and his sister in their Aberdeen bungalow. A wonderful couple and what I would give now for that shrewd banking brain to be still around to save me from all my rash investments.

Considerations of a more general nature now come to mind. Since my childhood, customs and behaviour in general have deteriorated. "Manners maketh man" is a well-known saying from yesteryear. The demands of the Women's Liberation Movement, together with a lack of training among our young, have resulted in the disappearance of common courtesies, that, as a boy, I was taught to uphold. My father always made a great display of lifting his hat to the ladies and my failure to get up, especially when ladies entered the room, would provoke a sharp rebuke from my parents. Giving up one's seat to ladies or walking on the outside of the pavement was second nature to us. Ironically, in this age, we are now likely to be rebuked by the ladies for not treating them as equals.

I am very conscious that in these memoirs I have not so far projected the profession of medicine as primarily a caring and sensitive calling. I have always found ludicrous the misconception expressed by many of my patients that doctors are born and not made. Apart from a small minority of religiously motivated doctors, I can scarcely remember, either during my time at University or during medical practice, a doctor displaying a sentimental approach to the job. It is therefore very difficult to evaluate the combination of reasons, both social and vocational, that brought the majority of us to study medicine. That many have a natural empathy with the needy and distressed is in my mind incidental because this seldom appeared to be the principal reason in defining our careers. It is certainly true however that those who are either soft-hearted or starry-eyed are unlikely to be enamoured with a profession that calls for gritty determination, staying power, common sense and above all, an acceptance that we do not wear the mantle of a God or even of a Florence Nightingale.

The field of astrology makes many of us hold our heads in exasperation, but still prepared to have a wee glance at it out of the corner of our eye. My mother had a natural affinity with the occult and had a wonderful flair for reading tea-leaves. Wherever we went socially, she was always in great demand and the ladies especially would sit around agog with expectancy. Hilarious sessions are recalled at Dunecht estate on our visits to Bill Smith's family when Mrs Smith and her daughters could never get enough of these imaginative sessions. The boys, Ronald and young Bill, later to be known as Wull, would have none of it, so I could then quietly slide away to follow boyish pursuits with Bill.

The old Gypsy's prediction of my mother's life proved to be so accurate that reading horoscopes in our house became a regular feature and reinforced my superstitions. It is interesting to note that horoscopes are big business nowadays. So I am reading *Sun Sign, Moon Sign* by Charles and Suzi Harvey and am truly amazed. Narrowing down my birthday to the actual time of birth 11.50 a.m. on 20th November 1928, I find that I am Sun Scorpio, Moon Aquarius. Straight away, I see that I share the exact time of birth with the philosopher Voltaire, so I am obviously in good company. However, the unsettling part is that if I had to describe my own strengths and specific weaknesses – my hopes and fears – my emotions and cynicism, they are all there as if I had described them myself. You say that this has been written so that anyone could fit the description? I reply, no. It is far too specific, describing my introspection to a tee. So, what does it all mean? Talk about me rationalising my doubts about religion. This is all too eerie for me even to start to understand. So perhaps that old gypsy and my mother were blessed with a power that makes speculation pointless.

The Deeside railway always fascinated me and watching the train pass from so many different perspectives along Deeside was part of my childhood. Waiting for it to come round the bend into Aboyne Station from the east, or appearing in a cloud of smoke out of the tunnel to the west, never failed to excite. It was a heart-rending experience to stand on the bridge at Peterculter Station with my little son in 1966 while we watched the last passenger train pulling out for Ballater. I was convinced at the time that the closure was a mistake for the future of Deeside but, along with many others, I never took any action, an omission that I now deeply regret. Supporting the infant *Royal Deeside Railway Preservation Society* now is the least we can do to compensate for our previous lethargy.

Spanning the River Dee at Cults, the "Shakkin" Brig stands forlorn and rusting with its staging disintegrated. It represents a monument both to our past and to our ineffectiveness in stimulating any action to restore it to its former beauty. Not only was it a means whereby Sunday worshippers could reach their kirk, but also it was a favourite traditional weekend walk for city dwellers, and was the local pride and joy for a generation past.

The "Shakkin" Brig at Cults in 1982.

Daughter Nicky views the Dee with the
Bridge still almost repairable - not now.

The fact that it has outlived its usefulness means that it should be either preserved like a listed building, or removed as both an eyesore and a hazard. Despite some local endeavours to rescue it, sufficient money was never forthcoming: and so it stands as a symbol of neglect and, along with much else around Aberdeen, does no credit to our City Fathers or to us.

Having been heavily involved in the Scouting movement throughout my formative years, I am sad that the message of clean, outdoor living and the tradition of helping your neighbour, as advocated by Baden Powell, has been somewhat diluted by the indifference of society. Those dated pictures in the old *Scouting for Boys*, showing a decadent youth slouching on a street corner with a fag hanging from his mouth, compared with the smart uniformed scout, were powerful propaganda even then. Somewhere this image has been lost; many say that it is no longer relevant to modern youth.

I find this conclusion disappointing and, in my naivety, I would like to see our young caught up again in a new movement reaching right down to the bottom of society and taking them off the streets to counteract loutish behaviour. The litter and chewing-gummed streets are a disgrace to a civilised nation and I would love to see this eliminated. I am certain that voluntary service, or even national service overseas, directed towards those in their late teens and early twenties would be beneficial to us as a nation; but where is the will?

In recording the past in these memoirs, I am very aware that my children have two sources of genetic inheritance. It therefore seems appropriate to append some of the history of my wife's family, especially as I regret not having given this full consideration in the past.

Kaye's grandfather David Angus, a Midmar contractor and timber merchant was a well-known pioneer in using traction engines for threshing and transporting, from back in the 1800's. A more detailed account of his life was given in an appreciation of him that appeared in the local press at the time of his death in 1935.

Obituary.

WELL-KNOWN MIDMAR MAN OF AFFAIRS.

Mr D. Angus, Contractor an Timber Merchant.

Midmar parish and the whole distric in very truth, writes a correspondent, hat lost their ''Gran Old Man'' by th death, at the O Schoolhouse, Mi mar, of Mr Davi Angus, contracte and timber me chant, at the ag of eighty-five.

Born at Bogs c Laithers, Turrif he went as a bo of sixteen with hi father to the farı ef Wateridgemui Midmar.

At the age o twenty-three year

Mr D Angus.

Exerpt from Appreciation of Traction Engine Pioneer – David Angus.

A red flag led the way to Aberdeen.

"Born at Bogs of Laithers, Turriff, he went as a boy of sixteen with his father to the farm of Wateridgemuir, Midmar. At age twenty-three, a mishap with his father's threshing mill, lost him his left arm and was the turning point in his career. The use of traction engines for both shifting about and driving travelling threshing mills was just beginning and he was among the first to see the field for such operations. Starting in 1875 with one engine and one mill, these were soon followed with three other complete units, of the best plant available and in the season, all working to capacity, in most of the district between Dee and Don, from Tarland to Aberdeen. At the same time, wagon after wagon was added to his road haulage plant and he carried out some remarkable feats in heavy road haulage. He soon grasped, too, the possibilities of the rubber-tyred steam and petrol driven wagons and made large use of both, in general road haulage all over the country, as well as in his own timber business."

My father-in-law, also David Angus, used to recount his own memories of those early days when, as a young boy, his father would make him walk in front of the traction engine with a red flag, on the road to Aberdeen. This was done in order to comply with the licensing regulation, for proceeding on a main thoroughfare. Kaye's father, a marine and motor engineer with his own business, had been in the Territorial Army before the First World War and served from 1914 to 1916 as a piper with the Gordon Highlanders in the trenches in France. He had suffered not only the discomfort of war, but also the spectre of death all around him and he himself had been gassed. He was totally phlegmatic about his experiences, but he often told me of the sudden death of his comrades, many often picked-off by German snipers. Raising a head above the trenches was the last act of many of his comrades. I never liked to intrude further into his other memories from that dreadful war. After his experience in the trenches, his laid-back attitude was well illustrated by the manner in which he dealt with the dangers threatening civilians in the Second World War. Kaye recalls the day the Heinkel bomber was shot down by two Spitfires into the Aberdeen ice-rink, not three hundred yards from their house. Her father stood out in the garden watching the dogfight, with debris falling around him, while everyone else dived for cover. Similarly, during the air raids, nothing would induce him to leave his warm bed for a cold damp air-raid shelter. I can well visualize him being totally immune to such 'trivial' dangers.

During the war, the hit-and-run raiders struck at Aberdeen both by day and night. Kaye recounts how she and her mother were walking home from the cinema one evening in the summer after watching *The Mill on the Floss*, when a Heinkel suddenly appeared, flying the length of Holburn Street just above the roof-tops, while machine-gunning indiscriminately. Kaye jumped on to the windowsill of an adjoining house while her mother threw herself flat down on the pavement. The plane was so low that she said she could distinctly see the crew in the cockpit as the plane passed her. Thankfully, living in the country, I was never subjected any such experiences.

For me, the only experience of war in Aberdeen was a visit to a minesweeper moored in the harbour in 1944. To term a small yacht a minesweeper seemed rather incongruous, but that was its function. I believe the boat had belonged to Lord Glentanar pre-war and was still manned by his old skipper. The skipper, a friend of my father, invited me down one evening from school to see over the boat and have supper with the four crewmen and the Lewis gunner. The tight security at the gate was reassuring and I felt it a real privilege to gain access. The yacht was being used as a magnetic mine detector having had its hull demagnetised and being so small, this was far easier than doing it to a full sized minesweeper. A year or so later, with the European war at an end, my next visit to Aberdeen harbour was in much more relaxed conditions, to view a surrendered U-boat, with the clouds of world conflict rolling away.

A great regret in later years was the loss of Grandfather Angus's leather-bound ledger detailing all the farms at which he had been employed with his threshing-mills. The ledger itemised tonnage and prices from all over the district over decades. After the death of Kaye's grandmother, the book came into her family when discovered during the clear-out of the Old Schoolhouse at Midmar. However, it did not come to my notice until after Kaye's father died. Her mother, intent on getting rid of junk, had gradually torn up the ledger over a period of months, and it was not until it had disappeared that I recognised that an irreplaceable piece of local history had been destroyed. Why I did not wake up to the loss beforehand, I shall never know; but it has come to be regarded as one of my most regrettable oversights.

Finally, I have always harboured a deep regret that I did nothing to mark the passing of my parents. With cremation and the scattering of ashes, there is no location that marks the spot where my loved ones are interred. The sentimental attachment that many people, including myself, have for graveyards and the pausing to remember those who have gone before, is very poignant. As far as I am concerned, I am denied that indulgence. Moreover, it has vaguely troubled me that my parents have passed this way through momentous times, yet there remains not a trace of either them or their story. In this book, I can salute them and, through the written word, leave some remembrance of them for future generations to read.

Chapter 20
A Pot-Pourri Of
Glen Tanar Memories

Seniority and retirement brings not only a sense of relaxation from a life of constant deadlines, but also the time to sit back and contemplate all that has gone before. It is not surprising that many of these reminiscences date back to childhood and, with time to ponder, there comes a greater understanding of those far-off years.

There is little doubt that estate life bred in all of us a distinct attitude, which would remain for the rest of our days. For many this meant a life of relative servility, as their opportunities to get out of the rut were almost impossible in that age of a class structure, which few dared to cross. Born into a labouring class and forced by financial circumstances to leave school at the earliest date possible, the best chance of progress was a good apprenticeship. That many would eventually break away from this narrow life-style was inevitable, especially as the war opened many eyes to the inequality of this way of life.

Looking around me in those early days, I found it amazing to view the differing attitudes of the workers. Some were forelock-tugging laird's men par excellence, while others just appeared to be going through the motions. Some were blatantly rebels and stood up for their rights – not that it did much good through the '30's, but all that changed in the '40's. On the other hand there appeared to be a sense in the wider district that those from the Glen were rather privileged to be on such an estate. Certainly at school we sensed our exclusiveness.

My parents always instilled in me to be gracious to our employers but to be in no way subservient. No burning rebellion to overthrow their aristocratic lives, but to get your education and to establish your own life away from this yoke of feudalism. This has led me to feel no bitterness over our class system, but I am acutely aware that it still permeates society at all levels. That it is present wherever you look in the UK, saddens me and I believe it demeans us all as citizens.

The class structure in those early days was really interesting. The estate pecking order from the factor down was clearly understood by every worker and child. We were intrigued, however, by our position in the village school set-up in Aboyne. Here we found that the village children were essentially from working class homes, with just above them the children from the shopkeeper class. The professionals, such as the doctor, the banker and at times the schoolmaster, were liable to look elsewhere for their children's education; while the minor gentry certainly looked down their noses at this ruffian's establishment. Above them, of course, the landed and titled rich could be patrons of the school, but they would never have considered sending their own children there. Layer upon layer of class existed with many trying desperately to ape the more elite strata above them.

In retrospect, so pathetic, but man seldom changes and many of us have since then been caught up unwittingly into this very web. At the bottom of the school class pecking order were those poor souls who hailed from anywhere near Tarland. The Stewart tinker's encampment was situated outside Tarland and over the years this was enough for us to keep up an unremitting barrage of insults at anyone remotely from that district with the cry "Tarland tinks, Tarland tinks". Oddly enough, my mother, so high and mighty at times, never turned away the odd tinker offering to sharpen knives or mend pots and pans. Likewise the little wizened old women enveloped in their traditional shawls and carrying those heavy wicker-baskets of wares always found a ready friend on our doorstep to buy some small article and exchange the gossip of the district.

The attitude of snobbery in this country which involves looking down on others is reprehensible, but the obsequiousness of looking up to those 'above' is equally undesirable. While the Americans with their 'can-do' attitude are dedicated to improving their standard of living, we in this country tend to disparage those that would attempt to better themselves. Nothing delights us more than when those who appear to have climbed a few rungs of the ladder come clattering down. Unhappily this is a viewpoint that is widely held and I am guilty myself at times of the same reaction when some unpleasant individual comes a cropper. That two of my grandchildren are growing up in the classless Australian society is therefore some consolation to not having them here with us.

Glen Tanar kids always seemed, in some odd way, unable to blend snugly into this class structure. We felt as if we were somewhat a race apart – nothing exotic but just somehow different. This could have stemmed from the fact that we came from outside the village and were living in a fairly close community. Certainly it had nothing to do with social standing as we were just as working class as our Aboyne brethren. But there always seemed to be a comradeship that made many of us feel quite superior and proud of our Glen Tanar association.

These days, when parents are anxious about letting their children walk half a mile to school and where their big off-road limousines clog up the approaches to our schools, it is interesting to remember the miles we walked and cycled all those years long ago. The journey to Glen Tanar School was two and a half miles away, so that in three years I must have walked about 3,000 miles, while cycling to Aboyne, four and a half miles away for six years, would be well over 10,000 miles. A total of 13,000 miles is an astonishing distance to contemplate and when one remembers that it was achieved in some atrocious weather, this makes it all the more commendable. I was very adequately clothed and fed and really did not suffer, and this says more for the less well equipped generations of tough Scottish children who were able to cope with such hardship. Now, when I look around at so many grossly overweight adults and children, I would love to turn the clock back and get them on their bikes or on their feet to do at least ten miles a day.

This experience was undoubtedly character building, but there are other conditions to which I would not wish to return. The idea that you can thrash knowledge into a child's head was widely prevalent in the old days. How barbaric this seems to us now. Even as a child I used to watch in dismay as some of my classmates were beaten when they failed to comprehend. I have no quibble over the use of the strap to keep control but, as an instrument of education, it must surely stop the learning process through fear and apprehension.

The Queen of Scottish Woods –
The Bonnie Birken Tree
Weathering and neglect threaten the heritage of these Glen Tanar Stones.

Listening to that rumbustious entertainer Billy Connolly on *Desert Island Discs* talking about his early school days, when he occupied the second row from the front, struck a chord with me. Billy outlined that the bright pupils were in the back row, those of average ability in the second, while the dunderheads occupied the front. He, along with his pals who were not too bright, but with some hope, occupied this second row. Only when this classroom structure was viewed through his eyes did I begin to understand how fortunate those of us who resided towards the back were.

Rote learning was the accepted method of training our memories to retain the basics. Chanting C-A-T and M-A-T and going over our multiplication tables ad infinitum seems on the face of it such a stolidly unimaginative exercise and yet, throughout life, those tables have been my salvation, as is the chanting of the days in the month. Modern method teachers may frown on this communal way of learning but with me it has certainly stood the test of time. Miss Pirie, with her pointer thrust out belligerently, was not one to be ignored and so we all put our hearts and souls into our responses to please this terrifying lady.

My lasting memory of that walk to school was the path through the piggery wood. Passing through the little iron gate and wending our way up through the birch trees on to the High Road always had a magical feeling about it. Little wonder that I am left with a profoundly sentimental attachment to our native birch. Wherever I perceive it now, it never fails to bring a warm glow into my heart. Whether in woodland or scattered thinly up some gully as we climb expectantly towards a distant peak, it makes me very conscious of our Deeside heritage.

Cycling to Aboyne has its own separate memories. Perhaps it was the spring ploughing time, when we would pass one man and his horse turning up the rich brown earth, to find him still there only half way across the field on our return at night. Or a bitter frosty morning, with the cold mist floating above the Tanar and a farm worker throwing neeps into a cart from a rime-covered field. That certainly drove home the message that we should stick into our books or that could be our lot in a few years' time. This lesson was further reinforced by seeing the farm workers in their dreich barren bothy after a hard day's work.

The memory of cycling home from Aboyne is dominated by the prevailing south-westerly wind which always seemed at its worst after we had endured a strenuous day. No, not from too much class-work, but from playing football for far too long after school. Coming past the Tower of Ess the road bends around the Swan's Neck corners and comes out on to higher ground towards Greystone and Kildoo. This is where the wind really hit us with full force and many were the nights that I cursed and swore over this long, boring road and my useless bicycle. In addition, here it was that the rutting stags made their presence felt. Their roaring, combined with the eeriness of the gloaming and a bicycle with a mind of its own, produced a level of frustration mixed with apprehension that is unsettling to recall.

Stone Carving at the Tower of Ess.

*Some autumn evenings the roaring
stags could make us very uneasy.*

Lord Glentanar was not frightened to test out new ideas on his estate and many of these drew wry comments from some of his employees who were convinced that none of them would work. Probably after the war, about 1947, he was the first in the district to experiment with a rudimentary electric car which could manage the trip to Aboyne and back at a leisurely pace before its batteries required recharging from the mains electricity supply. Some years before this, the laird suspected that the red deer harboured the tic that was affecting the sheep and the grouse numbers on the hill. Building a deer fence around the estate did not solve the problem of the deer already within the fence. In order to deal with them a large stockade was built at Kildoo, opposite the gamekeeper's cottage at Greystone.

With the deer down on the low ground in winter, an inviting trail, probably of turnips, was laid out leading into the stockade. During the night the deer would feed as far as the inside of the stockade, when a keeper would pull the rope from afar and the gate would close, trapping the animals. While cycling to school over a period of weeks we witnessed the culling as the gamekeepers, lying on a high bank, shot them all. This seemed to me at the time an unnecessary massacre and I was never very sure that anything positive came of this experiment as other estates, with large deer numbers and grouse moors, never took such drastic action. Also at Greystone above the road was a rough rocky piece of pasture land where the wheeling, diving plaintive peewits went beserk as we looked for their nests on our way home from school. The green plover seems so much rarer now and on my trips back to the Glen I note with sadness that they are nowhere to be seen in this old haunt.

"From Earth I Flow – Seaward I go"

Engraved Stone on Road to Eitnach.
All in danger of deterioration or lost among vegetation.

Another lasting memory from those former days was the thrill of rising early in autumn to run down to the field below the mansion-house to pick the small mushrooms that had sprung up overnight. Gathering the white fungi dotted all over the dew-covered grass was like uncovering gold nuggets. I can still conjure up a breakfast dream consisting of the aroma of sizzling bacon, eggs and fresh wild mushrooms now darkening in the frying pan. The taste and smell of these are a world away from the bland, commercially produced look-alikes that flood our supermarkets nowadays. Pocket money did not exist in our household in the early days and I am sure most of my chums would have had precious little to spend at any time. However, we must have had the odd halfpenny or penny to spend as the Cattanach's little sweetie shop, just over the Aboyne bridge on the south road, was a regular stopping place on our way home. Sherbet, candy, liquorice, coloured suckies and various fruit gums all for about a penny or less enticed us to recharge our batteries before the long pull home. Rarely did we have enough pennies for this indulgence, but I can still visualise all those goodies laid out invitingly on that cramped little shop counter.

The history of Glen Tanar includes some really serious fires to which I have made previous reference. Over the years a number of much smaller fires occurred, often the result of heather-burning which was carried out to produce succulent young heather shoots for the grouse to feed on. On many occasions extra help was required to extinguish such a fire which had got out of hand when the wind had strengthened. At other times smouldering peat had flared up when the keepers had left, thinking everything had been put out.

One such fire up the river Guerney gave me my one and only experience of this potential disaster. The fire had got out of control when the wind changed direction sending the flames into the nearby forest. The situation caused serious concern as the strong wind sent the fire raging through the branches. All available assistance was required and I, now a teenager, readily volunteered. Having battled throughout the night beating the flames with the heavy unwieldy wire brushes, we finally brought the fire under control as dawn broke. The women-folk bringing up food and drink throughout the night had given us some respite. However, I was totally exhausted with the exertion and excitement as we trekked down from the hill, but a long hot bath and a welcome breakfast did wonders. When I remember that the huge blazes of the past sometimes continued for weeks I can imagine the weariness those fire fighters must have experienced.

No memory of Glen Tanar is complete without mention of the Norwegian shelties, as we called them in the old days, but now better known as the Norwegian Fjord horse. Introduced to Glen Tanar by

The Norwegian Shelties.
A thread of memory back to my childhood.

the laird in 1929 - probably influenced from his Norwegian connections to his wife's birthplace, they were an integral part of our upbringing. As a breed we just took them for granted not realising they were almost unique to the UK, apart from those owned by the Duke of Westminster. The tradition, carried on by the laird's daughter, the Hon Mrs Jean Bruce, they continue to be one of the few remaining threads back to those days of opulent splendour when the estate exuded a timeless tranquillity linked to the confidence of wealth.

So, are all these memories just rather pathetic sentimentality? There is little doubt that as you get older the days of your youth are remembered with increasing appreciation and, no doubt, with some distortion. However, in my case, childhood experiences have never left me for one moment and now that I have come to write about them, it is simply the culmination of a lifetime of reminiscences.

September - 2003.

*Dr Jim Taylor makes his own Paradise
in Rhynie, Aberdeenshire.*

My old friend Jim Taylor, who branded me a cynic in our student days, has also returned to his roots in Rhynie of all places, after a career in England. His wife, June, an Edinburgh Royal Infirmary trained nurse, and probably one of my wife's closest friends, certainly has her doubts. But Jim loves his old stamping ground, that to me appears bleak and barren; but the associations in his mind obviously have nothing to do with appearances. Perhaps then all the beauty and freshness of my glen is also an illusion and just a part of my being.

If that is so, why then do my contemporaries from the same background appear to have feelings that are almost identical? No, I firmly believe that the Glen Tanar of my dreams is the Glen Tanar of reality and nothing will ever make me change my mind.

Chapter 21
Past, Present And Future

The years have rolled on from the late eighteen hundreds, roared through the last century and are already heading off into the future.

Now, let us rewind the imaginary video recording. I, a diminutive scruffy little boy, sit on my father's shoulder as he stands among a group of gaping peasants. We are looking at the dapper figure of a Nantes doctor as he tries in vain to start his ugly-looking vehicle in a blustery wind. The picture moves forward and I am still there on the shoulder; but who is this small elegantly dressed gentleman in the trilby hat? Looking out over Southampton Water towards the Isle of Wight, from the rail of the mighty *Titanic* my father cannot believe his luck, with the world agog over the maiden voyage of this great vessel...

Now, the thundering roar of the mighty howitzers destroy the cosy pre-war world of the Edwardians and I find myself for the first time breathing the bracing air of the Ayrshire coast, while millions perish in the mud of Flanders and the Somme. Now, the sound of cheering crowds in Trafalgar Square breaks eerily into the austere dimly-lit room in Hill Street as my father tries to translate from Dickens' *Bleak House*. Among the crowds a striking young woman with waist-length fair hair celebrates by dancing the night away...

The year is 1926. Stepping down uncertainly from the overnight sleeper in Aberdeen's Joint station is an elegantly dressed lady in striking London fashion. As she stares around at the cold, uninviting surroundings, with the rain streaking the dark grey granite buildings, I can feel her pangs of apprehension already...

A new cameo comes into focus as I see myself writhing in agony, while two large figures bend over me. One of them

Cannes - South of France 1925.

Aberdeen still way over the horizon. Mother and her constant companion, the Kerry Blue - Ruffian.

289

is a woman, whose anxious face seems to be suspended in a mist of antiseptic that overwhelms my senses...

The sun is shining and we are sitting in the heather by the lake. Two jam-jars with strings attached are in the water, while we wait for the bandies to explore these foreign objects. I shout, "Yes you've got one," as Alfie yanks his jar on to dry land, the bandie's little head bobbing against its prison walls. My mother laughs with pleasure to see the children so happy and this is how life should stay forever...

I imagine the preceding paragraphs earning a nod of approval from Mr Mair, my Aboyne headmaster, while Charles Forbes of the Grammar School, smiles gently, but with a quizzical look that seems to be saying – "Can the boy keep it up?"

The March of Time.
Drs. Geoff Gill and Alan Simpson in mid-career.

Rugby friends now in their Seventies.
Sandy Cheyne and Marshall Munn try to throw a Cushion.

I have no real desire to continue in this vein, but there is little doubt that I take pleasure in ideas, attempting to string them together sentimentally, while capturing an atmosphere. Not that I can ever attain the magic with words of my erstwhile Aboyne classmate, Alistair Taylor, but at least I can try. Some of my friends experience a similar pleasure from their many accomplishments, such as playing the piano. I still greatly regret that, because I opted out of piano lessons, I never achieved the enjoyment that is experienced from this musical skill. I envy my friends, Quintin Aitken, yet another old grammar school chum, and his wife Sadie, for their wonderful musical virtuosity; while to listen to my colleague, the surgeon John Cockburn, producing wonderful music from his clarinet, is sheer delight.

During the lifetime of my parents, advances were made that would have seemed impossible to earlier generations. The steam engine already existed, but the internal combustion engine was to astound my father. It would seem that Bleriot, having crossed the Channel in his flimsy machine had scaled the peak of technological achievement. But no, the iron warriors creeping across the battle-strewn wastelands of the Western Front had made the horse a relic and thus changed armies forever. Suddenly, Bleriot's aeroplane has become a real fighting machine and, before long, sleek birdlike aircraft appear in which increasing numbers of people are carried all around the world. Accelerating the advance, the mushrooms above Japan herald an uncertain nuclear age, while in no time at all, we have human beings walking across the face of the moon and destroying forever our children's belief that it is made of cheese.

My parents had experienced in one generation the greatest advances mankind had ever known. In all fields of science, engineering and medicine we have advanced to such an extent that nothing now seems beyond the reach of human endeavour. Computers, with their integrated circuits have revolutionised science, business and communications. I believe that by the time of their death, my parents had become so used to rapid advances that, if they had been told that little green men had landed in California from Mars, they would have shrugged it off as just another modern miracle.

What has not changed, of course, in their lifetime or indeed, in ours, is man's inability to live in harmony with his neighbour. Mother had vivid memories of the Boer War, the Great War and the Second World War, with the result that, when she was reminiscing in later years, one never knew to which war she was referring. For my father, the wars did not seem to have left any momentous memories except for seeing Zeppelins over London. However, he would have remembered being put in jail in Paris for a week on his first return to France in 1920. The charge was one of his being a traitor and a deserter. Eventually the documents turned up which showed that he was unfit for military service, having failed his medical in the UK. Nevertheless, he had to spend a very nervous week in the cells, anxiously wondering whether a revengeful nation might just put him in front of a firing squad.

My father did not become a naturalised British subject until 1947 so he was treated as an alien during the Second World War and had to regularly attend the police station in Aboyne to show that he was not harbouring Germans or planning the downfall of Glen Tanar estate. Such was the nonsense of war.

Glen Tanar from the High Road looking towards the Home Farm.

The High Road in my boyhood was a well-kept thoroughfare – no longer.

The advent of Hitler and Mussolini in the 1930's deeply affected my parents but, for me, life at Glen Tanar was still idyllic. But when, in 1939, Russia and Germany signed a pact that threw them together, I sensed that we were heading towards another world war.

The Second World War had finished, but the slaughter continued. Jews in Palestine killed Martin after he had survived being killed by Germans. He was the brother of Nessie Urquhart, who had made my first day at school so memorable. The senseless killings would continue over much of the globe. Conflict would spread like wildfire with the partition of India, and wars in Korea and Vietnam. Ethnic cleansing would blight Africa, the Balkans and elsewhere. Unbelievably, as it seems to some of us, British soldiers and Irishmen, looking and speaking so alike, continued to kill one another in the struggle for the right to rule Ireland. Religious differences between various Christian sects continue to encourage a savage and bloody conflict that no right-minded person, and certainly no humanist, can countenance.

I cannot understand how, in my lifetime, apparently civilised people can return to the primitive state in which they kill one another without reason. The Jews in Israel, who have suffered generations of degradation and the threat of extermination, seem to have learned nothing from their history. They, too, cause suffering to Arabs after having suffered so much themselves and now reap the harvest of revenge in return. It appears that mankind still continues to be unable to exist without invoking the support of some higher being. I believe that religious intolerance is the root cause of such discord, but I ask myself will this ever change? Is the human mind unable to move forward? Will mankind ever be free from these chains thus enabling him to evolve into a more tolerant being?

292

Past, Present And Future

The old order is passing and the gap between classes is narrowing. My father would have approved of the fact that Jack is now nearly as good as his master. The simplicity, security and sheer innocence of the old life on the estates are, for me, an experience that can never be bettered. Although I hail the prospect of the equality of man with enthusiasm, I am so grateful that this new age came after my time.

In those far-off days we seemed to live in a world of truly interesting characters, to be found at all social levels from the lairds down to the little itinerant tinkie woman with her shawl and wicker basket. The tradesmen and estate workers all had their nicknames, some of which we would not dare to say to their faces, but might shout out loudly behind their backs when we thought we were far enough away from them. In school, university and the hospital, the personalities abounded. In General Practice, the names of Philip o' Huntly, Taylor of Peterheed and Danny Gordon of Ellon, used to make us housemen jump to accept their emergency cases. There is a well-known local joke about the young nurse who was taking a call from a doctor who was demanding that a case be admitted to the ward. Asked by the resident house doctor who was calling, the nurse said a lady called Philippa Huntly who sounded mighty like some ill-tempered old man. Many of that generation of GPs were certainly puffed up with their own importance, being men of considerable standing in their own communities, but they were real characters none the less.

A World lacking Characters?
Not while Jimmy Oswald is alive.

*No longer the boisterous loon
from the Cabrach, but still capable
of twisting plenty tails.*

Talking of days gone by, allows me one other medical joke, recounted as totally genuine by Mr Alec Adam, retired orthopaedic surgeon and now cherished librarian of the Aberdeen Medico-Chirurgical Society. Mr Willie Anderson, renowned Aberdeen surgeon of the pre-NHS days, was taking a clinic of young medical students around the bed of a farm servant. Informing the budding doctors that this was a case of suspected bowel obstruction, he invited one of the girls in the group to ask a question of the patient that might help with the diagnosis. "Have you passed flatus?" asked the student earnestly. The man appearing quite bemused, Willie brusquely intervened. "No, no, to communicate with such a son of the soil you must talk to him in his own vernacular". Turning to the patient, "Have you farted?" demanded Willie. "Na, na, mannie, dinna blame me - it must hae been some o' you eens!" True Doric humour bridging all levels of social class and education, while still having the characters to go with it.

Looking around me now, it appears that I can scarcely identify any such character because most of us seem to have conformed to a common pattern of behaviour. Is this because we are all becoming more sensitive to the impression that we make on other people; and are we fearful of being held up to ridicule and regarded with suspicion for not conforming? Those people that remotely come to mind as being 'characters' are those who are refreshingly unselfconscious, perhaps a little eccentric, and who go through life untroubled or unaware of what others think of them.

The trams have gone from Aberdeen, as have many of the distinctive qualities of our ancient city. The oil industry has in many ways improved the infrastructure of the town, but the wonderful Union Street of my youth is but a memory. 'Walking the mat' was the term used to describe regular parading up and down Union Street. As schoolboys and students, it was our habit to walk up one side of the street and down the other to eye up all the 'talent.' Meeting at the 'Monkey House' in Union Terrace was the recognised custom for generations of Aberdonians; and, we, as students, would congregate there to decide which cinema queue to join.

The volume of traffic has now increased so much that it has made life almost intolerable for some. Residential streets, which were once leafy havens, are now clogged with cars on both sides. The installation of 'sleeping policemen' to calm speeding traffic has disfigured and defaced many lovely streets. These are hazardous to enter, while their broken and uneven pavements make them a total disgrace to the city fathers. Gray Street is a case in point. Yet, many of our friends live there contentedly, especially Dr Vivienne Watson, my fellow resident from our Maternity Hospital days. They have developed a community spirit and a harmonious atmosphere, blending many of the residents together in a way that is welcoming to newcomers and is an example to the rest of us.

Saying farewell to the twentieth century in this country heralds an exciting new age of endeavour, wealth and tranquillity; but, looking around the world there is an uneasy sense that there are still potential sources of suffering and upheaval for millions of people. Man appears no nearer living with his fellow man in peace than he has for generations past, and the hazards looming on the horizon for my children's children look ominous. We can only hope, for their sake, that the desire for self-preservation coupled with common sense will prevent the advent of a devastating holocaust.

What then is the future of the Fouin name in Britain? My son, Peter and his wife, have two female children so that, if marriage survives as a social process, the name will die out. Only if they stay single and name their children after themselves can the name Fouin possibly endure. In Australia, the surname Meyer has already displaced Fouin, although the latter remains among the Christian names of Nicky's two children. In France the name is found principally in Brittany and further computer searching reveals that only one hundred and sixty are recorded in the whole of France. I discovered in 1990 that, among my direct family in France, females are predominant and only two boys at that time remained to preserve the name.

Typical Cunliffe-Brooks engravings on
water trough near Aboyne.

The intertwined WCB initials are present on
many of his inscribed stones.

Worldwide, it would appear that the family was among the first French to settle in Canada in the early 1600's. Driven south by the invading British a generation later, they appear to have settled in Lafayette, Louisiana. So far, my attempts to contact any members of the family have met with no response, but I have high hopes that I will be able to put this right if I make a trip to South Carolina in the future.

The bedrock of this book has been my upbringing on Glen Tanar estate and my continuing close affinity with this secluded glen. Time has ravaged the dream of Cunliffe-Brooks to make his Highland paradise; but still, if you know where to look, his eccentric wells and stones have become part of antiquity. Reading Ian R Mitchell's book, *On the Trail of Queen Victoria in the Highlands*, I find myself broadly in agreement with his pessimism about land usage and even with much of his Marxist outlook.

However, I tend to disagree with his implied criticism of Cunliffe-Brooks converting the estate into an "English rural vernacular." I believe Brooks left much that was a huge improvement on the past and, while many of his plaques may appear to be enigmatic, they at least make one pause and think. The estate buildings and houses are a credit to the artisans of over a hundred years ago, and I believe the estate workers of those days would have been delighted to be housed in such comfort as I experienced as a boy much later on. Yes, I totally agree with Ian Mitchell about the unfairness of it all and would hate to see a return to such inequality, but yet I would not trade one day of my youth for the life-style of my own children or grandchildren.

In her lifetime, I often held my mother in rather grudging respect with empathy and sympathy some little way behind. To find in her latter years, that very empathy with her grand-daughter which she had so missed with her own son, gave her great satisfaction. That she could share her love of poetry and the fullness of life with Nicky surprised me, until I realized that these were her very own genes jumping a generation. In this salute to my mother and also to her grand-daughter, the following is one of the many poems which meant so much to her from those far off days. This was sent by Mother to her youngest sister, my aunt Isobel, in 1914, just as the first clouds of war descended over their young innocent lives.

"In Memory of the Old Days"

When twilight comes across the quiet land,
I crave your presence, you who understand.
The comradeship of word, of look, of smile,
The gentle talk and laughter afterwhile.
The homeward walk across the wave-worn sand,
How will it be, I wonder, when the grand
full, muddy glow of life has vanished?
The sun's last rays have fallen and coldly on the dial,
When twilight comes.

Oh that we two, together, still may stand
Undone, perchance, the deeds we hoped and planned.
Tired and maybe old, yet missing nought
Of tenderness of olden word or thought.
God grant that life may leave us hand in hand.
When twilight comes.

Have I done justice to the past, or are there other areas where friends and family will say I have failed to paint an accurate picture? Memories keep coming to me in my quieter moments, and many have filtered into these pages as an afterthought; but somewhere I have to stop and say, enough is enough. Old contacts have been renewed with people who probably never believed they would hear of me again, and it is heart-warming to know that so many of my memories are also theirs.

These memoirs now draw to a close, but life moves on and, even as I revise some of the facts, the picture has changed as friends and acquaintances die. I have even been almost induced to reconsider some of my basic beliefs. The mind just accepts the inevitability of birth and death which neither prayer nor rebellion can change. In my twilight years, it seems sensible just to get on with life and to regard every new day simply as a bonus to be accepted with gratitude. Those Glen Tanar images heralded my introduction and with those self-same memories I now complete this saga with deep satisfaction.

Epilogue

This book has turned out to be a labour of love, uncovering long forgotten details and unwrapping carefully stored memories that have occasionally brought a lump to my throat. The experts advise you never to write your memoirs, unless you are rich or famous. I have ignored that advice and have written this account of my life for the benefit of my progeny. Those of my friends who read this will, I trust, derive some pleasure from its contents. Nothing very unusual has occurred, which millions of others have not also experienced; but while photographs in the family album represent static individuals, so this book is an attempt to bring them to life and to describe the events surrounding our family during the twentieth century.

I hope that, by revealing some previously hidden anxieties and also the hopes and fears from my past, I will not surprise too many. The memories of some episodes are as vivid today as when I first experienced them. In addition, I am grateful for the comments of friends who have refreshed my memory of those events that we shared from so long ago. At the same time, however, the more I discuss our past with different people the more I sense that all our visions are self-selective and none of us seem to remember exactly similar things. I fully realise, therefore, that this is my story, based on my personal impressions, and possibly distorted by not a little hindsight on occasions. Many will see themselves as I saw them in my childhood, while others will recognise family members and friends who may no longer be with us. I trust that I have neither besmirched anyone's memory nor misrepresented too many facts in these reminiscences.

The Glen Tanar association has, of course, formed the kernel of these memoirs. I can still go back from time to time to try and recapture the sparkle and freshness of all those years ago. My children, Peter and Nicola, spent some weeks grouse-beating on the estate when they were young students. Thus, I was able to pass on some of the magic that is the Glen for them to savour. Also, having scattered my mother's ashes along the road to Eitnach, there will always remain a part of us all in that wonderful setting. Just before you reach the Black Ship, deep in the pine forest, you will see by the roadside, one of Sir Cunliffe Brooks' many inscribed stones. These very simple, but for me atmospheric lines, resonate so much that this will remain forever the glory of my past and of that Glen Tanar of old.

The Pine is King of Scottish Woods,
And the queen - Ah who is she?
The fairest form the forest kens,
The Bonnie Birken Tree.

Appendix One
Personal View

British Medical Journal.
Volume 287 - 2 July 1983.

There is no doubt about my parochialism. It has changed in character over the years, but I remain basically highly insular despite the various broadening influences of experience and travel. My provincial foundations, however, were first shaken in 1939, when a small Aberdeenshire village was invaded by barbaric hordes of evacuees from the east end of Glasgow. These cheerful gregarious urchins proceeded to threaten the whole fabric of our world with their physical aggression, quick wittedness, and accounts of a life hitherto undreamed of by us. Gang warfare, religious intolerance, Rangers and Celtic, all became a frightening reality in our rural lives. The Glasgow influence persisted many years later when as a national service medical officer I had the responsibility of a Royal Army Service Corps unit composed of larger editions of these self same evacuees. Sergeant Bilko would have struggled in such company as every trick was perpetrated to achieve passes to visit non-existent sick grandmothers in the Gorbals, evade foreign postings, or simply be excused normal ablutions.

On entering general practice my prejudice against any hint of a Glasgow twang was well established. Scottish nationalism was acceptable to me for the east coast, but if it incorporated Strathclyde I would rather link up with the devil. English accents also evoked differing responses when making decisions in the surgery. Geordies stirred distant memories of my Morpeth ancestry and were treated as kindred spirits. Cockneys were viewed with extreme wariness, while cultured public school English was a source of deep suspicion evoking that sense of inferiority that has so often dogged the Scot in other spheres.

All that has changed with the passage of time, some maturity, and, of course, the North Sea oil boom. Now the dialects of the United Kingdom make little impression other than to trigger off in my subconscious the intellectual level at which I may have to conduct the consultation. If, however, my parochialism has broadened to accept patients from mainland Britain I still find difficulty bridging the seas and oceans.

The North American accent halts my scribbling pen in mid-air. I sit back and view my adversary intently to get some clue about what form the duel will take. Do I gather a hint of prior knowledge in the use of our National Health

Service or is this a new arrival simply asking for the pointing finger to the nearest paediatrician? I find myself immediately caught up in a contest of wits. Is it to be a worthwhile battle for re-education or shall I simply acquiesce to the request on the basis that this is a worthless transient - here today and gone tomorrow? I am only too aware that all my prejudices are alerted and I fight to achieve a rational conclusion to the interview without resorting to some sly jibe about American medicine.

Of course, the American approach evaporates as my Canadian patient indignantly disowns any association with his southern neighbour. To the Scot most Canadians are long lost brothers, and the consultation simply serves to cement the ties of good will. Australians and South Africans are viewed with much more initial caution but the New Zealander, enhanced by his country's unstinting support during the Falklands crisis, is given the red carpet treatment.

Among the Europeans, and despite my Breton blood, I view the French with great coolness. Like the Americans they seem the product of their medical system, with, in my view, an unreasonable expectancy of medicine associated with extensive investigations unrelated to need and a rather clawing dependency on their own doctors. Unlike the Americans, however, they give the impression of being totally wedded forever to their system and can see British medicine only as second best. Time does not seem to change their attitudes, and I am not surprised when they fly back to Paris for a second opinion, usually gynaecological, the day after seeing our local specialist. Add to this the partial barrier of language and an apparent lack of our type of humour, and I find myself experiencing at times a very unsatisfactory doctor/patient relationship. I recognise this, however, as being as much about my own difficulties of carrying a French name in a Scottish setting as about my Gallic countryman.

The German, inflated by my super race image of him, is a disappointment with his low blood pressure and health anxieties, while the Pole with lurid descriptions of his disease processes contrasts so vividly with north east understatement as to seem completely unrealistic. The accolade for my favourite European in the surgery undoubtedly goes to the Dutch. Their coolness, dry sense of humour, and stoical outlook on life so mirror our own population that I immediately feel a warmth of comradeship towards them. They seem unconditioned by their previous medical experiences and usually make open minded patients, gauging advice and treatment without any sign of national prejudice.

That blood bath in Ireland sends niggles of doubt through my mind about my attitude towards the Irish as a whole. I only hope I am not detecting a sense of increasing exasperation, and surely not intolerance, in my counselling technique towards them in their time of need. On the other hand, the bronzed fair haired Norwegian exudes the feeling of wellbeing that refreshes my soul. You can sense the bracing air, the blue fjords, and snow capped mountains – a small nation of independent thought and deed so welcome in our age of super powers and cruise missiles.

These various nationalities ebb and flow through the surgery daily, and even the most unimaginative of us must somehow be affected by their presence. Has the experience widened our horizons and stimulated our minds to the benefit of our own indigenous population, or is this an area of little clinical importance and so unworthy of much thought or discussion? If, however, we are attempting to instil the rational approach in our trainees how may we achieve this if we ourselves remain a mass of conflicting and often unperceived prejudices and emotions? Even with the experience of 24 years in general practice why do I still feel tempted to challenge patients' beliefs or attitudes and find my approach biased by their backgrounds? Surely I should have matured enough not to label strangers - after all, I now realise the average Glaswegian is one of the kindliest in the country, but somewhere deep down I still view him as a potential mobster.

Perhaps this whole subject squeezes into that ill defined arena of racial discrimination and the shadow of an Act of parliament immediately stifles us from frank debate. For the next generation, however, the advent of diagnostic electronics may eliminate our human foibles, but then predictably my day will be incomplete if contact with this grossly obese Texas oilman is reduced to a computer read out.

Peterculter, Scotland UK.

PIERRE FOUIN,

General Practitioner.

Appendix Two
Individual Details

Additional information on some individuals
mentioned in the text.

Aitken, Quintin & Sadie - retired garage proprietors, Peterculter, Aberdeen. *(Chapter 21)*

Anderson, Graham M. - late of his family firm of George Donald & Sons Ltd. ("Potty" Donalds to Aberdonians for decades). My art connoisseur. *(Chapter 13)*

Archibald, William (Bill) - retired from Royal Navy. Sadly lost track of... *(Chapters 2, 3, 6, 7, 8, 11, 13 and 18)*

Bell, Millicent (Misty) - Teacher of Domestic Science. Married Norman Donald, Headmaster, Insch, Aberdeenshire *(Chapter 8)*

Cheyne, Dr Alexander I (Sandy) - retired Glasgow consultant psychiatrist and almost still farming. *(Chapter 14)*

Clark, Dr Francis - prominent Aberdeen business man, "A legend to generations of medical students with his audacious pranks and ploys" *(Chapter 14)*

Cockburn, John S - cardio-thoracic surgeon, Aberdeen Hospitals, "Clarinettist supreme". *(Chapter 21)*

Davidson, Dr James - Director of Radiology, Hamilton, Ontario, Canada, "Bright as a button". *(Chapter 14)*

Dawson, Alfred G (Alfie) - retired service electrician, Aberdeen Construction Group. Orchid grower and bonsai addict, a master at keeping track of old acquaintances! *(Chapters 2, 3, 4, 8, 9, 10, 11, 13, 18 and 21)*

Emslie, Dr Michael J - retired GP Eastbourne with Banchory roots. Flamboyant entrepreneur, bon vivant and only classmate who could boast of having a pheasant shoot with birds flying in off the sea. *(Chapter 14)*

Farr, Dr Val - retired paediatrician, Aberdeen Sick Children's Hospital. An expert in male psychology thus keeping her happily single. *(Chapter 14)*

Fouin, F L Pierre - MB ChB (University of Aberdeen 1954), DRCOG, FRCGP. Retired GP and University Lecturer.

Fouin, Kathleen R. (Kaye), née Angus - RGN, Theatre sister Ward 9, Aberdeen Royal Infirmary and handmaiden to my bête noire, the late Mr George Mavor. *(Chapters 5, 12, 14, 19 and 20)*

Fouin, Peter R (son) - BSc (Hons) Arch. Dip. Arch. Fouin & Bell Ltd, Architects, Leith Walk, Edinburgh. *(Chapters 2, 15, 17, 19, 20 and Epilogue)*

Fouin, Nicola D (daughter) - BEd. Dunfermline College of PE, BSc (Physiotherapy), Queen's University, Glasgow. Resident in Mildura, Victoria, Australia. *(Chapters 2, 15, 17, 20, 21 and Epilogue)*

Gill, Dr Geoffrey M - MBE, retired GP, Inverurie, Aberdeenshire and lifelong Scouter. Husband of Philip o'Huntly's daughter, Dr Margaret Philip. *(Chapters 14 and 21)*

Halley, Evelyn M (cousin) - married Capt. Arthur Scott, MN. Lives in Alderney, Channel Islands. *(Chapters. 8 and 9)*

Halley, Will - married to my aunt, Isobel Watson (Evelyn's father). Was Scottish circulation manager for The Mail on Sunday, also established Halley's Deliveries (Pantechnicon-vans). Died 1939.

Hepburn, James - one of "the three disciples". Retired ghillie, Ballater, Aberdeenshire. *(Chapter 2)*

Jason, Aileen, née Reay, MA (Hons) - teacher of English at Inverurie Academy and Aberdeen High School for Girls. *(Chapter 14)*

Jason, Dr A Charles - retired Physicist, Assistant Director, Torry Research Station, Ministry of Agriculture, Fisheries & Food. *(Acknowledgements)*

Leslie, George E, BSc (Hons) - long service RAF (navigator). Honeywell Electronics. *(Chapters 14 and 15)*

Longmore, Dr Herbert J A - retired GP, Lochmaben, Dumfries. "Head down and at 'em Herb and don't dare let me exaggerate how good we are." *(Chapter 14)*

Masson, Fred - (1922 - 2003) - electrical contracts manager, Peterculter, Aberdeen. *(Chapter 4)*

McDonald, Dr George A - retired consultant haematologist. Glasgow Royal Infirmary. *(Chapters 14 and 16)*

Mitchell, Dr M James (1930 -1985) - GP, Crieff, Perthshire. "What are YOU doing Here?" *(Chapter 12)*

Mitchell, Ian R - writer and historian whose Marxism strikes a chord with an estate loon. *(Chapter 21)*

Munn, Dr J Marshall - retired GP, Stirling. "Nippiest scrum-half in the North-east." *(Chapter 14)*

Newbigging, Marie (Tink) - well known breeder and judge of Shetland ponies. Married Dr Ian (Bruno) Brooker, retired GP, Shetland. "Tom Patey's secret weapon to make us forget our fear." *(Chapters 11 and 14)*

Pattillo, Dr John - retired GP, Shrewton, Salisbury. "Steak, peaches and cream - pure joy!" *(Chapter 14)*

Raitt, Bett - MBE, retired nursing officer, Aberdeen Royal Infirmary. "The Manhattan drink's Queen." *(Chapter 12)*

Reid, Dr Ian W C (Boom) - GP and Politician, Alberta, Canada. Past solicitor-general and labour minister in the Province. *(Chapter 14 and 19)*

Simpson, Dr Albert A - served as a flyer in the First World War with the RFC. Thereafter qualified as a doctor at Aberdeen University. GP in Muswell Hill, London to outbreak of war. Served in RAF as an MO before returning to London, then to emigrate to Canada to settle in Digby, Halifax, Nova Scotia up to his death. Father of my old friend and colleague, Dr Alan W Simpson, also in Canada, consultant anaesthetist, Kitchener, Ontario. *(Chapter 12)*

Smith, Bob - ex-editor, Aberdeen Evening Express. One of the North-east's best known authors. *(Chapter 6)*

Smith, Mrs Annie, née Halley - sister of Will Halley (my uncle). Wife of Bill Smith (late head gardener Dunecht estates & writer on horticulture). Mother of Ronald (Springfield Nurseries) and Bill junior (Market gardener, Lyne of Skene). *(Chapters 8 and 19)*

Smyllie, Dr Gordon H (1926 -1999) - Bacteriology Senior Lecturer, University of Aberdeen. *(Chapter 14)*

Stewart, George A M - retired schoolmaster, Dumfries. George Formby Maestro. *(Chapters 12 and 14)*

Strang, John - Garage Proprietor and Haulage Contractor, Kincardine O'Neil, Aberdeenshire. *(Chapters 3, 4 and 15)*

Strang, Peter Jnr (1926 -1997) - Hotelier and Plant Hire Operator. *(Chapters 4, 8 and 10)*

Stuart, Dr Douglas - one of "the four musketeers." Retired GP Nottingham. *(Chapter 14)*

Taylor, Dr James F - Chloride Electrical MO, Manchester. Retired to Rhynie, Aberdeenshire. "First to diagnose the cynic - but who is the greatest cynic now?" *(Chapters 14, 18 and 20)*

Tullet, Dr Adam - graduated 1956. Practised as a GP in Kilmarnock. "Sinking pints and opposing forwards - none better." *(Chapter 14)*

Watson, Dr Vivienne - retired GP, Aberdeen. Twin sons, both GP's - great satisfaction. *(Chapter 21)*

Watson, Isobel - Mother's youngest sister. Married to Will Halley, mother of cousin Evelyn.

Watson, Mary (Molly) - Mother's oldest unmarried sister. Deputy Superintendent, Soldier's, Sailor's & Airman's Institute, Edinburgh.

Webster, Jack - journalist and well respected author who keeps the North-east in his heart. *(Chapter 7)*

Wood, Dr John - retired consultant obstetrician and gynaecologist, Nanaimo, Vancouver Island, Canada. *(Chapters 11 and 14)*

Wright, Donald Bodgener (1915-1984) - Banker and talented musician. Husband of Alice (Ashie) Angus - Kaye's Aunt. Personification of an English gentleman - delightful friend and sailing companion. Both buried in Midmar churchyard. *(Chapter 15)*

Young, Douglas, BSc - College of Agriculture Adviser. Retired to Fortrose, Ross-shire. *(Chapters 3, 6, 12 and 19)*